Interventionist Research in Accounting

This book is the first comprehensive methodological guide for accounting researchers on Interventionist Research (IVR). It provides all the fundamental components needed for understanding what IVR is and how to plan, design, and conduct legitimate intervention studies, which can endure the scrutiny of institutions and peer review. This text systematically opens the 'black box' of an alternative research paradigm seeking to contribute simultaneously to theory and practice through direct and collaborative engagement with organisations, practitioners, managers, and professionals. It mobilises the production of innovative and theoretically grounded research for academe and of practical relevance or usefulness and interest to the field of practice.

Interventionist Research in Accounting: A Methodological Approach unpacks current thinking on IVR to forge a confident path ahead for IVR through adopting a forward-thinking approach. This book recognises the remedial potential of IVR to address the research-practice-relevance gap in accounting research and deliberates the challenges of IVR in accounting. It addresses the design, development, and implementation of interventions critical to solving real-world problems as well as guiding readers in planning an IVR project, including budgetary and ethical aspects, utilising suitable research methods and data collection techniques, and establishing validity and reliability. Further, it offers guidance on selecting and managing the research team and recruiting, accessing, and retaining intervention participants; these two components are crucial to creating collaborative relationships required for effective intervention.

This book is a guide serving as a valuable resource for accounting researchers conducting intervention studies, for doctoral and other research students undertaking accounting research, and academics working in universities and business schools or teaching courses in accounting and research methodology.

Vicki C. Baard is Senior Lecturer in the Department of Accounting and Corporate Governance at Macquarie University, Australia. Previously, she has held senior managerial roles as a practicing management accountant in Banking, Entertainment, and other related global service organisations. Vicki's doctoral thesis centered on interdisciplinary interventionist research, considered as pioneering doctoral work, which ultimately led to her joining academe. Dr Baard is a qualitative and quantitative interdisciplinary researcher in interventionist research and management accounting.

John Dumay is Associate Professor in the Department of Accounting and Corporate Governance at Macquarie University, Australia. Formerly a business consultant, he joined academia after completing his PhD in 2008. His thesis won the European Fund for Management Development and Emerald Journals Outstanding Doctoral Research Award for Knowledge Management. John researches intellectual capital, knowledge management, accounting, corporate reporting and disclosure, research methodologies, and academic writing. John is a highly cited scholar who has published over 100 peer-reviewed articles, book chapters, and books. He is the Associate Editor of the highly regarded *Accounting, Auditing and Accountability Journal*, and *Meditari Accountancy Research*, and Deputy Editor of *Accounting & Finance*.

Routledge Studies in Accounting

For more information about this series, please visit www.routledge.com/
Routledge-Studies-in-Accounting/book-series/SE0715

Interventionist Research in Accounting

A Methodological Approach

Vicki C. Baard and
John Dumay

Routledge
Taylor & Francis Group

NEW YORK AND LONDON

First published 2021
by Routledge
52 Vanderbilt Avenue, New York, NY 10017

and by Routledge
2 Park Square, Milton Park, Abingdon, Oxon OX14 4RN

Routledge is an imprint of the Taylor & Francis Group, an informa business

British Library Cataloguing-in-Publication Data
A catalogue record for this book is available from the British Library

Library of Congress Cataloging-in-Publication Data
Names: Baard, Vicki, author. | Dumay, Johannes, author.
Title: Interventionist research in accounting : a methodological approach / Dr. Vicki C. Baard, DTech and Dr. Johannes Dumay, PhD.
Description: New York : Routledge, 2020. | Series: Routledge studies in accounting | Includes bibliographical references and index.
Identifiers: LCCN 2020018943 (print) | LCCN 2020018944 (ebook) | ISBN 9781138579163 (hardback) | ISBN 9781351262644 (ebook)
Subjects: LCSH: Accounting—Research. | Intervention (Administrative procedure)
Classification: LCC HF5630 .B23 2020 (print) | LCC HF5630 (ebook) | DDC 657.072—dc23
LC record available at https://lccn.loc.gov/2020018943
LC ebook record available at https://lccn.loc.gov/2020018944

ISBN: 978-1-138-57916-3 (hbk)
ISBN: 978-1-351-26264-4 (ebk)

Typeset in Sabon
by Apex CoVantage, LLC

Contents

Figures

Tables

Preface

Interventionist Research (IVR) in Accounting introduces accounting scholars to the exhilarating, challenging and immensely rewarding world of linking academic research to practice. We explore how accounting academics can conduct research and develop the outcomes from their research efforts to be relevant to social systems as constructed by people, organisations, and societies to address real, everyday practical challenges in today's dynamic global environment. We discuss IVR as a methodology, a contemporary counterpart to qualitative and quantitative research methodology, with significant potential to generate research that empowers people to solve problems and to manage everyday challenges, thus, satisfying the need for practically and socially useful research. The book contemplates the science and the art of designing, creating, implementing, and disseminating interventions to achieve significant positive impact on social system competence, effectiveness, and overall well-being.

Interventionist research (IVR) was conceived by Kurt Lewin in the early part of the 20th century. It is an approach to research grounded in his scholarly endeavours on field theory, group dynamics, discrimination toward minority groups, and the process of change. We follow Lewin's governing principles of social practice research, which he termed "a type of action research". We also draw heavily on intervention theory constructed by Chris Argyris (1970), who was a student and associate of Lewin. Additionally, we introduce the Interventionist Research Framework, adapted from Rothman and Thomas's (1994) practical approach to IVR in social work, for use in accounting IVR, specifically to provide methodological guidance for doing IVR in the field.

IVR begins with solving a problem that is of interest to both scholars and society. It is about learning what strategies, practices, policies, and technologies work best to produce outcomes that make a difference in what matters most to researchers and the social system under study. Although creating, developing, and testing interventions may be a challenging process, establishing an effective intervention that solves a real-world problem or makes an overall improvement to a situation can be personally and professionally rewarding. Interventions may be aimed at social systems and may be directed, for instance, at financial account-ing practices and policies, management control systems, social system behaviours and functioning, or social environments. In our experience, and in writing this book, we draw on research conducted in the social and human science disciplines. Therefore, our approach to conducting accounting IVR is interdisciplinary.

Over 14 chapters, we offer a comprehensive guide to IVR for accounting researchers, divided into four parts, where each chapter initiates discourse on critical considerations in IVR. The three chapters of Part 1 provide a rich context that introduces readers to the scope of IVR. In Chapter 1, we introduce readers to the nature of IVR, including what IVR is, what it produces, its origins, and how IVR differs from other methodologies. In Chapter 2, we discuss the potential of IVR as a remedy for two persistent and ongoing accounting problems: the (often) irrelevance of accounting research and the gap between research and practice. We also set out the elements that support IVR's legitimacy as a standalone methodology, which we call the 'good' of IVR. Chapter 3 discusses the challenges and risks that IVR presents to accounting scholars by its very nature. Along with the good, those who engage in IVR need to be aware of these 'bad' and 'ugly' elements. Being forewarned is being forearmed and knowing about these elements means scholars can be prepared for and manage the challenges and risks.

In Part 2, five chapters outline the 'Methodological Foundations and Design', being IVR's pillars of authenticity. Chapter 4 presents a discourse on the philosophical and theoretical pillars of IVR and shows how these two pillars complement each other to provide a legitimate foundation for the methodology. In Chapter 5, we outline the Interventionist Research Framework (IRF), originating from the human sciences, specifically social work. The IRF is a practice-oriented framework tailored for accounting IVR that embraces Kurt Lewin's governing IVR principles and explicitly operationalises Argyris' (1970) theoretical principles. The IRF offers a universal, yet flexible approach to undertaking IVR and unambiguous methodological transparency on how IVR is accomplished. Chapter 6 explicates ethical and budgetary considerations, IVR planning, and pro-tecting intellectual property associated with an IVR project. Given that intervening and interventions are fundamental to IVR, Chapter 7 explores methods for collecting, storing, and analysing IVR data, followed by approaches to ensuring IVR's reliability and validity in Chapter 8.

Part 3, 'People, Social Systems and Interventions', positions scholars in the real world, outside the comfort zone of academic ivory towers, by connecting and collaborating with social systems and a diverse collec-tion of people inhabiting a range of social systems in the field. Chapter 9 enhances our understanding of social systems that are both the context and the subject of an IVR study. Social systems constitute accounting IVR's participants, and thus are a starting point for the recruitment process. Hence, this chapter emphasises the importance of and shares strategies for recruiting, approaching, and retaining participants. Chapter 10 guides scholars on selecting and managing an intervention team essential for effective and successful IVR. Chapter 11 provides guidelines and offers a case example on designing and constructing interventions for implementation into real-world contexts.

Part 4, 'Intervention Implementation and Dissemination' also places accounting scholars in touch with the reality of the world, which they would normally observe and examine without immersing themselves in the field, to actively help resolve a practical problem. Chapter 12 offers alternative approaches to intervention implementation and presents case examples from successful and unsuccessful implementation efforts. Chapter 13 begins by providing advice on publishing in academic journals and professional magazines, while not forgetting about engaging with professionals through presentations and writing up a research report for the host organisation. Chapter 14 completes the book with our thoughts and reflections on the future of accounting IVR.

We have made every effort to create a book that integrates conceptual, methodological, and practical aspects of IVR consistent with the IVR's theoretical, practical, and societal outputs. We aspire to stimulate the utilisation of IVR in future accounting research endeavours directed at developing its theoretical foundations and best practices that can make a difference in the everyday lives of people, organisations, communities, and societies.

Acknowledgements

A very special mention to our wonderful proofreading team of Jemima and Nate from WordByWord Proofreading. You always help polish the diamond and we would be lost without you.

Part 1

Interventionist Research—Why It Matters and Why You Should Care

1 An Introduction to Interventionist Research

We begin this book by discussing the nature of IVR. Although we recognise that some scholars reading this book may be familiar with or currently undertaking IVR, others may be unfamiliar with or have reservations about this approach as a methodology. IVR is a reliable and valid methodology, but likely any methodology is not without its challenges and risks. Hence, this chapter provides an understanding of IVR's origins and the governing principles essential to undertaking IVR in today's world. This understanding includes the output that IVR can produce and the significance of that output to researchers and people in organisations.

We also recognise that IVR is one of many methodological choices for accounting researchers. Therefore, this chapter also addresses the fundamental differences between IVR and other more traditional forms of research. However, rather than argue for IVR as a substitute to more traditional paradigms, we regard it as a contemporary counterpart to positivist and interpretivist methodologies. IVR has great potential to solve real-life problems experienced by people in organisations and of interest to researchers. It also brings meaning and value from an empirical and theoretical perspective to accounting research. IVR is an evolving methodology and given its unique nature, embraces theory as a critical component to delivering theoretically relevant and legitimate research. Hence, in this chapter we also discuss theory, in a general sense, as a critical component of IVR.

The Nature of IVR

IVR is a methodological approach that originated from Kurt Lewin's (1946, 1947b) notion of a 'type of action research' in the social sciences (Baard & Dumay, 2018; Lukka & Vinnari, 2017). In the absence of a definitive definition of IVR, we refer to Dumay and Baard (2017) who define IVR as:

> a research methodology based on case study research, whereby researchers involve themselves in working directly with managers

in organisations to solve real-world problems by deploying theory for designing and implementing solutions through interventions and analysing the results from both a theoretical and practice perspective.

Intervening is the essence of IVR (e.g., Argyris, 1970; Rothman & Thomas, 1994; Gitlin & Czaja, 2016). Therefore, to enhance our understanding of what IVR is, we must consider what it means to intervene and what constitutes an intervention. Argyris (1970, p. 15) states that "to intervene is to enter into an ongoing system of relationships, to come between or among persons, groups or objects for the purpose of helping them." Carkhuff (1983, p. 63) defines an intervention as:

> both a response and an initiative. It is a response to a situation that defines a need. It is a response to a deficit or what is not present. At the same time, it is an initiative to influence that situation—to fill in what is not present, to transform the deficits into assets. In short, an intervention is an attempt to make a difference.

Fraser *et al.* (2009) refer to interventions as one or more actions with the purpose of: changing social system behaviours, attitudes, or beliefs; altering social system variables, such as culture, leadership, social structures, policies, etc.; and/or ameliorating real-world problems. Social systems embody individuals, families, peer groups, teams, intergroups, work units, businesses, schools, universities, government agencies, national or multinational corporations, and communities (Bruhn & Rebach, 2007). We follow Argyris' (1970) interpretation of intergroups as interdependent groups that draw on important resources and interactions to achieve a superordinate goal. Social system actors refer to people inhabiting a social system, for instance, employees; managers; group, intergroup, or team members; accountants, auditors, and other accounting-oriented practitioners; and standard setters and policymakers. We refer to social systems and social system actors throughout this book as a proxy for research participants. Thomas and Rothman (1994) state that the aim of an intervention should be to improve organisational or community life and wellbeing by developing practices and/or products that are effective in real-life contexts. Inherently, that means involving a coordinated effort of research participants who are experiencing the problem. Mullen (1994, p. 167) concurs, arguing that interventions should result in a social technology that solves a social problem and inspires change in a situation brought about by a social problem.

These definitions of 'intervening' and 'intervention' have some key features that further inform us about what IVR is. For instance, each demand that researchers physically inhabit a social system in the field to construct an understanding of the situation; this is consistent with Lewin's governing principle of doing research in the field. Immersion in real-life events is fundamental to IVR (e.g., Merchant, 2012). Additionally, that researchers collaborate with actors in a coordinated effort to focus on a problem or problematic situation is another feature of the methodology. Inevitably, when researchers undertake IVR, they must adopt a managerial perspective, which allows them to experience and understand how accounting influences the everyday lives of all the research participants (Cullen *et al.*, 2013). Fundamental to all these definitions is that IVR is oriented toward problem-solving, where researchers respond to a need in a social system. Greenwood and Levin (2007) argue that researchers might stimulate change by attempting to solve or solving problems when conducting IVR (see also Baard & Dumay, 2018). Developing solutions through interventions is essential for solving practical problems. Designing, developing, and implementing workable solutions is an important catalyst for social system change. Solutions to problems and the knowledge they contribute to practice is an IVR output.

Two of Lewin's governing principles include problem-solving and seeking change in the social system being researched. Baard and Dumay (2018) view change as a singular concept, incorporating social and organisational change, where the interaction of both forms potentially stimulate positive changes in social system actors with respect to social values and power. In this way, IVR can potentially emancipate a system's actors or indeed the system itself (Boog, 2003). Thus, IVR's emancipatory potential positions accounting research to serving the needs of diverse social systems. This is societally relevant research (Lukka & Suomala, 2014), which in part characterises the 'good' of IVR (see Chapter 2).

IVR and Accounting

In the context of accounting, IVR is referred to as a qualitative methodology (Parker, 2014). Its use is most dominant in the management accounting discipline using a longitudinal case study method (Lukka & Vinnari, 2017; Merchant, 2012). IVR's association with management accounting may be because management accounting owes its existence to real-world practice and functional issues (Mitchell, 2002). IVR is also evident in critical accounting (e.g., Neu *et al.*, 2001) and in business information systems research (Baard, 2010). Lewin (1946, 1947b) refers to IVR as a form of field experimentation and, based on our review of the literature, we find most accounting researchers have interpreted IVR as case study research. Although IVR incorporates some elements from other methodologies, it is different from traditional research. Later in this chapter, we contrast IVR with non-IVR methodologies.

Since Lewin's early work using this kind of action research, diverse scholarly interpretations of his work have given rise to several variations of the methodology (Baard, 2010). Accordingly, IVR can be thought of as an umbrella concept incorporating these variants, for example, action research, action science, clinical research, design science, and constructivist research (Jönsson & Lukka, 2007). More recently, Lukka and Suomala (2014) introduced engaged scholarship as an additional variant of IVR. Baard and Dumay (2018) and Jönsson and Lukka (2007) argue that the many different interpretations of IVR are problematic because they create confusion about what IVR is and what it produces. In turn, this undermines the scientific and practical value of the methodology and jeopardises scholarly attempts to forge a path ahead for IVR. These many variations are one of the 'bad' aspects of IVR we discuss further in Chapter 3.

In reflecting on IVR as an umbrella concept, Baard and Dumay (2018) argue for researchers to adopt a 'purist' form of IVR to preserve the original intentions and scientific value of the methodology. The purest form of IVR is one that closely follows Lewin's governing principles and Argyris' (1970) intervention theory (see also Baard, 2010; Dumay & Baard, 2017). In our discourse so far, we have identified several of Lewin's governing principles. Another governing principle, relevant to the idea of IVR in a 'purist' form, is that the methodology must produce theoretical and practical outcomes. He referred to this as the duality of output, which constitutes an important feature of IVR, and may present in varying forms—especially given the diverse scholarly interpretations of IVR that have been developed since. An IVR study that achieves the duality of output is research that simultaneously contributes knowledge to theory and practice (Lukka & Suomala, 2014). Recent examples of accounting IVR studies fulfilling this goal include Cullen *et al.* (2013), Campanale *et al.* (2014), and Chiucchi (2013). Achieving IVR's duality of output also positions the methodology to generate research with theoretical and practical relevance. IVR's remedial potential to address the irrelevance of accounting research and the research-practice gap reside in this duality (Evans *et al.*, 2011; Jönsson & Lukka, 2007). This remedial potential in part characterises the 'good' of IVR (see Chapter 2).

We acknowledge that accounting scholars' decision to adopt a 'purist' form of IVR or one of its variations is one each researcher must make for themselves. We also recognise that sometimes this decision will depend on the research aims, the research question, and the desired research outcomes. Scholars choosing the purist form are encouraged to refer to their methodology as IVR, while scholars choosing a variation should not muddy the IVR waters and instead use the actual name of the variation. This, after all, is basic scientific precision and rigour. Further, regardless of any approach taken, it is wise for researchers to always go back to the "methodological drawing board" when following any research methodology (Parker & Roffey, 1997).

Several scholars have attempted to argue for IVR's potential value for accounting researchers (e.g., Cullen *et al.*, 2013; Parker, 2014; Lukka & Vinnari, 2017). However, its use in the accounting literature is still limited, and we find a protracted sense of academic reluctance to engage with it.

In part, this reluctance may be due to the risks and challenges sometimes encountered in IVR's perilous landscape; awareness of them means one can avoid them (see Chapter 3).

The Origins of IVR

Kurt Lewin (1890 to 1947), a social psychologist whose work is grounded in social science, is recognised as the founding architect of IVR (Greenwood & Levin, 2007; Jönsson & Lukka, 2007; Adelman, 1993; Peters & Robinson, 1984; Foster, 1972). Lewin was a scientific pragmatist whose main interest was to conceptualise the "general laws of life", generate social change in the field using his governing principles, and integrate science into practice (Dickens & Watkins, 1999; Sandelands, 1990; Adelman, 1993; Peters & Robinson, 1984). Kleiner and Maguire (1986, p. 12) refer to Lewin as a "theorist, methodologist and a practitioner". As a theorist, Lewin set high standards, arguing that theory in social science should not be surrendered, nor should theory's relationship to practice be lost (Argyris *et al.*, 1985). Sandelands (1990, p. 248) argues that Lewin worked hard to unite theory and practice because he viewed the development of both as the same: "good theories are practical because they are built through practice". As a methodologist, Lewin (1946) conceived notions, proposed ideas, and published articles on action research. At every turn, he advocated for a change in research toward field studies and quasi-experiments in real-life social systems, always with the aim of addressing practical, social problems. As Bargal (2006, p. 383) states:

> He deviated from the common methodological norm, which focused on the positivistic paradigm and enabled ivory tower scholars to 'intrude' in the realm of practitioners. By introducing action research as a methodology, Lewin essentially obliterated the boundary that existed between research and practice, and highlighted their interdependence.

As a practitioner, Lewin approached his work with a view to making things happen. He focused on practical problems, such as social conflict, discrimination, group dynamics, and factory production, and he worked to mobilise action that would make a difference to individuals, groups, organisations, and communities (Sandelands, 1990). In this section, we discuss the origins of IVR, centring on field theory, WWII as an IVR catalyst, dual IVR objectives and outcomes, the iterative process of IVR, and IVR as a stimulant for change.

The Idea of Field Theory

Lewin's concept of action research is heavily influenced by his own life experience. As a Jewish academic in Nazi Germany, Lewin emigrated to the United States a few years prior to WWII, where he was viewed as a member of a minority group. Discrimination and marginalisation stimulated his interest in finding an instrument to influence intergroup relations (Bargal, 2006). He established a research centre at the Massachusetts Institute of Technology (MIT) specifically dedicated to exploring group dynamics with a view to solving social problems (Lewin, 1945a), and his work at this centre led him to his answer—a new research methodology, followed by intervention theory and, ultimately, action research (Bargal, 2006; Lewin, 1946).

At that time, Lewin had already spent 25 years developing field theory as an explanation for the forces at play in social situations (Cartwright, 1951; Burnes & Cooke, 2013; Adelman, 1993). Based on influences from forcefield theory from physics and gestalt psychology, field theory was to become the key theoretical foundation of action research. Field theory views social situations as a life space (also referred to as a psychological environment, a perceptual environment, a psychological field, social field, or force field) (Bargal, 2006). A life space is a full, but discrete environment, in which a behaviour manifests (Bargal, 2006), for example, home, work, the gym. Lewin recognised that individuals and groups are social units (Bargal, 2006) with separate life spaces for all their different activities (Burnes & Cooke, 2013); thus, the rationale behind field theory is that behaviour is the result of forces in the relevant life space and, more specifically, that the behaviour of an individual or group is a function of the interactions between a person and their environment. Wrapped up within this theory is the notion that individuals and groups tend to maintain a constant behavioural equilibrium—a process that may be disrupted by dynamic field forces.

Field theory helps us to understand that there are forces which sustain undesirable behaviours. So, to change extant behaviours into desired behaviours, those forces need to be destabilised or other forces need to be reinforced. Lewin asserts that behavioural change occurs as a result of changes to the psychological forces in the life space and, therefore, to bring about change, researchers must understand both the life space and the forces within it (Cartwright, 1951). Lewin viewed field theory as a means for integrating scientific exactitude and practical relevance by presenting a theory-based approach to analysing behaviour and a practical method for changing behaviour (i.e., interventions) through permitting individuals and groups to better understand their actions (Burnes & Cooke, 2013).

WWII—An Important Catalyst for IVR

Arguably, WWII was a catalyst in Lewin's path from field theory to action research. In 1943, the U.S. government was looking for ways to change civilian meat consumption habits in light of meat shortages and their priority to reserve what little meat there was for their fighting forces (Greenwood & Levin, 2007). In 1943, Lewin undertook a study on food habits commissioned by the National Research Committee to examine: why people eat what they eat; how those habits could be changed; and thus, interventions that might achieve the desired results (Lewin, 1943). Four main outcomes from this research came to shape the nature of IVR.

First, Lewin introduced the notion of the gatekeeper as a critical participant in IVR studies. Gatekeepers are the project controllers who can either prevent or allow researchers to achieve their objectives (Lewin, 1943). Housewives were the gatekeepers in Lewin's food study; they were the people in control of what food the family would eat. Therefore, a key objective was to reprogram women's meat supply habits by, say, promoting meat substitutes or considering inferior cuts of meat. Understanding the social situation and the factors influencing the decisions of the gatekeeper has a significant influence over the success of the intervention. It is also important to understand the nature of the gatekeeper, for example, their values, attitudes, social habits, knowledge, and skills, if a researcher is to gain sufficient access to the social system to effect change.

Second, Lewin used interviews to gather valid and useful information, he used theory to help him think about the problems he aimed to solve, and he used field experiments in natural settings to derive and test methods of change (Lewin, 1943). Third, he motivated people to change by helping them understand the need for change and providing enough psychological safety for them to engage in the change process. Engaging in change extends to adopting ownership of the change, reinforcing, and committing to it as enduring change. Argyris (1970) adopted this notion of enduring change as the third principle of his intervention theory, calling it "internal commitment". Four, cooperation between the researcher and the research participants has taken its place as the vital ingredient for ensuring both theoretical and practical outcomes (Cartwright, 1951). From cooperation emerged one of Lewin's governing IVR principles, namely the essentiality of collaboration between researchers and research participants. Foster (1972) interprets Lewin's idea of collaboration as one where researchers and participants are equal partners, sharing mutual respect and equality. Here the values, objectives, and power needs of everyone involved in the IVR study are considered and decisions about the project and its interventions are made democratically.

The Idea for IVR's Duality of Output

Lewin's (1946) further research on minority groups was an endeavour in action research to improve intergroup relations and to assist practitioners in evaluating the interventions used on minority groups. Hence, his action research model is viewed as a direct response to the problems he perceived involving the social actions of social systems. Lewin was very explicit that social research should pursue two main objectives—the study of "general laws" (i.e., theory) and the diagnosis of a social situation. Several aspects of this research inform contemporary IVR, the first being that he realised that the old research approaches would not do. He needed a new approach (Lewin, 1946, p. 35):

> The research needed for social practice can best be characterised as research for social management, or social engineering. It is a type of action research, comparative research on the conditions and effects of various forms of social action, and research leading to social action. Research that provides nothing but books will not suffice. This by no means implies that the research needed is in any respect less scientific or 'lower' than what would be required for pure science in the field of social events.

Bargal (2006) clarifies Lewin's use of the term social engineering, derived from engineering, as using knowledge and techniques to bring about change in a physical world. Further, Bargal asserts that in using the term, Lewin never intended to present an impersonal view of or undermine the human aspect of people in the field. Lewin (1946, p. 36) also distinguishes between academic knowledge and the knowledge required for practice as follows:

> Social research concerns itself with two rather different types of questions, namely the study of general laws of group life and the diagnosis of a specific situation. Problems of general laws deal with the relation between two possible conditions and possible results. They are expressed in 'if so' propositions. The knowledge (general) laws serve as guidance for the achievement of certain objectives under certain conditions . . . . the engineer or surgeon . . . has to know too the specific character of the situation at hand. This character is determined by a scientific fact-finding called diagnosis. For any field of action both types of scientific research are needed.

From Lewin's argument for a new scientific research approach for social practice, the need for both theoretical and practical outcomes emerged. The knowledge needed for practice outcomes is derived from the social situation or life space, and academic knowledge is the general laws that emanate from research.

IVR—An Iterative Process

Lewin (1946) outlines that intervening and acting is a systematic and cyclical process that consists of fact-finding, planning, execution (action), and evaluation; this is Lewins' final governing principle of IVR. Fact-finding means to ascertain the character of the research situation and to diagnose the problem (Lewin, 1946). For example, collecting and analysing data is part of the fact-finding stage (Dickens & Watkins, 1999). Argyris (1970) interprets the idea of fact-finding as generating valid and useful information—the first principle of his intervention theory. Planning involves generating solutions to the problems or undesirable behaviours, which allows researchers and social system actors to gather new insights on the benefits and weaknesses of their solutions (Lewin, 1946). Interventions or intervening follows the planning stage and is characterised from engaging in some form of action aimed at solving the problem. Another fact-finding stage, intervention evaluation follows intervention. Lewin (1946) emphasises that it is essential for interventions to be properly evaluated because, without evaluation, researchers and participants will not know the extent to which their research objectives have been achieved nor whether a social system change has even occurred. However, with evaluation, interventions can be tweaked to maximise the positive outcomes. In an examination of Lewin's work on action research, Dickens and Watkins (1999) outline that several iterations of an action research process might be needed before a problem is finally solved.

IVR and Change

Lewin's (1947a) first paper on group dynamics outlines an approach to social change. He viewed the iterative action research process as a means to bring about actual change in the field. He observed the field as a "constellation" of social events; social systems and their relationships and values; and the forces in the field that sustain undesirable and desirable behaviours (p. 32). Lewin (1947b) conceptualises change as a sequential and discrete three-step process where the current social equilibrium needs to be changed to bring about a desired state of affairs. When changing the status quo, researchers must consider the field holistically, which includes individuals and groups, their relationships, value systems, attitudes, social habits, and customs. Some considerations can be obstacles to change, such as a social habit that creates inner resistance to the desired change. Other considerations might be leveraged, such as value systems that support similar notions of 'what's good'.

Lewin (1943) also indicates that any conditions in the life space that influence human behaviour should promote change, not restrict it. Lewin describes this as a process of "unfreezing". At Level 1 (L^1), the participants recognise the need for change. At L^2, change is beginning to happen—new behaviours, values, attitudes, competencies, or patterns of thinking are beginning to emerge. Lewin (1945b) uses the term re-education to outline a change that is not only about acquiring new knowledge, habits, or skills, but it also encompasses changes in self-perceptions and mobilising people to overcome their inner resistance to change. For both Argyris (1970) and

Lewin, freedom of choice is an important aspect in one's willingness to change and, in turn, their ongoing commitment to making that change enduring. In fact, Argyris' (1970) second principle of intervention theory is using free and informed choice for decision-making. Our interpretation of the idea of free choice is based on Bargal's (2006) discourse and Lewin (1945b; p. 53), where he states:

> the creation . . . of an atmosphere of freedom and spontaneity. Voluntary attendance, informality of meetings, freedom of expression in voicing grievances, emotional security, and avoidance of pressure may lead to changes in the individual's self-perception and social perceptions.

Additionally, in support of the notion of free choice, Lewin (1945b, p. 52) states that:

> A factor of great importance in bringing about a change in sentiment is the degree to which the individual becomes actively involved in the problem. Lacking this involvement, no objective fact is likely to reach the status of a fact for the individual concerned and therefore influence his social conduct.

The third phase of the change process involves stabilising the change. Termed "freezing" by Lewin, this means returning the social system to a steady state with the new values, beliefs, attitudes, habits, etc. as the dominant, normative behaviours. From a social system perspective, accomplishing change means that the system has increased its adaptive capacity, its ability to innovate, and its autonomy (Dickens & Watkins, 1999).

What Happened Next?

After Lewin's passing in February 1947, Chris Argyris continued to investigate organisation and group development in Lewin's tradition by developing and testing a model of action research described by Peters and Robinson (1984) as Lewinian. Argyris argued tirelessly for researchers to embrace both theory and practice as the only real option for making a difference in the world (Edmondson, 2011; Adelman, 1993). However, Adelman (1993) notes that the merits associated with action research after Lewin's passing have risen and fallen in esteem since the 1950s. This wavering trend is still evident today given the criticisms of the approach (e.g., Baard & Dumay, 2018; Jönsson & Lukka, 2007).

IVR versus Other Non-IVR Methodologies

Non-interventionist approaches often examine the 'what' of events or phenomena, i.e., what has already occurred or what has influenced prior events. In answering a what question, researchers typically use a positivist or quantitative approach to data collection, such as a survey for example, which then needs to be generalised to capture its meaning in other contexts. When attempting to answer 'how' and 'why' questions with a non-interventionist methodology, many researchers will turn to an interpretive or qualitative approach, such as case studies and/or critical reviews of the literature.

Broadly speaking, IVR is no different to most other methodologies: its goal is to explain a phenomenon, the genesis of the research is usually motivated by a theoretical research question, and many of the same methods are used for data collection and analysis, such as case studies and experiments, observations, interviews, focus groups, and surveys. Therefore, given these similarities, how is IVR different?

Two key criteria set IVR apart from the rest. First, the researcher is directly involved with the system and actors being studied. Second, the researcher does not avoid influencing the system—in fact, quite the opposite. Direct involvement with a phenomenon lends itself to ethnographic methods, such as observations and/or interviews (Jönsson & Lukka, 2007). Therefore, in this sense, IVR is akin to a case study because, generally, interventionist researchers do tend to focus on a single social system. However, in a case study, the researcher holds an etic stance, examining the issues experienced by research participants from the outside. Their goal is to collate and interpret enough data about the social system to develop a deep understanding of the phenomena as they are. Whereas, in IVR, the researcher immerses themselves in the social system to actively help ameliorate the problem being studied. It is this immersion that specifically distinguishes IVR as a methodology.

Whatever the level of the immersion, the researcher becomes an active participant as a social system actor. They become a competent and trustworthy 'insider' to the real-time processes of the entity. This is an emic stance that has a substantial impact on both data collection and data analysis. Not only is data collected empirically but also the researcher is regarded by research participants as "being one of us", which influences the data collected (Jönsson & Lukka, 2007, p. 376). Hence, as much as the researcher must have the ability to become an insider, they must also be able to take a step back and remove themselves from the inside to pause and reflect upon the intervention in real time.

Directly influencing the subject of a study is a controversial topic in the social sciences. However, applying an intervention is like any experiment. It is a practical test, or a series of small tests, to determine whether a proposed solution fixes an identified problem (Dumay & Baard, 2017). This is a key feature of IVR and the singular most important influence over whether the study achieves practical relevance for society. For the intervention to be valuable, the participants must gain a benefit and they must commit to taking action to get it. Benefits may come in the form of positive change, improved practices, solutions to annoying problems, and so on. Unlike IVR, non-IVR does not ask its participants to commit to constructing a new reality.

Jönsson and Lukka (2007, p. 374) also view IVR as a "kind of field experimentation" because the researcher does not have control over what naturally occurs in the field. Rather, the researcher "seeks to determine the experimental situation through observation, acts on that situation in concert with the host organisation, observes processes and outcome, and analyses findings in view of the relevant literature". Melnyk and Morrison-Beedy (2012) observe that IVR is also known as experimental research because it allows researchers to draw conclusions about relationships between the intervention and the outcomes of the intervening. Thinking about IVR as a form of experimentation emphasises the need for evidence, both for accounting researchers and for non-academics. In making sense of the research results and analysing the findings, the researcher may adopt an etic stance once again. Therefore, during the normal iterative process that constitutes IVR, the researcher will adopt etic and emic stances, moving "there and back again" between academia and practice. The need for researchers to accomplish iterative journeys between the etic and emic world presents specific challenges in the field. It requires the researcher to possess diverse and unique qualities if the challenges are to be addressed effectively (see Chapter 3, 9, and 10).

Outputs of IVR

As mentioned previously, IVR must produce both theoretical and practical outputs for it to be considered pure and legitimate. Practical outputs include solutions to problems, behavioural changes, or deeper insights into the social system resulting from the intervention or, indeed, the researchers intervening. For example, intervening in an organisation may result in changes to the organisation's structure, technology, controls, strategies, and accounting systems that enhance an organisation's health and wellbeing, including its actors.

Further, in solving practical problems, IVR has the potential to stimulate social change, which further adds to IVR's practical output (Baard & Dumay, 2018). Social change has a more intense focus on individuals and groups enhancing their competencies, achieving autonomy, equitably distributing social values, or changing their power or status than organisational change (Baard & Dumay, 2018; Sweetman *et al.* 2013; Greenwood & Levin, 2007). These notions of change are normally viewed as beneficial, but Jönsson and Lukka (2007) caution IVR researchers that change may also cause harm to research participants, especially if the change was unintended. Sweetman *et al.* (2013) provide one particularly harrowing example of negative change, being the personal humiliation or exclusion that can occur if interventions are not designed with due concern for its participants (see ethical considerations in Chapter 6). Thus, accounting researchers should proceed cautiously when undertaking IVR and familiarise themselves with a full and complete picture of the social situation as defined by Cartwright (1951).

IVR and its associated change can also achieve societal relevance through emancipating individuals and groups (Lukka & Suomala, 2014). Research shows that IVR has emancipatory intentions attributed to Kurt Lewin's (1946) work on minority groups or other social system actors in a social situation (Huault *et al.* (2014). In the workplace, emancipation usually relates to people seeking freedom and autonomy through liberation from social or political constraints (i.e., restrictive policies), exercising free choice, empowerment to exercise independence and self-assertion (Baard & Dumay, 2018), and promoting self-advocacy, self-actualisation, and self-consciousness (Boog, 2003). Boog (2003, p. 426) states that IVR:

> is designed to improve the researched subjects' capacities to solve problems, develop skills, increase their chances for self-determination, and to have more influence on the functioning and decision making processes of organisations and institutions from the context of which they act.

We posit the same could be true for social systems. However, Boog (2003, p. 434) also cautions researchers that their interventions may also "de-emancipate research subjects" or cause unintended change. Note that we are not stipulating that accounting researchers must have an emancipatory vision when undertaking IVR. Rather, empowerment and/or emancipation is one area where accounting scholars could generate research with societal relevance.

Accounting IVR's theoretical outputs contribute to the literature on theory by either testing, illustrating, or developing a theory in a specific context or generally. These contributions could be made either to 'theories with status' and 'theories of practice', which includes intervention theory (Llewellyn, 2003). In a review of the literature, Peters and Robinson (1984) could not find a unified theory or set of methodological principles directly related to action research. In fact, they found quite the opposite; hence, their research highlights the inconsistencies and incongruities in the various interpretations of action research by different scholars. Therefore, a contribution to the literature in relation to intervention theory, as conceived by Argyris (1970) and underpinned by Kurt Lewin's original notions of action research, also constitutes an IVR output. In keeping with the fundamental tenets of IVR, Corley and Gioia (2011) also argue for research to be both theoretically relevant and provide practical utility.

IVR—The 'So-What' Factor

Associated with most positions a researcher holds within a research study is the notion of 'so what' and 'why should we care'. These notions are particularly important given several 'bad' and 'ugly' aspects of IVR. The first bad aspect, previously mentioned, relates to the variants of IVR that create an ambiguity about what IVR is and does. Second, IVR is difficult to accomplish compared to other established research methodologies, where it is moderately easier to maintain a stable and ongoing publication record (Merchant, 2012). Third, given IVR's nature as a methodology, it can take a long time to complete a study and requires a range of highly developed competencies (Markides, 2007; Dumay & Baard, 2017). The 'ugly' of IVR is its association with researchers as 'consultants', which adversely influences its reputation (Baldvinsdottir *et al.*, 2010; Lukka & Suomala, 2014). Coupled with this stigma is the perception that IVR yields second-rate research (Scapens, 2008).

Melnyk and Morrison-Beedy (2012, p. 3) call for potential interventionist researchers to use the 'so what' factor as their foundation for IVR. 'So what' positions IVR to focus on problems that require solutions or situations amenable to change. It informs the research design, ensuring both theoretical and practical outcomes. And it reduces the risk of generating research findings that are only disseminated to academics through academic channels but largely do not reach the actual beneficiaries of the findings. Given Lewin's governing principle of IVR achieving both practical and theoretical outcomes, we incorporate some theoretical considerations when using the 'so what' factor in IVR. Below are some useful questions to consider when undertaking IVR:

- *So what* is/are the aim(s) of your IVR? Is/are the aim(s) unique? Does your IVR project challenge existing ideas and theories?
- *So what* is the research question? Does this IVR project have an important research question that addresses a significant problem in real-world social systems and will advance theoretical knowledge? Is the research question feasible, innovative, and focused on a discipline-specific topic that you are passionate about?
- *So what* is the research problem? For whom is it a problem, and why does the problem persist? Has this problem been previously researched? Is the problem or the problematic conditions resolvable or modifiable by using an intervention?
- *So what* is the intervention you intend to apply to the problem at hand? Is the intervention novel? If so, how and why? Will the intervention need to be designed and developed from scratch or is an appropriate intervention already available?

  (see Chapter 4 for theoretical intervention types and Chapter 11 on intervention design and construction)

- *"So what"* difference or impact will your IVR study make with respect to policies, practices, strategies, costs, processes, actor emancipation, learning and development, etc.?
- *"So what"* is the probability of your intervention being adopted and implemented by the participants and/or those facing similar issues?

  (see Chapter 12 on implementing interventions)

- *"So what"* are the likely practical and theoretical outcomes of your IVR project once complete? What are others outside of the participants in your current project, including yourself, likely to do with the research outcomes?
- *"So what"* actions will you perform to transform your findings into real-world contexts?

  (see Chapter 13 on IVR dissemination)

In raising the 'so what' factor associated with IVR, we offer some ideas on how to position an IVR study to generate practical relevance and to a lesser extent to generate theoretical relevance. Using IVR for purely practical purposes is not beneficial to either practitioners or researchers (Jönsson & Lukka, 2007; Lukka & Suomala, 2014; Baard & Dumay, 2018). Similarly, without theoretical relevance, prestigious academic journals will not publish IVR studies, and scholars will continue to question IVR's legitimacy as a methodology. Hence, we discuss IVR and theory next.

IVR and Theory

Baard (2010) argues for IVR to be a "standalone" methodology on the basis that IVR is underpinned by IVR philosophy and intervention theory (see Chapter 4) and is operationalised by an Interventionist Research Framework (see Chapter 5) adapted from Rothman and Thomas' (1994) IVR framework used in social work. She asserts that, without these three pillars, IVR has questionable scientific value, legitimacy, and capacity for utility in future accounting research. Some criticise IVR for not integrating theory to the same extent as other non-interventionist approaches.

Theory is critical to IVR because it underpins everything: the research question, the problem being researched, intervention design and construction (i.e., will it work?), implementation (i.e., how does it work in real-life settings?), and evaluation (i.e., why does it work?)(Gitlin & Czaja, 2016; Bruhn & Rebach, 2007). Gitlin and Czaja (2016) argue that interventions without a theoretical foundation will not advance a researcher's understanding of change. Nor will it show how and why an intervention achieved specific outcomes, the means through which it was effective, or the causes of its failure. In other words, interventions grounded in theory are more effective than those without. Fleury and Sidani (2012) state that theory and theoretical frameworks are essential for IVR because it helps researchers to understand: a) the complexity of the situation under research; b) the factors causing the problem and, therefore, the problem itself; c) the nature of the intervention required to solve the problem, including its design; d) the inputs and conditions needed to implement and operationalise the intervention; e) the mechanisms underlying the transformative change processes that the intervention is likely to produce; and f) why the expected outcomes did or did not occur. Operationalising an intervention refers to "activities or strategies that constitute the intervention; they represent what is to be done and what is necessary, sufficient, and optimal to produce the desired outcomes, to create change and/or desired outcomes" (Fleury & Sidani, 2012, p. 24). Bruhn and Rebach (2007) argue that practice influences how theories are constructed and developed, and that theory and practice together ameliorate social problems by offering "the possibility of social change" (p. 9).

Given the need for an IVR study to have a theoretical foundation and for accounting IVR to deliver a theoretical contribution, we must revisit what theory is. Corley and Gioia (2011, p. 12) define theory as "a statement of concepts and their interrelationships that shows how and/or why a phenomenon occurs". Kerlinger (1986, p. 9) defines theory as "a set of interrelated constructs, definitions, and propositions that present a systematic view of phenomena by specifying relations among variables, with the purpose of explaining or predicting phenomena". By these definitions, at a basic level, theory organises, describes, explains, and predicts why a phenomenon exists or why it exists in the way that it does. In more practical terms, theory refers to a methodical way of understanding events, behaviours, experiences, and situations by applying a series of explanatory or predictive interrelated concepts, meanings, and schemes.

Theories differ based on scope, levels of abstraction, and specificity. Further, they can be categorised into one of three levels: broad, mid-range, and micro (Gitlin & Czaja, 2016). Llewellyn (2003) considers "what counts as theory" in qualitative accounting research by identifying and examining five levels of theorisation. She starts with metaphor theories (Level 1), then progresses to differentiation theories (Level 2), concept theories (Level 3), and theorising settings (Level 4), ending with theorising structures (Level 5). The literature seemingly does not offer consensus on the different levels of theories, nor which theories should be included at each level, but scholars are offered insights into different forms or types of theories for use in research. We have opted to follow Llewellyn (2003) and, for each theory level, we: a) provide a definition; b) identify the sorts of empirical issues that are likely to be examined; and c) show the different methodologies associated with each level. These criteria can be used as a way forward for accounting IVR to ensure and advance its theoretical contributions, consistent with IVR's duality of output.

Grand Theories

Beginning with the broadest level of theory (Gitlin & Czaja, 2016), sometimes referred to as context-free grand theories, which occurs in the "world of ideas" rather than the "world of practice" (Llewellyn, 2003, p. 676). For example, critical theory is an example of a grand theory. Grand theories enjoy extremely high levels of abstraction, emphasising structural, impersonal, and large-scale aspects of the social domain, such as social institutions, culture, hierarchies of class, and the distribution of power and resources (Gitlin & Czaja, 2016; Llewellyn, 2003). These theories normally do not have definitions, and the relationships among constructs and propositions are vague. They typically emphasise that social conditions (i.e., external or macro conditions) influence social action and attempt to explain things in terms of a wider framework of concepts. Snyder (2009, p. 227) asserts that social action is grounded in Kurt Lewin's approach to social research and defines social action as "real people engaging in real actions on behalf of real causes". He views social action as an individual phenomenon involving actions of individuals where they reflect on their own values, motives, and personalities. Additionally, as a social phenomenon that groups, organisations, or communities engage in to collectively perform activities to serve the greater good. The actions of research participants are explained with regards to external social forces. Thus, individual motivations and reasons for their actions or endeavours are not investigated or considered to be important. Similarly, organisational issues, group interactions, and collective achievements are not depicted as contexts for action. Llewellyn (2003) states that the structural phenomena associated with social realms are not directly observable in interviews, focus groups, or generally through qualitative research methods. Hence, grand theories typically rely on rational arguments rather than empirical realism. Llewellyn (2003) argues that, for this reason, grand theories are unlikely to receive attention in the accounting discipline. Accordingly, we concentrate our discourse on micro-level and mid-range theories, as discussed next.

Micro-Level Theories

Micro-level or situation-specific theories have a narrow scope and level of abstraction and tend to focus on specific populations, fields, or phenomena (Gitlin & Czaja, 2016). Theorists at this level normally emphasise that their frameworks concern the social interactions of individuals or small structures, such as families, couples, and peer groups (Bruhn & Rebach, 2007). Empirical issues relating to micro-level theories include examining reasons, actions, motivation, and social processes (Llewellyn, 2003). According to Gitlin and Czaja (2016), theories applicable at this level include social exchange theory (i.e., the values of benefits and costs of social relationships), social phenomenology (i.e., the role of human consciousness in constructing social situations), and symbolic interactionism (i.e., contemplates relationships or patterns of interaction among people in society). Using our interpretation of Gitlin and Czaja's (2016) micro-level theories, we view Llewellyn's (2003) theories on metaphor and differentiation as being reasonably consistent with micro-level theories. In metaphor theories, the metaphor represents a person's "structural form of experience" (Llewellyn, 2003, p. 667). It means people engage with, organise, understand, and apply meaning to the world they inhabit by fashioning a picture of their world that gives their life, their organisation, and their experiences meaning and importance. However, differentiation theories describe how people relate to the world through dualities. For instance, subjective/objective; politics/rebellion; bureaucracies/clans; thinking/doing; and relevance lost/relevance gained (Llewellyn, 2003). Here, people provide order to the world and create meaning and importance by establishing contrasts. The insight is that metaphors are the point of origin for concepts, whereas dualities divide and categorise concepts.

Micro-level theories may also be associated with ethnographic studies originating from anthropology, as ethnography aims to encapsulate the beliefs, values, and motivations of research participants via researcher immersion in the field. It seeks the "native's point of view" and attempts to find "thick descriptions" of everyday life (Llewellyn, 2003, p. 692; Jönsson & Lukka, 2007). Consistent with Gitlin and Czaja (2016), Llewellyn (2003) states that ethnographies are theorised through both metaphors and differentiation.

Mid-Range Theories

Mid-range theories can be derived from grand theories and are composed of definitions, defined constructs, and propositions that may be testable (Gitlin & Czaja, 2016). Concepts are instruments used in social science and social practice to "observe and represent the world and to act and work in it" (Llewellyn, 2003, p. 672). When new concepts come to the fore, they represent diverse ways of thinking and acting in the world. Additionally, concepts are critical to practice, which is one of the main linkages between people and social structures. Hence, because practice is theorised through concepts, mid-range theories encompass theories of practice. Following our interpretation of Gitlin and Czaja's (2016) mid-range theories, we view Llewellyn's (2003) concepts and context-based theorising structures consistent with mid-range theories. Concept theories observe social practice to formulate ideas that represent the world or that work and act in it, such as accountability, decision-making, and power (Llewellyn, 2003). Empirical issues covered by concept theories include agency, which is about how things are accomplished in practice (Llewellyn, 2003). For example, a study may explore how people use resources to effect change, solve a problem, or enhance their competencies with organisations as the empirical unit of analysis. So, although ethnography is mostly associated with micro-level theory, it can be a more suitable choice than concept theory when examining individual or group beliefs (Llewellyn, 2003). That said, Llewellyn (2003) argues that ethnomethodology relates to concept theories because its domain centres on 'doing' instead of 'thinking'. It involves exposing the expectations and implicit rules that regulate ordinary life and examining social orders, membership, and accountability.

Context-based theorising links concepts and differentiations to create a cognitive framework, i.e., a schema, that helps to organise and interpret information. At this level, it means focusing on specific social, organisational, or individual phenomena in situ, such as social loafing in teams, emancipation in organisations, or organisational conformance to a government policy. The goal is to elicit an understanding of the interplay between the phenomena and the social settings where human activity occurs (Llewellyn, 2003). Hence, although this level of theory is all about practices, the social conditions in which these practices occur are not ignored. This is consistent with Lewin's idea of field theory, where he emphasises the need to consider the social conditions surrounding the enquiry when undertaking IVR (Cartwright, 1951). As a case in point, accounting is a technical practice, but it is deeply embedded in a social system that cannot be separated from practice.

Context-based theories that are frequently used in accounting research include contingency, institutional, legitimacy, and resource-dependency theory. The types of empirical issues likely to be associated with Level 4 theorising is where researchers examine the social organisation of relationships between individuals, organisations, and the communities in which they operate. When investigating phenomena within a real-life context, Yin (2017), promotes direct contact with research participants through field research. However, Llewellyn (2003) stipulates that case studies focused on individuals or specific events are related to micro-level theories and concept theories. Conversely, case studies concerned with the "conditions and constraints under which social action is organised" are related to context-based theories (p. 693). So which theory do we use for accounting IVR?

French *et al.* (2012) state there are no criteria or guidance that outlines how researchers can select theories or conceptual frameworks to guide IVR. Yet Gitlin and Czaja (2016) state that behavioural IVR will typically need to rely on more than one theoretical framework as interventions are potentially multifaceted. Additionally, researchers may need to address previously unspecified needs or complex problems, situations, and behaviours. When using more than one theory, Gitlin and Czaja caution researchers to provide a transparent account of how their chosen theories link together and how each theory contributes to the intervention overall.

In the context of accounting IVR, this is important because the extant literature on how theories are applied and evaluated as the foundation of an intervention is extremely limited (Fleury & Sidani, 2012). Given scholarly concerns that IVR may not consider theoretical aspects or that practical aspects outweigh theory, we think it is important to emphasise and be explicit on this point. Table 1.1 outlines a series of questions that may be helpful to accounting scholars when evaluating the potential of theories to suit their IVR research.

In the IVR accounting literature, the role of theory is acknowledged, and persuasive rationales for theoretical relevance prevail (Lukka & Vinnari, 2017; Baard, 2010; Malmi & Granlund, 2009). Another way of looking at the levels of theories is to view them as 'theories with status', whose role is to help explain accounting issues of interest to accounting scholars. Theories with status are "applied to explain causes, effects and various interrelationships" of accounting, and they emanate from

Table 1.1 What Theory Should I Use?

What theories have been used in prior accounting research, including those based on IVR?

Which theories are conceptually clear, which means they can be reliably measured?

Which theories have conceptual definitions that are consistent with your underlying research assumptions?

Which theories may inform you about the complexity of the situation to be studied and to what extent?

Which theory explains the research problem in the least complex way?

To what extent are the theoretical concepts relevant to the study metrics?

Which theories can inform you about the nature of the intervention required to remedy the issue?

What theory or theoretical concepts in your study have already been examined through IVR?

Which theories can help you design a useful and effective intervention?

What theories have prior research identified that specify the critical inputs and conditions needed for operationalising and implementing interventions?

What theories address the change desired from your intervening?

What theories have theoretical concepts that help to explain change resulting from an intervention?

Does prior research hold any theoretical claim consistent with evidence that explains why a change did or did not occur in your IVR study?

What theories may explain why the expected change did or did not occur and to what extent?

To what extent does the theory(s) generate contributions to our current knowledge, novel research questions, and ideas for future advancements?

the economics, organisation theory, sociology, and psychology disciplines (Malmi & Granlund, 2009, p. 602). Examples include agency, structuration, actor-network, and goal-setting theory (Malmi & Granlund, 2009). Mid-level theories, specifically concepts that may be construed as theories of practice, constitute "a map or recipe or instructions manual which provides [a] means by which we can do things in the world or cope with events" (Sayer, 1992, p. 113). Llewellyn (2003) also discusses 'theories with status' and 'theories of practice' and observes that, in the social sciences, there is a dearth of practice theories that show what and how research results in accomplishments. In her discourse, she notes action research as a potential methodology for implementing concept theories; this potential has not been wholly realised. Llewellyn (2003) refers to Lewin's (1946) original intentions for his 'type of action research' as a research methodology to solve pressing social problems and stimulate change by bringing both researchers and participants together to set the research agenda. She also links action research to theories of practice. When discussing IVR or any of its variations, the issue of consulting always comes to the fore. Llewellyn (2003) finds that the perceptions of a correlation between IVR and consultancy cannot be traced to Lewin's original vision of the methodology. Lewin's intent was to initiate change through inquiry into important and urgent problems arising from WWII, which places action research squarely in the realm of solving societal problems, not the problems of one or a few entities (Dickens & Watkins, 1999).

Reflecting on the current argument for accounting researchers to generate theoretically informed IVR, we find that there is limited use or even acknowledgement of intervention theory (IVT). Lewin's untimely passing in 1947 meant that there was no opportunity to debate his action research views with his peers, leaving his contemporaries to produce varying interpretations of his work and no unifying theory (Peters & Robinson, 1984; Dickens & Watkins, 1999). Argyris (1970) developed IVT to offer methodological guidance on conducting IVR with the aim of supporting, understanding and explaining social action, agency, and change (see Chapter 4). Following the theoretical arguments presented by Gitlin and Czaja (2016) and Llewellyn (2003), we view IVT as a theory of practice (see also Baard, 2010) and argue for IVT's potential as an umbrella theory of IVR (see Baard & Dumay, 2018). IVT is not a new theory, but we posit that its rare use in accounting IVR positions interventionist researchers to test and refine IVT to intensify IVR's theoretical relevance. Theory must drive the practice of IVR just a 'theories with status' must underpin theorising in the accounting discipline and its socio-technical role in society. Baard and Dumay (2018) call for accounting researchers engaging in IVR to: a) procure visibility of the theoretical potential of their IVR project early in the research design; b) theoretically problematise experiences and events; c) construct theoretically motivated research questions and informed interventions; d) theoretically frame the practical outcomes of the research; and e) use IVT to theoretically guide IVR. Accordingly, accounting interventionist researchers have opportunities to provide theoretical contributions to theories with status and intervention theory—these theories of practice have potential to be used and developed in an upward spiral.

In Summation

IVR is an exciting methodology aimed at solving real-life problems for a range of social systems and the people that inhabit them. It is about learning what strategies, practices, policies, and technologies work best to produce outcomes that make a difference in what matters most to researchers and the social systems under research. IVR is complex and the research process risky and challenging. Yet, research participants benefit from being involved with an IVR project by experiencing outcomes such as positive social change, emancipation, learning, problem-solving, enhanced decision-making, and knowledge development. Researchers, placed in the shoes of the practitioner, generate knowledge and develop insights into how social systems grow, develop, and create value for their futures. The 'good' of IVR is explored next in Chapter 2.

References

Adelman, C. (1993). Kurt Lewin and the origins of action research. *Educational Action Research*, 1(1), 7–24.

Argyris, C. (1970). *Intervention theory and method: A behavioural science view*. Reading, MA: Addison-Wesley Publishing Company.

Argyris, C., Putnam, R., & McLain Smith, D. (1985). *Action science—Concepts, methods, and skills for research and intervention*. San Francisco, CA: Jossey-Bass Inc. Publishers.

Baard, V.C. (2010). A critical view of interventionist research. *Qualitative Research in Accounting and Management*, 7(1), 13–45.

Baard, V.C. & Dumay, J. (2018). Interventionist research in accounting: Reflections on the good, the bad and the ugly. *Accounting and Finance*, Advance online publication. https://doi.org/10.1111/acfi.12409

Baldvinsdottir, G.F., Mitchell, F. & Nörreklit, H. (2010). Issues in the relationship between theory and practice in management accounting. *Management Accounting Research*, 21, 79–82.

Bargal, D. (2006). Personal and intellectual influences leading to Lewin's paradigm of action research. *Action Research*, 4(4), 367–388.

Boog, B.W.M. (2003). The emancipatory character of action research, its history and the present state of the art. *Journal of Community & Applied Social Psychology*, 13, 426–438.

Bruhn, J.G. & Rebach, H.M. (2007). *Sociological practice: Intervention and social change*. New York, NY: Springer Science.

Burnes, B. & Cooke, B. (2013). Kurt Lewin's field theory: A review and re-evaluation. *International Journal of Management Reviews*, 15, 408–425.

Campanale, C., Cinquini, L., & Tenucci, A. (2014). Time driven activity-based costing to improve transparency and decision making in healthcare. *Qualitative Research in Accounting & Management*, 11, 165–186.

Carkhuff, R.R. (1983). *Sources of human productivity*. Amherst, MA: Human Resource Development Press.

Cartwright, D. (Ed.). (1951). *Field theory in social science: Selected theoretical papers by Kurt Lewin*. London, UK: Social Science Paperbacks.

Chiucchi, M.S. (2013). Intellectual capital accounting in action: Enhancing learning through interventionist research. *Journal of Intellectual Capital*, 14, 48–68.

Corley, K.G. & Gioia, D.A. (2011). Building theory about theory building: What constitutes a theoretical contribution. *Academy of Management Review*, 36(1), 12–32.

Cullen, J., Tsamenyi, M., Bernon, M., & Gorst, J. (2013). Reverse logistics in the UK retail sector: A case study of the role of management accounting in driving organisational change. *Management Accounting Research*, 24, 212–227.

Dickens, L. & Watkins, K. (1999). Action research: Rethinking Lewin. *Management Learning*, 30, 127–140.

Dumay, J. & Baard, V. (2017). An introduction to interventionist research in accounting. In Z. Hoque, L.D. Parker, M.A. Covaleski, & K. Haynes (Eds.), *The Routledge companion to qualitative accounting research methods* (pp. 265–283). New York, NY: Routledge.

Edmondson, A.C. (2011). Crossing boundaries to investigate problems in the field: An approach to useful research. In S.A. Mohrman & E.E. Lawler III (Eds.), *Useful research: Advancing theory and practice*. Retrieved from: https://learning.oreilly.com/library/view/useful-research/9781605096018/xhtml/ch02.html

Evans, E., Burritt, R., & Guthrie, J. (2011). *Bridging the gap between academic accounting research and professional practice*. Sydney, Australia: Institute of Chartered Accountants Australia.

Fleury, J. & Sidani, S. (2012). Using theory to guide intervention research. In B.M. Melnyk & D. Morrison-Beedy (Eds.), *Intervention research: Designing, conducting, analysing, and funding* (pp. 11–36). New York, NY: Springer Publishing Company LLC.

Foster, M. (1972). An introduction to the theory and practice of action research in work organisations. *Human Relations*, 25(6), 529–556.

Fraser, M.W., Richman, J.M., Galinsky, M.J., & Day, S.H. (2009). *Intervention research*. New York, NY: Oxford University Press.

French, S.D., Green, S.E., O'Connor, D.A., McKenzie, J.E., Francis, J.J., Michie, S., . . . Grimshaw, J.M. (2012). Developing theory-informed behaviour change interventions to implement evidence into practice: A systematic approach using the theoretical domains framework. *Implementation Science*, 7(38). Retrieved from: https://implementationscience.biomedcentral.com/articles/10.1186/1748-5908-7-38?report=reader

Gitlin, L.N. & Czaja, S.J. (2016). *Behaviourial intervention research: Designing, evaluating, and implementing*. New York, NY: Springer Publishing Company LLC.

Greenwood, D.J. & Levin, M. (2007). *Introduction to action research: Social research for social change*. Thousand Oaks, CA: Sage Publications.

Huault, I., Perret, V., & Spicer, A. (2014). Beyond macro-and micro-emancipation: Rethinking emancipation in organization studies. *Organization*, 21, 22–49.

Jönsson, S. & Lukka, K. (2007). There and back again: Doing interventionist research in management accounting. In C.S. Chapman, A.G. Hopwood, & M.S. Shields (Eds.), *Handbook of management accounting research* (Vol. 1, pp. 373–397). Oxford, UK: Elsevier.

Kerlinger, F.N. (1986). *Foundations of behavioural research* (3rd ed.). New York, NY: Holt, Rinehart & Winston.

Kleiner, R. & Maguire, F. (1986). Lewin's sphere of influence from Berlin. In E. Stivers & S. Wheelan (Eds.), *The Lewin legacy: Field theory in current practice* (pp. 12–20). New York, NY: Springer-Verlag.

Lewin, K. (1943). Forces behind food habits and methods of change. *Bulletin of the National Research Council*, 108, 35–65.

Lewin, K. (1945a). The research center for group dynamics at the Massachusetts Institute of Technology. *Sociometry*, 8, 126–136.

Lewin, K. (1945b/1997). Conduct, knowledge and acceptance of new values. In G.W. Lewin (Ed.), *Resolving social conflicts & field theory in social science* (pp. 48–55). Washington, DC: American Psychological Association.

Lewin, K. (1946). Action research and minority problems. *Journal of Social Issues*, 11, 34–46.

Lewin, K. (1947a). Frontiers in group dynamics: Concept, method and reality in social science: Social equilibria and social change. *Human Relations*, 1(1), 5–41.

Lewin, K. (1947b). Frontiers in group dynamics: ll. Channels of group life: Social planning and action research. *Human Relations*, 1(2), 143–153.

Llewellyn, S. (2003). What counts as "theory" in qualitative management and accounting research? Introducing five levels of theorising. *Accounting, Auditing & Accountability Journal*, 16(4), 662–708.

Lukka, K. & Suomala, P. (2014). Relevant interventionist research: Balancing three intellectual virtues. *Accounting and Business Research*, 44(2), 204–220.

Lukka, K. & Vinnari, E. (2017). Combining action-network theory with interventionist research: Present state and future potential. *Accounting, Auditing & Accountability Journal*, 30, 720–753.

Malmi, T. & Granlund, M. (2009). In search of management accounting theory. *European Accounting Review*, 18(3), 597–620.

Markides, C. (2007). In search of ambidextrous professors. *Academy of Management Journal*, 50, 762–768.

Melnyk, B.M. & Morrison-Beedy, D. (2012). Setting the stage for intervention research: The "so-what" factor. In B.M. Melnyk & D. Morrison-Beedy (Eds.), *Intervention research: Designing, conducting, analysing, and funding* (pp. 1–10). New York, NY: Springer Publishing Company LLC.

Merchant, K.A. (2012). Making management accounting research more useful. *Pacific Accounting Review*, 24(3), 334–356.

Mitchell, F. (2002). Research and practice in management accounting: Improving integration and communication. *European Accounting Review*, 11(2), 277–289.

Mullen, E.J. (1994). Design of social intervention. In J. Rothman & E.J. Thomas (Eds.), *Intervention research: Design and development for human service* (pp. 163–193). Binghamton, NY: Haworth Press.

Neu, D., Cooper, D.J., & Everett, J. (2001). Critical accounting interventions. *Critical Perspectives on Accounting*, 12, 735–762.

Parker, L.D. (2014). Qualitative perspectives: Through a methodological lens. *Qualitative Research in Accounting & Management*, 11, 13–28.

Parker, L.D. & Roffey, B.H. (1997). Methodological themes: Back to the drawing board: Revisiting grounded theory and the everyday accountant's and manager's reality. *Accounting, Auditing & Accountability Journal*, 10(2), 212–247.

Peters, M. & Robinson, V. (1984). The origins and status of action research. *The Journal of Applied Behavioural Science*, 20(2), 113–124.

Rothman, J. & Thomas, E.J. (Eds.). (1994). *Intervention research: Design and development for human service*. Binghamton, NY: Haworth Press.

Sandelands, L.E. (1990). What is so practical about theory? Lewin revisited. *Journal for the Theory of Social Behaviour*, 20(3), 235–262.

Sayer, A. (1992). *Method in social science: A realist approach*. London, UK: Routledge.

Scapens, R.W. (2008). Seeking the relevance of interpretive research: A contribution to the polyphonic debate. *Critical Perspectives on Accounting*, 19, 915–919.

Snyder, M. (2009). In the footsteps of Kurt Lewin: Practical theorising, action research, and the psychology of social action. *Journal of Social Issues*, 65(1), 225–245.

Sweetman, J., Leach, C.W., Spears, R., Pratto, F., & Saab, R. (2013). I have a dream: A typology of social change goals. *Journal of Social and Political Psychology*, 1, 293–320.

Thomas, E.J. & Rothman, J. (1994). An integrative perspective on intervention research. In J. Rothman & E.J. Thomas (Eds.), *Intervention research: Design and development for human service* (pp. 3–23). Binghamton, NY: Haworth Press.

Yin, R.K. (2017). *Case study research: Design and methods* (6th ed.). Thousand Oaks, CA: Sage Publications.

2 The 'Good' of IVR— Relevance and Remedy

The 'good' of IVR is evident in three main constituents embodying the potential value of IVR that make it a desirable approach to undertake accounting research. First, IVR has the capacity to produce research with theoretical, practical, and societal relevance due to its unique duality of both theoretical and practical output and its capacity to effect social change. Second, IVR is a methodology underpinned by Lewin's governing principles informed by his research and sound philosophical and theoretical foundations, mobilising it to 'scientifically' deliver research relevance. Third, IVR's theoretical foundations are operationalised using a practical interventionist research framework providing methodological guidance on conducting IVR. These three constituents make IVR capable of producing accounting research with relevance and offering a remedy for the research-practice gap.

Two of the most relentless and contentious debates in the accounting literature centre on two ongoing accounting problems: accounting research relevance and the research-practice gap. But what does relevance mean and for whom does research relevance matter? Accounting research relevance is multifaceted. Hence, we discuss the different meanings and perspectives on research relevance. We also explore the possible reasons for the gap between research and practice. With this background in place, we turn to the 'good' of IVR and its utility as a potential remedy for these two ongoing problems.

The Meaning and Importance of the Relevance of Accounting Research

Accounting is a social science with many diverse sub-disciplines—for instance, financial accounting and reporting, management accounting, corporate accounting, international accounting, forensic accounting, sustainability accounting, accounting information systems, taxation, auditing and assurance, corporate governance, professional ethics, and more. However, Quagli *et al.* (2016) refine these many streams of research into three broad areas: financial accounting, management accounting, and non-financial accounting. No matter the division, accounting research is an applied social science because it examines, critiques, and develops "technologies and technical practices used by accounting practitioners in social and organisational settings" (Parker *et al.*, 2011, p. 5), such as accounting standards, policies, budgets, costs, and performance. We digress briefly to clarify what we mean by the term 'practitioner' because based on our review of the literature there is ambiguity surrounding its meaning. Leisenring and Johnson (1994) refer to a practitioner as any "accountant other than an academic" (p. 74). Quagli *et al.* (2016, p. 33) state the term can refer to "public and private standard setters, consulting and auditing firms, developers of accounting software, private professionals, . . . individual managers involved with accounting". We, therefore, consider practitioners to include management and financial accountants; accountants focused on information systems, sustainability, international, forensic, corporate social responsibility, environmental, taxation, and other specialist forms of accounting; auditors; and managers with a significant involvement in accounting. We exclude managers with a minimal involvement in accounting, e.g., customer service managers, logistics, and supply chain managers.

Some scholars argue that the primary aim of accounting research is to improve practice or provide new insights for practice, rather than critiquing or explaining it (e.g., Ittner & Larcker, 2002). Moreover, they assert that, to clarify the impact of their research, accounting scholars should establish clear links between research output and its benefits to practice and society. This need for impact, or influence as it is often called, has led to rigorous scholarly debates on whether and how to make accounting research more relevant. Much of the dialogue distils 'research relevance' down to its practical relevance for accounting practice, as measured through its scientific rigour and applicability. This makes sense given accounting research is an applied discipline and, therefore, we argue that practical relevance should be one of its distinguishing features. But that begs the question: What does 'relevant' and 'relevance' mean in the accounting context?

The Meaning of Research Relevance in Accounting

Debates over definitions and perceptions of the terms 'relevant research', 'research relevance', and 'research usefulness' in the literature are rife (e.g., Tucker & Parker, 2019; Butler *et al.*, 2015; Evans *et al.*, 2011). But relevant and relevance are among those overused, catch-all terms that are used ambiguously, interchangeably, and typically without precision (e.g., Tucker & Parker, 2019; Rautiainen *et al.*, 2017; Broadbent, 2016; Kieser *et al.*, 2015; Butler *et al.*, 2015; ter Bogt & Van Helden, 2012; Quattrone, 2009; Nicolai & Seidl, 2010). As Nicolai and Seidl (2010) state, the ambiguous nature of relevance is problematic because, without a clear understanding of what relevance means, how can we understand the fundamental debate, let alone the conflicting associations between science and practice, or how the various notions of relevance relate to each other. Therefore, if IVR is to be relevant, have relevance, or be useful, we need to be specific about what these terms mean to IVR.

Leaving usefulness aside for the moment, first, it is important to note that relevant is an adjective and relevance is a noun. The *Macquarie Encyclopaedic Dictionary* (2011, p. 1051) defines relevant as "bearing upon or connected with or to the purpose, or pertinent to the matter in hand". We interpret this as meaning: A is relevant to B when A makes a difference to B. In the accounting context, this means research is relevant to practice when it solves a real-world practice problem. In IVR, this translates to: intervention A is relevant to social system B when intervention A solves problem(s) and produces change in social system B. Academic research that frees individuals to solve future problems for themselves means it is relevant to the social system they inhabit. Butler *et al.* (2015) suggest that research is relevant when it has academic rigour and produces 'actionable knowledge', which, by their definition, means knowledge that can be transferred to practitioners. Citing the definition given by one of their respondents, Tucker and Parker (2019) concur with this interpretation, claiming relevant research "is research that makes a difference by delivering economic, societal benefits, creating new knowledge and informing public policy". Therefore, accounting research is relevant when its outcomes can be transformed into knowledge actionable by those in the social system that has valuable or important benefits or produces positive change.

From a slightly different standpoint, the *Oxford Advanced Learner's Dictionary* (2019) defines relevant as "having ideas that are valuable and useful to people in their lives and work". Beer's (2011) explanation falls closer to this definition with the argument that actionable knowledge should offer guidance to managers about how to approach "solving organisational effectiveness, commitment and performance problems". The correlation between research being relevant and research offering ideas and important benefits to a social system is still present, but this definition also introduces the notion of usefulness, discussed further in this section.

So relevant is an adjective and relevance is a noun but, beyond grammar, is there any real difference between the two? Surely, it's reasonable to use these words interchangeably based on the syntax of a sentence. Scaratti *et al.* (2017) do not agree, stating that relevance is an outcome of research that encompasses collaborative processes, generates conversation between academics and practitioners, and co-generates knowledge. Hence, relevance is associated with the research process. Scaratti *et al.* (2017) define relevance as issues of importance, such as problems, knowledge requirements for resolving problems, or understanding the value assigned to context in a practitioner's daily work experiences. Tucker and Parker (2014, p. 105) frame the notion of relevance as "its use or usefulness to 'practice' or 'practitioners'" (see also Lukka & Suomala, 2014). However, they later revise their definition to "enquiry that informs professional, business and government practice" (Tucker & Parker, 2019). Leisenring and Johnson (1994) state that neither relevance nor relevant are appropriate terms to use for accounting research. Rather, 'useful' is a far better term. Using financial accounting standards to justify their stance, they speak of decision-makers and how accounting information must extend beyond the reliable and relevant to include the understandable (International Accounting Standards Board, 2018). Theirs is an obvious but, arguably, too often neglected maxim: accounting information that is not understandable is not useful. Hence, we further explore the idea of information or knowledge generated by accounting research as useful rather than having relevance.

The *Macquarie Encyclopaedic Dictionary* (2011, p. 1355) defines the adjective useful as "serving some purpose, serviceable, advantageous, helpful, or of good effect, practical use as for doing work or producing material results". Beer (2011) states that actionable knowledge is useful because it helps managers solve problems. The inference is that, when accounting scholars transfer actionable knowledge effectively, it (should) produce material results like solving problems, imparting learning, or making a significant contribution to the greater good of the social system. Additionally, research is useful when it informs practice and mobilises accounting technologies for 'good effect'.

Among the other scholars with views on useful research and research relevance, Unerman and O'Dwyer (2010) describe useful as practice research that provides long-term business and societal benefits or informs the development of new accounting practices to meet changing business and societal needs. They cite several historical failures of accounting, such as Enron and WorldCom, to demonstrate by way of absence and failure how important accounting and accounting practices are to society (Unerman & O'Dwyer, 2010. For practitioners, Malmi and Granlund (2009) suggest that accounting research is useful for analysing the performance implications of organisational decisions. Mitchell (2002) indicates that accounting research is useful when it informs, develops, and improves practice through effective communication between researchers and practitioners, and when it actualises successful solutions to solving practical problems (see also van Helden & Northcott, 2010). Edmondson (2011) states that for research to be useful, the problem under study must be compelling and consequential to people in organisations experiencing the problem. Naturally, the research should therefore help to solve the problem. Beer (2011) argues that focusing research on a social system problem is critical to producing relevant and useful knowledge. Bolton and Stolcis (2003) state that useful scholarly research should satisfy two criteria. First, the outcome of academic research must improve someone's understanding of a social system, and it must lead to practice improvement. Second, the outcome of academic research must produce theoretical contributions and incrementally contribute to the extant body of accounting knowledge. Here, we find the notion of useful interesting because it is consistent with IVR's aim to solve social system problems and its premise of duality of output. Further, this leads us to what usefulness means in the context of theory.

For scholars, knowledge is useful when research contextualises the extant literature and prevailing theories or when it provides a deeper understanding of situations that prompts the need for a new or revised theory. Yet theory for theory's sake is of little use. Theory must apply to practice to be useful. This requires researchers to go into the field and construct an understanding of the social system and its influencing variables in situ. It requires a collaboration between scholars and practitioners and between scholars of many disciplines to draw diverse perspectives, expertise, and novel insights into the phenomena under study. All these things increase the opportunity to produce actionable knowledge. Beer (2011) argues that working collaboratively with non-academics, i.e., practitioners, managers, and other professionals, is critical to positioning scholars to produce useful, actionable research. Moreover, collaboration with non-academics leads to important conversations about issues in the field, which can draw attention to both known and unforeseen practical issues, as well as contribute to richer theoretical descriptions.

In summary, we find that accounting scholars use the terms relevant research, research relevance, and useful research interchangeably. Each term enjoys a subtle difference, but we acknowledge that interpretations of their meanings may result in overlaps, thus creating difficulties in disentangling the meaning of each term. Scholars produce relevant accounting research when: a) it makes a difference to the social system and its actors by offering valuable ideas, solving a problem, or producing positive change; and b) knowledge is transformed into actionable knowledge and transferred to non-academics. Accounting research has relevance when it informs professional and organisational practices of any form outside of academe, or it is considered useful to practice. Accounting research is useful when it: a) occurs in the field in collaboration with non-academics with a focus on social system problems; b) helps managers to implement solutions to problems that produce 'good' effects; c) meets societal and business needs; and d) produces theoretical contributions and mobilises practice improvement.

Research Relevance: Engagement and Impact

Tucker and Parker (2019) find that relevance is a multidimensional concept and that it is challenging to differentiate between terms such as 'engagement' and 'impact'. Within the context of research relevance, a broad definition of engagement is "working collaboratively and in participation with non-academics". The Australian Research Council defines engagement as "as the interaction between researchers and research end-users outside of academia, for the mutually beneficial transfer of knowledge, technologies, methods or resources" (ARC, 2019). These definitions of engagement are consistent with Lewin's (1946, 1947) IVR principle of collaboration, essential to the methodology of IVR.

Impact is formally defined as "the influence or effect exerted by a new idea, concept or ideology" (Macquarie Encyclopaedic Dictionary, 2011, p. 619). Again, Tucker and Parker (2019) take a literal interpretation that impact is the capacity for research to effect change in policy, practice, or theory, or is a consequence or outcome of the research. Scaratti *et al.* (2017) define impact as the transformative aspects of knowledge generated from research that may lead to change. We view impact as the extent to which actionable knowledge effectively transfers from scholars to non-academics, and the extent to which actionable knowledge produces 'good' not 'bad' material results for social systems.

The concept of impact is pervasive in organisations that fund research (Broadbent, 2016). Statements by the Australian Minister of Education (Birmingham, 2016) and various Australian government papers (e.g., Watt, 2015; Department of Education and Training, 2015) have highlighted a shift in attention towards the relevance and impact of university research. Many governments measure research impacts, but each tends to define impact in different ways. For example, the United Kingdom's Research Excellence Framework (REF) defines impact as "an effect on, change or benefit to the economy, society, culture, public policy or services, health, the environment or quality of life, beyond academia" Broadbent (2016, p. 19). Sweden, Denmark, Austria, the Netherlands, Germany, and Canada measure impact on similar criteria (Parker *et al.*, 2011). Whereas, Australia's Excellence in Research (ERA) currently defines impact as "the contribution that research makes to the economy, society, environment or culture, beyond the contribution to academic research" (ARC, 2019).

As part of the National Innovation and Science Agenda, the Australian government has committed to investing approximately $3.5 billion in university research. It also intends to introduce a national engagement and impact assessment scheme that includes outcomes beyond academia (Cooper & Guthrie, 2017). The hope is that the new national evaluation system will demonstrate how universities are translating their research into economic, social, and environmental impacts (ARC, 2019). Unlike the past, publication points will no longer be a key driver of what and who gets funded and what and who does not. In the future, engagement, impact, and research income on its economic and social benefits will be the most likely criteria for government funding (Martin-Sardesai *et al.*, 2019).

These research management systems are the lifeblood of academia. They rate and rank the quality of research across universities, faculties, and departments, which typically becomes the only benchmark of an institution's reputation. According to Broadbent (2016), the UK's REF bases its ratings on two main factors: 'reach', meaning the extent and diversity of the research's influence on social systems and their beneficiaries; and 'significance', which is the extent of influence over policy and practice. Although many issues surround impact, one of the main issues is that impact is more evident and tangible for disciplines such as physics, medicine, or engineering, whereas, for accounting, the impact may be less obvious (Quagli *et al.*, 2016). Given that impact is such a critical consideration in funding decisions and an academic's reputation, remuneration, and career prospects, accounting scholars have to work harder or against what's necessarily good for the discipline to meet a universal definition of impact or risk to avoid being penalised for not measuring up (Martin-Sardesai *et al.*, 2017). In sum, given the nature of IVR, we view the methodology to help accounting scholars achieve research relevance through engagement and impact across a range of social systems.

Research Relevance: For Whom?

A final aspect related to understanding what relevant or relevance means in accounting research is asking the question for whom the research is relevant beyond academics and practitioners (ter Bogt & van Helden, 2012). We believe that this is important for understanding why the theoretical, practical, and societal perspectives of research relevance are all different and, fundamentally, why a research-practice gap prevails. Tucker and Parker (2019) state that practitioners (see our definition) are just one group of knowledge consumers for academic research; there are many and diverse others with multiple viewpoints that have a legitimate interest in scholarly output (e.g., Rautiainen *et al.* 2017). Therefore, producing research with relevance must consider *all* its potential beneficiaries from the very beginning—from the research questions to the objectives, methodology and methods, findings, and dissemination of those research findings. The Interventionist Research Framework (IRF) encompasses the entire IVR process, enabling accounting researchers to think about the research beneficiaries from the beginning (see Chapter 5).

Jönsson and Lukka's (2007) notion of the etic and emic realms is pertinent here. These two realms can be viewed as different 'communities of practice' with different agendas, cultures, and sensibilities (Kieser *et al.*, 2015; Malmi & Granlund, 2009). They also hold different knowledge and unique sets of expertise (Laughlin, 2011). The etic realm is the domain of pure logic where, regardless of discipline, science, rigour, theoretical foundations, and formal methodologies come together to generate knowledge that singularly provides "rational arguments for why we are justified in considering a certain claim true" (Jönsson & Lukka, 2007, p. 378). Moreover, scientific knowledge builds theories that generalise phenomena based on reasoned principles and causal relationships underpinned by objectivity and criticism (Van de Ven & Johnson, 2006).

In the emic realm, the domain of practice or world of practical reason is where we find the non-academics—the decision-makers, problem-solvers, and takers of action who assume responsibility and accountability for their actions. Here, we find the problems people face in their everyday lives. Knowledge relevant to non-academic actors includes wide-ranging insights on what they should know and do to solve practical problems (Beer, 2011; Edmondson, 2011). But, to be relevant, its insights must be accompanied by actionable knowledge in the research's contextual setting. It must guide those in the emic realm to achieve their desired outcomes (Beer, 2011). Consequently, non-academic knowledge in the emic realm is "customised, connected to experience, and directed to the structure and dynamics of a particular situation" (Van de Ven & Johnson, 2006, p. 806).

Tucker and Lowe (2014) state that the difference between academic and non-academic communities of practice lies in their competences, values and beliefs, and career interests and needs. It is the distinctiveness of academics and non-academics and the etic and emic worlds they inhabit that gives rise to the notion of research and practice and the tensions between the knowledge and practices. Here is where the gap between research and practice exists (see Bolton & Stolcis, 2003). Therefore, it helps to think about the differences between these two realms when thinking about who an accounting study might be relevant to, who it has relevance for, and who will find it useful.

Different Perspectives on Accounting Research Relevance

In searching for an understanding of research relevance, we find various accounting research relevance perspectives, namely theoretical, practical and societal relevance (e.g., Flyvbjerg, 2001; Lukka & Suomala, 2014), decision relevance (Nicolai & Seidl, 2010), and value relevance (Barth *et al.*, 2001). Knowing and thinking about all these different perspectives helps to balance the diverse interests of academics and non-academics (e.g., Lukka & Suomala, 2014). Moreover, it opens the discussion on relevance to include all areas of accounting.

Theoretical Relevance

Aristotle's intellectual virtue 'episteme' in the context of scientific knowledge corresponds to 'know why' types of questions (Flyvbjerg, 2001) or the formal knowledge revealed in the quest to answer theoretical questions (Van de Ven & Johnson, 2006). For the purposes of our discourse here, episteme relates to theoretical relevance (Lukka & Suomala, 2014), also referred to as academic relevance (Rautiainen *et al.*, 2017). Theoretical relevance is a fundamental aspect of all scholarly research (e.g., Lukka & Suomala, 2014; Corley & Gioia, 2011), where researchers follow generally accepted research methodologies and methods (e.g., Rautiainen *et al.*, 2017) to ensure a link between research findings and a theoretical framework (Jönsson & Lukka, 2007). Theoretically relevant research can include incremental contributions to the extant literature, revisions or extensions to theory, or original theories (e.g., Corley & Gioia, 2011; Whetton, 1989). Corley and Gioia (2011) argue that for theoretically relevant research to be useful, it must have both scientific and practical utility (see also Lukka & Suomala, 2014). Scientific utility means that theory helps researchers to identify what concepts we should study and the relationships between them. Practical utility arises when scholars apply theory to the problems that confront social systems. However, Van de Ven and Johnson (2006) take their argument a step further, highlighting that both theoretical and practical knowledge has the potential to offer complementary, not competing, understandings of reality. Accounting research that is only theoretically relevant contributes to the research-practice gap.

Practical Relevance

Aristotle's 'techne' reflects practical instrumental rationality or 'know-how' questions (Flyvbjerg, 2001), refers to technical, instrumental, or tacit knowledge exemplified in action (Van de Ven & Johnson, 2006), and refers to practical relevance (Lukka & Suomala, 2014). Generating research with practical relevance requires scholarly awareness of the explicit contribution they can make when engaging with the non-academic community without compromising the research's academic merit (Chapman & Kern, 2012). Ter Bogt and van Helden (2012) view practice-relevance as scholars connecting with practice when they are doing research that is interesting to practitioners and other social system actors. In reflecting on the meaning of research relevance and usefulness, we interpret research with practical relevance as research that: a) connects scholars with non-academics to examine issues of interest to all stakeholders involved; b) enables the production and transfer of actionable knowledge to social systems outside of academe; c) occurs in collaboration with non-academics to produce material results or significant, positive outcomes for social systems; d) develops innovative accounting practices; and e) informs professional and organisational decision-making. Consequently, IVR is well-positioned as a methodology to produce accounting research with practical relevance.

Societal Relevance

Aristotle's 'phronesis', translated as 'prudence' or 'practical common sense' is context-dependent, is associated with value rationality, and involves power issues and judgements in specific contexts (Flyvbjerg, 2001, pp. 55–57). Further, it involves ethical knowledge and wisdom about the behaviours and actions required in ambiguous social situations (Van de Ven & Johnson, 2006). Hence, the outcomes of social science that adopt phronesis as their foundation should be significant to society (Flyvbjerg, 2001). As a social science, accounting is closely connected to social systems, and is therefore well-placed to respond to societal issues beyond organisations and micro-level (i.e., individuals) social systems.

Within the context of accounting research, societal relevance is a relatively unexplored concept. As far back as 1980, Burchell *et al.* (1980) called for accounting researchers to undertake more studies on accounting's social role. However, very few have answered. Modell (2014) finds that most management accounting research still focuses on issues related to organisational performance rather than wider societal issues, such as external reporting standards, corporate governance practices and regulations, social justice, social and environmental regulations, and economic and political reform. Consequently, he argues for more examination on how management accounting practices influence a wider range of constituencies, including customers, interest groups, regulators, and politicians. He also calls for researchers in auditing, financial accounting, and corporate governance to develop this broader forum of discussion. However, to produce research with social relevance, researchers must move out of their methodological comfort zone and consider alternatives such as IVR (Modell, 2014). Baard and Dumay (2018) argue that, by its nature, IVR has the potential to produce qualitative research with social relevance that enables social system change and emancipation.

Decision Relevance

Nicolai and Seidl (2010) discuss different forms of practical relevance in the context of management research and practice and, specifically, decision-making in practical situations, which is one type of managerial behaviour. Decision-making is a significant aspect of accounting practice. Nicolai and Seidl (2010) posit that scientific knowledge should influence decision-making and, therefore, scientific knowledge can have practical relevance. Barth *et al.* (2001) argue that accounting information has decision relevance if it makes a difference to the decisions made by those who are using accounting information.

Nicolai and Seidl (2010) view decision relevance from conceptual, instrumental, and legitimative relevance perspectives. First, conceptual relevance refers to the extent that scientific knowledge influences our perceptions and modifies our understanding of the decision situation. Our interpretation of what Nicolai and Seidl mean by the decision situation is: a) a social system problem that needs a solution; b) any other situation that has a 'bad effect' on social system effectiveness because it cannot achieve its objectives or accomplish work; c) the social system's current ability to adapt to its external environment; and d) the overall social system health in terms of its stability and survivability. People in social systems are likely to need relevant knowledge to advance their understanding of the decision situation and its scope. Thus, accounting scholars should generate scientific knowledge, transform it into "knowledge for understanding", and effectively transfer this knowledge to a practical situation (e.g., Beer, 2011). In practical situations, a social system actor can cognitively use this knowledge to change their perception and understanding of the decision situation by enriching their capacity for sense making. Then, they are better able to identify and support potential solutions or alternatives to address the decision situation.

Second, scientific knowledge transformed into actionable knowledge has an indirect form of influence because it influences the course of actions actors select. Thus, scientific knowledge has 'instrumental relevance'. Nicolai and Seidl (2010) state that instrumental relevance consists of schemes, technological rules, and forecasts. Schemes are derived from, or substantiated by, theories. They help structure scientific thinking and, thus, help define the various alternatives when deciding. Technological rules or recipes guide actors on how to go about selecting from the various courses of actions, whereas forecasts help to predict distinct consequences of choosing among the alternatives (Kieser *et al.*, 2015). Instrumental relevance, achieved through the effective transference of actionable knowledge, helps actors to reduce any complexity surrounding their options—often this is by process of elimination.

Third, scientific knowledge can be used to justify a selected course of action to the decision-makers and to others in a social system. Thus, scientific knowledge can have 'legitimative relevance'. Knowledge that is rigorous, scientific, and underpinned by theory is, usually, a more credible form of legitimacy than a choice made for preference (Kieser *et al.*, 2015). For instance, an online retailer collaborates with interventionist scholars to resolve a decision situation concerning a serious reverse logistics problem (e.g. Cullen *et al.*, 2013). The retailer is currently contending with dissatisfied customers and significantly increased logistics costs. After exploring several solutions to this problem, the outcome of the IVR project is that the retailer implements a supplier, customer, and performance-driven approach to managing reverse logistics. The solution results in significant cost reductions, faster and more efficient product returns, and increased customer satisfaction. Further, all these performance improvements increase the firm's value. However, the key is that the scientific knowledge within accounting technology was used to legitimate the course of action taken by the retailer.

In reflection, we find the various perspectives on decision relevance interesting, as it offers accounting scholars research prospects to examine conceptual, instrumental, and legitimative relevance in accounting IVR.

As far as we know, little or no IVR on decision relevance in accounting prevails. Thus, these perspectives help accounting researchers from all three broad areas of accounting to potentially produce research with practical relevance.

Value Relevance

Barth *et al.* (2001) find that value relevance provides prolific insights for accounting standard-setters. They define value relevance as an accounting amount that has a predicted and significant association with equity market values. Moreover, they assert that academic research on value relevance examines the extent to which accounting amounts reflect the information used by investors in valuing a firm's equity but not necessarily in estimating a firm's value. Thus, in accounting research, value relevance refers to something that has a material influence on an organisation's value (Rautiainen *et al.*, 2017). Barth *et al.* (2001) also consider the notion of decision relevance, where the information conveyed by an accounting amount is relevant if it can make a difference to the decision-makers using that information. The association between value relevance and decision relevance arises because, in the long term, managerial decisions influence a firm's performance, which influences the firm's value. However, Rautiainen *et al.* (2017) argue that producing evidence of a material influence on an organisation's value is difficult. In part, this is because everyone has different perceptions of what is valuable, and therefore what has value relevance. The public sector expects value for society; the private sector expects profits or cash flows; customers expect quality products and services, and on it goes. For Rautiainen *et al.* (2017), such a diversity of demands may prove problematic for the value relevance of IVR. However, we do believe that no such obstacle applies to IVR's potential for value relevance.

The International Financial Reporting Standards (IFRS) state that the aim of general purpose financial reporting (i.e., financial statements or other means) is to "provide financial information about the reporting entity that is useful to current and potential investors, lenders, and other creditors in making decisions relating to providing resources to the entity" (Deloitte, 2019, p. 17). They also state that the usefulness of financial information increases if this information is comparable, verifiable, timely, and understandable (Salim, 2019). In the context of financial reporting, decision-making relates to, among other things, trading equity and debt instruments, loans and other credit forms, employing voting rights, and allocating resources (Salim *et al.*, 2019). Further, IFRS state that the financial information found in financial reports, both words and numbers, is useful if the information meets the characteristics of relevance and faithful representation (Deloitte, 2019). Financial information has value relevance to decision-making if it can predict future outcomes. And if it can confirm, refute, or revise previous predictions, it has confirmatory value. According to (Salim *et al.*, 2019, p. 31), financial information must be "complete, neutral and free from error" to be a faithful representation of financial information. Accordingly, we find that value relevance for accounting research means that the knowledge produced from the research findings is scientific, verifiable, and will influence decisions for the 'good' of the social system.

Barth *et al.* (2001) state that scholars are both producers and consumers of research with value relevance, and therefore non-academics are not its primary audience. Rather, non-academics require a knowledge transfer in the form of, say, professional forums or articles in practitioner journals. As mentioned previously, for research to be useful, and particularly decision-useful, it must be understandable (Barth *et al.*, 2001). Therefore, research outcomes need to be translated into explicit implications for practice, and the knowledge produced must be organised and presented in a form that gives its users insights into the operations and outputs of their social system. This transfer of knowledge is critical; otherwise, accounting research is unlikely to have value relevance. Further, thinking about value and decision relevance as they apply to standard setters makes visible another perspective of research relevance that financial accounting scholars undertaking IVR could pursue.

In summary, IVR has significant potential to produce accounting research with theoretical, practical, societal, decision, and value relevance for a range of social systems and their actors. Thus, accounting scholars conducting accounting research from all broad areas of accounting are presented with prospects for doing useful and impactful IVR research through engagement with social systems and non-academics.

The Accounting Research-Practice Gap

The relentless debate on the research-practice gap does not only apply to accounting but to many practice-based disciplines, for example, public health, organisational psychology, nursing, education, human resources, management, economics and finance, and management information systems (e.g., Kieser *et al.*, 2015; Tucker & Lowe, 2014; Corley & Gioia, 2011; Nicolai & Seidl, 2010; Markides, 2011; Bolton & Stolcis, 2003). In accounting, Evans *et al.* (2011) state that the research-practice gap is evident in auditing, financial accounting and reporting, and sustainability (see also Broadbent, 2016; Quagli *et al.*, 2016; Higson & Kassem, 2016). Scholars claim that accounting research is not adequately innovative and has become overly detached from the interests of social systems and their actors (Baard & Dumay, 2018; Merchant, 2012; Evans *et al.*, 2011; Baldvinsdottir *et al.*, 2010; Markides, 2011). Scholars also argue that accounting research is preoccupied with research methodologies and methods, which do not encourage practically relevant outcomes (e.g., Higson & Kassem, 2016; Tucker & Parker, 2014; van Helden & Northcott, 2010).

Mostly, scholars adopt a positivist approach, where the researcher "looks, sees and records" as opposed to an ethnographical or anthropological approach, where the researcher "goes native . . . [and] becomes an actor rather than a researcher" (Laughlin, 2011, p. 26). Hence, when accounting research lacks relevance, the work of scholars and the work of practitioners do not effectively influence each other, and there is little or no connectivity between them; only a gap. Chalmers and Wright (2011, p. 59) assert that:

> The research gap is never wider than when practitioners fail to turn to the accounting academy and its research findings for the development of practices, or when the academy fails to turn to practitioners for inspiration in identifying and developing research questions or interpreting results and contemplating their implications.

Therefore, accounting is "worlds apart" from practice (Laughlin, 2011, p. 21). In our vernacular, this means accounting research is irrelevant.

Why Does the Research-Practice Gap Persist?

Based on our research, we find that four main issues contribute to the refusal of the research-practice gap to budge. We do not claim that these are the only contributing issues, but rather the main ones based on our synthesis of the accounting literature.

First is the tension between the two different domains—academics and their sphere of logic and non-academics with their experiential praxis (Kieser *et al.*, 2015; Tucker & Lowe, 2014; Tilt, 2010). However, this problem is not as two-dimensional as it appears on the surface. It is a multi-faceted issue that cannot be solved overnight. Accounting scholars are generally methodologically driven, rigorous, independent, motivated by aspirations to expand knowledge in their field, and limited only by their reputation (Chalmers & Wright, 2011). They produce incremental knowledge, supported by data and rigorous analysis, that, little by little, adds to a repository of all knowledge—'another brick in the wall'. But how this knowledge is transformed for consumption outside academia is not always evident (Markides, 2011).

Additionally, the nature of accounting research emphasises positivist accounting issues that exclude practice or real-world contemplations (Chambers, 2005). Some scholars argue that accounting research should retain an arms' length approach, where critiquing, reflecting, questioning, and debating issues in organisations and communities are the order of the day (Parker *et al.*, 2011). Supporting professional practice is not necessarily the aim; indeed, accounting research may not be relevant to practitioners at all (Chalmers & Wright, 2011). Bolton and Stolcis (2003) observe that non-academics are guided by research based on common-sense case studies, which makes this type of research more likely to have impact outside the ivory tower. Case studies contrast with the positivist approach, which mostly yields scientific utility.

Many practitioners have a view that scholars are detached from the real-world and, accordingly, have little of value to offer (e.g., Tucker & Parker, 2014; Laughlin, 2011; Malmi & Granlund, 2009; Baldvinsdottir *et al.*, 2010). Unsurprisingly, therefore, they are not motivated to pay much attention to research findings, let alone collaborate with scholars (Laughlin, 2011). These practitioners may not be wrong in their opinions either. Tucker and Lowe (2014) find that academics typically know little of practitioner views—about their work or about their views on academic research. Nor are they aware of the (lack of) value that their research offers to practitioners, or how practitioners might use the research they produce. Ter Bogt and van Helden (2012) offer a somewhat contentious view that perhaps accounting researchers are fearful of being too norma-tive or, alternatively, being regarded as consultants. Therefore, scholars tend to focus on understanding how accounting tools and technologies operate in practice, rather than generating new or improved technolo-gies that align with practice. We agree that ter Bogt and van Helden (2012) may have a point, but we also argue that management accounting researchers are more disposed to applied research and problem-solving, which covers a fair amount of common ground with consultants. Baard and Dumay (2018) state that, for accounting academics, the fear of being labelled as a consultant is founded because it may negatively impact one's reputation. Hence, academics can be reluctant to admit that they engage in practice-relevant research. Yet this is something of a no-win situation because, if they do not address issues of interest to practitioners, they are dubbed as detached, valueless Philomaths.

Kieser *et al.* (2015) find that scholars have little or no practical experi-ence, and therefore may not thoroughly understand real-world organ-isational problems. Plus, they may not have the competences needed to find and solve problems in organisations (see also Quagli *et al.*, 2016). Markides (2007) also views this competences issue as a dilemma that con-tributes to the research-practice gap but extends his argument to include the unique values, attitudes, and mindsets needed to conduct rigorous, managerially relevant research. Markides (2007) argues that most schol-ars are trained to conduct rigorous research, e.g., reviewing literature, astute data collection and analysis, and embedding theory into research design, and that rigour is a self-perpetuating convention. Therefore, they draw reputational worth and a sense of identity from rigour in the eyes of other scholars, which reinforces rigour as a key measure of research qual-ity. Conversely, researchers focussed on accomplishing managerially rel-evant research must be able to interact with both the etic and emic realm.

They must ask interesting questions that are relevant to non-academics. Further, those questions must lead to theoretically interesting outcomes that can be tested in the emic realm. Dealing with the emic and etic is a difficult task to accomplish if you are a career scholar with no practical working experience. This is another contributory factor to the research-practice gap (Markides, 2007; see also Higson & Kassem, 2016).

Second is the issue of communication. Academic accounting research mainly focusses on other scholars, rather than practitioners, managers, and other professionals (Markides, 2007). This is evidenced in the conversations that academics hold. Mostly, those conversations are between scholars through articles published in journals or conferences, which excludes practitioners (Laughlin, 2011). Communicating research to non-academics in this way is a problem because academic research articles are often complex and difficult to read (Kieser *et al.*, 2015). These 'private conversations' make it more difficult for practitioners to connect with academic research and, likewise, for scholars to connect with practitioners (Chalmers & Wright, 2011). Additionally, non-academics often find it difficult to extract the actionable knowledge relevant to them from the research findings largely due to the theoretical terminology and jargon found in academic papers (Merchant, 2012; Parker *et al.*, 2011). Also, the contents of these articles are usually not organised, presented, and translated into an understandable form (e.g., Markides, 2011). This inaccessibility of research is a significant barrier to research relevance (Kieser *et al.*, 2015; Merchant, 2012). Hence, research findings must be translated into "practitioner language" and published in non-academic channels (Kieser *et al.*, 2015, p. 153); for example, reports or forums on the internet, submissions to regulators, newspaper articles, professional journals, and so on (e.g., Tucker & Lowe, 2014; ter Bogt & van Helden, 2012; Scapens, 2012). When research is more understandable, and its findings are explicitly applicable to a social system, non-academics may find accounting research more useful (Bolton & Stolcis, 2003).

Third, highly ranked academic journals are not always open to publishing research that demonstrates practical and societal relevance (e.g., Quagli *et al.*, 2016; Laughlin, 2011). Ter Bogt and van Helden (2012) find that the editors of some leading accounting journals view practical and theoretical relevance as complementary, but theoretical advancement is an essential component of a study, and therefore given a higher weighting. Unerman and O'Dwyer (2010, p. 15) observe that peer-reviewed academic journals are mainly interested in "technocratic accounting research" that does not investigate the influence or implications of accounting practices. Numerous accounting researchers adopt the view that articles published in academic journals diminish the value of applied research with practical relevance (Chalmers & Wright, 2011).

Four, academics experience intense pressure to maintain ongoing research productivity. They must publish in high-quality journals,

secure research funding, teach under- and post-graduates, and super-
vise the research of tomorrow's academics (de Villiers & Dumay, 2014).
Also, academic reward systems and promotion decisions surrounding
accounting academics are exemplified by attaining publications in high-
quality journals. Therefore, accounting researchers are more likely to
be deterred from engaging in practically and societally relevant research
and from generating and transferring knowledge to non-academic users
(Martin-Sardesai & Guthrie, 2018). Academic reward systems are
institutionalised by regulatory frameworks, such as REF and the ERA.
Markides (2011) states that academic reward systems and associated
incentives serve the university's best interests at the expense of relevant
research and the needs of stakeholders outside of the ivory tower of
academia (Markides, 2011). The link to reward systems is understandable given that monetary inflows are a valuable and scarce resource for
universities and that securing grants is contingent on performance. The
consequence of the current tertiary management climate is that scholars
are not always rewarded for producing research relevant to accounting practice (Chalmers & Wright, 2011; Stevenson, 2011). Although
academics have teaching and service goals, their primary objective is
publishing articles with discipline-specific knowledge, not on solving
organisational and community problems (Dumay, 2010). Hence, the
research-practice gap remains.

How Do Accounting Scholars and Practitioners Address the Research-Practice Gap?

To say that scholars have views on how to address the research-practice
gap is an understatement. Many different scholars have many different
views, and just a sample of them follow. Evans *et al.* (2011) argue that
accounting research must: focus on social, political, and organisational
settings; be informed by theory; and encompass interdisciplinarity and
long-term thought. Moreover, they assert that it is necessary for scholars
and social system actors to collaborate; otherwise, the focus will swing
to accounting technologies and practices, obscuring a broader societal
contribution. Merchant (2012, p. 340) argues that accounting researchers must get closer to practice to "understand what they do, what they
are trying to accomplish, how they operate and what issues they are
struggling with". A way forward is to potentially collaborate with non-
academics to convert research findings into something that can, in Malmi
and Granlund's (2009, p. 598) words, "be used by someone to accomplish
something". Thus, there is a need for greater methodical and meaningful
encounters between accounting scholars and organisations, communities,
and their actors. Laughlin (2011) states that accounting research must
focus on developing ideas directly related to specific and pressing problems experienced by practice to render it relevant (see also Merchant,

2012). Markides (2011) argues that for academic insights to be useful to non-academics, it is critical to transform relevant research findings into a knowledge structure that makes sense.

Unerman and O'Dwyer (2010) recommend that leading academic journals should encourage the submission of accounting research that meets the changing needs of society (see also ter Bogt & van Helden, 2012). In doing so, editors are likely to reduce the risk of accounting research losing its credibility in terms of its value in serving society's needs. Given that 'society' foots much of the bill for general research, editors would be wise to consider this aspect of their credibility more carefully. Further, Unerman and O'Dwyer claim that editors occupy a powerful position with the ability to influence what is considered relevant and what is not. Therefore, they should actively pursue academic work that addresses practical and societal concerns. Scapens (2008, p. 917) sees this issue in a slightly different way. He accepts journal rankings, citation counts, and impact factors as an inescapable aspect of academic life. However, he also counsels academics to try and find a balance between publishing research that does "carry research assessment points" with research that has relevance to non-academics. Quagli *et al.* (2016) suggest that publishing in professional journals, presenting at practitioner conferences, and implementing interventions at the professional association level are all ways to share research outcomes beyond the walls of academia. We argue these channels are direct and two-way, which makes them particularly suited to sharing research interests, exchanging views, and creating a perception that research is relevant. After all, history tells us that the only peaceful way to overcome a divide between two cultures is to communicate.

The accounting literature discussed above certainly offers some helpful remedies, prescriptions, and strategies for addressing the accounting research-practice gap. However, it offers very little support for the idea of IVR as a potential remedy to this persistent problem.

IVR—An Underutilised Remedy

The debate over the research-practice-relevance gap offers constructive ideas on how to resolve this issue. However, it does not present IVR as a legitimate methodological instrument with potential to reclaim accounting research relevance and address the research-practice gap. Some notable accounting scholars make a case for IVR to enhance practical research relevance (Lukka & Suomala, 2014; Merchant, 2012; Van Helden & Northcott, 2010; Quattrone, 2009; Scapens, 2008; Jönsson & Lukka, 2007). IVR has remedial potential to provide relevance to accounting research that extends beyond the practical relevance in management accounting to include theoretical and societal relevance (Baard & Dumay, 2018; Lukka & Vinnari, 2017).

Theoretical Relevance

Theory adopts a multifaceted role in IVR through supporting theoretical relevance (Lukka & Vinnari, 2017), accomplishing methodological legitimacy for IVR, and differentiating IVR from consulting (Baard & Dumay, 2018). In Chapter 1, we went to great lengths to demonstrate that theory is critical to IVR because it underpins every facet of the methodology. We also showed how theories differ based on scope and categorisation, the empirical issues they examine, and their associations with various research approaches and methods. With intervention theory, developed by Chris Argyris (1970), IVR is supported by a theory of practice from which methodological guidance to inform the practice of IVR may be derived (see Chapter 4). Moreover, intervention theory provides theoretical insights on the types of interventions researchers are likely to use in IVR. Intervention theory is not new but using intervention theory when conducting IVR is rare. Therefore, critiquing, using, testing, and refining intervention theory provides accounting researchers with significant potential to arrive at a contemporary theory of practice that can open the black box of IVR (Baard & Dumay, 2018) and address the lack of theories of practice currently persisting in the social sciences.

Further, in Baard and Dumay (2018), we state that theories with 'status', such as institutional, agency or actor-network theory, help us to explain accounting issues of interest to scholars in the context of IVR (see also Chapter 1). We provide evidence that Kurt Lewin used theory to analyse social system actions and behaviours and to discover the 'general laws of life'. Thus, his type of action research never ignored theory. Malmi and Granlund (2009) consider IVR to producing accounting theories that can be used to generate theoretically informed innovations and solutions to practical problems. Hence, there is also scope for IVR to support theoretical advancements to theories with status. Reflecting on the current argument for theoretically-informed IVR and the potential for IVR to contribute to the theoretical relevance of accounting research, we find that IVR has potential to strengthen the theoretical relevance of accounting research through its use and focus on theories of practice and status.

Practical Relevance

One of Lewin's IVR governing principles requires scholars to do research in the field and move beyond the role of observer by immersing themselves in a social system. Philosophically, this means that researchers move out of their etic domains where they adopt an expert role offering scientific knowledge and touch down in the emic world. Thus, scholars 'cross the divide' from pure logic or theory to a practical logic of real problems, making decisions about potential solutions and taking actions. Another principle requires scholars to collaborate with people in the social system where they adopt the role of a team member to achieve the collaborative work. Scholars agree that for research to be relevant to practical issues, scholars must go out into the field and collaborate (e.g., Kieser *et al.*, 2015; Merchant, 2012; Edmondson, 2011).

As per intervention theory, collaborative work may involve generating valid and useful information on diagnosing and analysing a prevailing problem and a range of solutions for solving the problem (Argyris, 1970). Part of being an active participant in the field, researchers seek to solve real-world practical problems (another governing principle) that other research traditions do not support. Merchant (2012) argues that real-world problems tend to be multidimensional, so when accounting scholars help practitioners to solve their problems, they themselves are introduced to new ideas and theories (see also Scapens, 2012). Conversely, when practitioners relate to scholars, they are more open to sharing and being influenced by scholars. Intervention theory supports participant engagement through championing the necessity for participants to make free and informed decisions and realising internal commitment during IVR. Chapman and Kern (2012) state that practitioner engagement is fundamental to IVR. Such an intrinsic role positions IVR to assume an important role in addressing the research-practice relevance gap.

IVR aims to generate interventions that add practical and social value to a social system. Whereas IVR philosophy introduces two types of interventions, intervention theory offers a more useful detailed conceptualisation of three intervention types most interventionist researchers are likely to use. We say useful because Argyris (1970) describes the intervention types, outlines the implications of using them to solve problems, and identifies what competences researchers need to design, develop, and implement each intervention. Thus, interventions are underpinned by intervention theory, a theory of practice. Additionally, the IRF identifies critical objectives and practical work researchers need to accomplish to design and develop interventions with sound prospects of successfully solving practical problems (see Chapter 5). Designing and developing interventions is the collaborative remit of both researchers and the people inhabiting social systems. Cullen *et al.* (2013) argue that using IVR enables researchers to engage with practitioners and obtain a sense of the issues prevalent in practice and appreciate the usefulness of IVR in providing managerially relevant solutions. Again, increased relevance helps to close the research-practice gap.

Societal Relevance

IVR's notable potential to produce accounting research with societal relevance may elevate IVR's dual output to an output trilogy, should accounting researchers opt to include a societal perspective on their research agendas. In our view and by our definitions of relevant, relevance, and useful, practical relevance may lead to or influence the societal relevance of accounting research. Modell (2014) argues that research should influence the broader society outside organisations, and we agree with his argument. However, organisations consist of organisational structures and mechanisms, and people or what we refer to as 'micro-societies' (i.e., individuals, groups, teams, and intergroups). These micro-societies engage in social interactions, they influence each other, and their behaviours, competences, capacity for self-management, social values, power, and status (i.e., social aspects) are regulated by organisational structures and mechanisms. Thus, we should not discount micro-societies for whom IVR can also provide societal relevance.

IVR's remedial potential extends beyond practical relevance. Interventionists use IVR to stimulate change (another governing principle) through solving social system problems (e.g., Baard & Dumay, 2018; Lukka & Suomala, 2014; Jönsson & Lukka, 2007; Greenwood & Levin, 2007). Baard and Dumay (2018) present a singular notion of change that incorporates both organisational and social change. Organisational change means modifications to organisational structures and mechanisms, such as reporting relationships, job design, strategy, technology, and control structures, that are likely to lead to changes in social aspects of micro-societies—referred to as social change. Interventionist researchers, interventions, and research participants are the instruments of change. In our recent paper (Baard & Dumay, 2018) we state that the positive changes in social value and power distribution for individuals and groups generate emancipatory prospects for these social system actors. [Moreover, we present a detailed account of the association between IVR, change, and emancipation, including cautionary notes on harmful unintended change and 'de-emancipation'.] Thus, to achieve societal relevance for accounting IVR, researchers should address the social aspects of accounting technologies and practices.

In Summation

Bridging the research-practice gap is essential to IVR and is a constituent of its 'good'. In delving into the meaning and different perspectives of accounting research relevance and the nature of the research-practice gap, we exemplify the 'good' of IVR to reclaim accounting research relevance and its sound remedial potential to reduce the accounting research-practice gap. In Chapter 1 we signposted some bad and ugly aspects of IVR, and here we note, IVR can also have some unintended consequences that, if not properly considered, have an equal chance of being good, bad, or ugly. Hence, in Chapter 3, we wash the rose-colour off our glasses and open our eyes to the bad and ugly aspects of IVR. We anticipate the result is a picture of IVR that is rich in dimension.

References

Argyris, C. (1970). *Intervention theory and method: A behavioural science view.* Reading, MA: Addison-Wesley Publishing Company.

Australian Research Council (ARC). (2019). *Engagement and impact assessment 2018–19*. Retrieved from: https://dataportal.arc.gov.au/EI/NationalReport/2018/pages/introduction/index.html?id=definitions

Baard, V.C. & Dumay, J. (2018). Interventionist research in accounting: Reflections on the good, the bad and the ugly. *Accounting and Finance*, Advance online publication. https://doi.org/10.1111/acfi.12409

Baldvinsdottir, G., Mitchell, F., & Nørreklit, H. (2010). Issues in the relationship between theory and practice in management accounting. *Management Accounting Research*, 21(2), 79–82.

Barth, M.E., Beaver, W.H., & Landsman, W.R. (2001). The relevance of the value relevance literature for financial accounting setting: Another view. *Journal of Accounting and Economics*, 31, 77–104.

Beer, M. (2011). Making a difference and contributing useful knowledge: Principles derived from life as a scholar-practitioner. In S.A Mohrman & E.E. Lawler III (Eds.), *Useful research: Advancing theory and practice*. Retrieved from: https://learning.oreilly.com/library/view/useful-research/9781605096018/xhtml/ch02.html

Birmingham, S. (2016). *Taking action to unlock the potential of Australian research*. Retrieved from: https://ministers.education.gov.au/birmingham/taking-action-unlock-potential-australian-research

Bolton, M.J. & Stolcis, G.B. (2003). Ties that do not bind: Musings on the specious relevance of academic research. *Public Administration Review*, 63(5), 626–630.

Broadbent, J. (2016). The "real" impact factor: Reflections on the impact of the research excellence framework. *Financial Reporting*, 1, 15–28.

Burchell, S., Clubb, C., Hopwood, A., Hughes, J., & Nahapiet, J. (1980). The roles of accounting in organisations and society. *Accounting, Organizations and Society*, 5(1), 5–27.

Butler, V., Delaney, H., & Spoelstra, S. (2015). Problematizing "relevance" in the business school: The case of leadership studies. *British Journal of Management*, 26, 731–744.

Chambers, R. (2005). Positive accounting theory and the PA cult. *Abacus*, 29(1), 1–26.

Chalmers, K. & Wright, S. (2011). Bridging accounting research and practice: A value adding endeavour. In E. Evans, R. Burritt, & J. Guthrie (Eds.), *Bridging the gap between academic accounting research and professional practice* (pp. 59–68). Sydney, Australia: Institute of Chartered Accountants Australia.

Chapman, C. & Kern, A. (2012). What do academics do? Understanding the practical relevance of research. *Qualitative Research in Accounting & Management*, 9(3), 279–281. https://doi-org.simsrad.net.ocs.mq.edu.au/10.1108/qram.2012.31409caa.004

Cooper, B. & Guthrie, J. (2017). *Post the Watt review: Australian business schools and collaboration with industry*. Sydney, Australia: Chartered Accountants Australia and New Zealand.

Corley, K.G. & Gioia, D.A. (2011). Building theory about theory building: What constitutes a theoretical contribution. *Academy of Management Review*, 36(1), 12–32.

Cullen, J., Tsamenyi, M., Bernon, M., & Gorst, J. (2013). Reverse logistics in the UK retail sector: A case study of the role of management accounting in driving organisational change. *Management Accounting Research*, 24, 212–227.

Deloitte. (2019). *IFRS in your pocket*. Retrieved from: www.iasplus.com/en/publications/global/ifrs-in-your-pocket/2019

Department of Education and Training. (2015). *Turnbull government response: Review of research policy and funding arrangements*. Retrieved from: https://docs.education.gov.au/documents/turnbull-government-response-review-research-policy-and-funding-arrangements

de Villiers, C. & Dumay, J. (2014). Writing an article for a refereed accounting journal. *Pacific Accounting Review*, 26(3), 324–350.

Dumay, J. (2010). A critical reflective discourse of an interventionist research project. *Qualitative Research in Accounting and Management*, 7(1), 46–70.

Edmondson, A.C. (2011). Crossing boundaries to investigate problems in the field: An approach to useful research. In S.A. Mohrman & E.E. Lawler III (Eds.), *Useful research: Advancing theory and practice*. Retrieved from: https://learning.oreilly.com/library/view/useful-research/9781605096018/xhtml/ch02.html

Evans, E., Burritt, R., & Guthrie, J. (2011). *Bridging the gap between academic accounting research and professional practice*. Sydney, Australia: Institute of Chartered Accountants Australia.

Flyvbjerg, B. (2001). *Making social science matter: Why social inquiry fails and how it can succeed again*. Cambridge, UK: Cambridge University Press.

Greenwood, D.J. & Levin, M. (2007). *Introduction to action research: Social research for social change*. Thousand Oaks, CA: Sage Publications.

Higson, A. & Kassem, R. (2016). Accounting research: Relevance lost. *Financial Reporting*, 1, 59–76.

International Accounting Standards Board. (2018). *IFRS® conceptual framework project summary*. London, UK: International Accounting Standards Board.

Ittner, C. & Larcker, D. (2002). Empirical managerial accounting research: Are we just describing management consulting practice? *European Accounting Review*, 11(4), 787–794.

Jönsson, S. & Lukka, K. (2007). There and back again: Doing interventionist research in management accounting. In C.S. Chapman, A.G. Hopwood, & M.S. Shields (Eds.), *Handbook of management accounting research* (Vol. 1, pp. 373–397). Oxford, UK: Elsevier.

Kieser, A., Nicolai, A., & Seidl, D. (2015). The practical relevance of management research: Turning the debate on relevance into a rigorous scientific research program. *The Academy of Management Annals*, 9(1), 143–233.

Laughlin, R. (2011). Accounting research, policy and practice: Worlds together or worlds apart? In E. Evans, R. Burritt, & J. Guthrie (Eds.), *Bridging the gap between academic accounting research and professional practice* (pp. 21–30). Sydney, Australia: Institute of Chartered Accountants Australia.

Leisenring, J.J. & Johnson, T. (1994). Accounting research: On the relevance of research to practice. *Accounting Horizons*, 8(4), 74–79.

Lewin, K. (1946). Action research and minority problems. *Journal of Social Issues*, 11, 34–46.

Lewin, K. (1947). Frontiers in group dynamics: ll. Channels of group life: Social planning and action research. *Human Relations*, 1(2), 143–153.

Lukka, K. & Suomala, P. (2014). Relevant interventionist research: Balancing three intellectual virtues. *Accounting and Business Research*, 44(2), 204–220.

Lukka, K. & Vinnari, E. (2017). Combining action-network theory with interventionist research: Present state and future potential. *Accounting, Auditing & Accountability Journal*, 30, 720–753.

Macquarie encyclopaedic dictionary. (2011). Sydney, Australia: Australia Heritage Publishing Company Pty Ltd.

Malmi, T. & Granlund, M. (2009). In search of management accounting theory. *European Accounting Review*, 18(3), 597–620.

Markides, C. (2007). In search of ambidextrous professors. *Academy of Management Journal*, 50, 762–768.

Markides, C. (2011). Crossing the chasm: How to convert relevant research into managerially useful research. *Journal of Applied Behavioural Science*, 47(1), 121–134.

Martin-Sardesai, A. & Guthrie, J. (2018). Human capital loss in an academic performance measurement system. *Journal of Intellectual Capital*, 19(1), 53–70.

Martin-Sardesai, A., Guthrie, J., Tooley, S., & Chaplin, S. (2019). History of performance measurement systems in the Australian higher education sector. *Accounting History*, 12(1), 40–61.

Martin-Sardesai, A., Irvine, H., Tooley, S., & Guthrie, J. (2017). Accounting for research: Academic responses to research performance demands in an Australian university. *The Australian Accounting Review*, 27(3), 329–334.

Merchant, K.A. (2012). Making management accounting research more useful. *Pacific Accounting Review*, 24(3), 334–356.

Mitchell, F. (2002). Research and practice in management accounting: Improving integration and communication. *European Accounting Review*, 11(2), 277–289.

Modell, S. (2014). The societal relevance of management accounting: An introduction to the special issue. *Accounting and Business Research*, 44(2), 83–103.

Nicolai, A. & Seidl, D. (2010). That's relevant! Different forms of practical relevance in management science. *Organization Studies*, 31(9 & 10), 1257–1285. https://doi.org/10.1177%2F0170840610374401

Oxford Learner's Dictionaries. (2019). Retrieved from: www.oxfordlearners dictionaries.com/definition/english/relevant

Parker, L.D., Guthrie, J., & Linacre, S. (2011). The relationship between academic accounting research and professional practice. *Accounting, Auditing and Accountability Journal*, 24(1), 5–14.

Quagli, A., Avallone, F., & Ramassa, P. (2016). The real impact factor and the gap between accounting research and practice. *Financial Reporting*, 1, 29–58.

Quattrone, P. (2009). "We have never been post-modern": On the search of management accounting theory. *European Accounting Review*, 18(3), 621–630.

Rautiainen, A., Sippola, K., & Mättö, T. (2017). Perspectives on relevance: The relevance test in the constructive research approach. *Management Accounting Research*, 34, 19–29.

Salim, A., Bakker, E., Balasubramanian, T.V., Bharadva, K., Chaudhry, A., Coetsee, D., . . . van der Merwe, M. (2019). *Wiley interpretation and application of IFRS standards*. Cornwall, UK: John Wiley and Sons.

Scapens, R. (2008). Seeking the relevance of interpretive research: A contribution to the polyphonic debate. *Critical Perspectives on Accounting*, 19, 915–919.

Scapens, R. (2012). How important is practice-relevant management accounting research? *Qualitative Research in Accounting & Management*, 9(3), 293–295. https://doi-org.simsrad.net.ocs.mq.edu.au/10.1108/qram.2012.31409caa.009

Scaratti, G., Galuppo, L., Gorli, M., Gozzoli, C., & Ripamonti, S. (2017). The social relevance and social impact of knowledge and knowing. *Management Learning*, 48(1), 57–64.

Stevenson, K. (2011). Leveraging academic research to improve financial reporting: A standard-setters view. In E. Evans, R. Burritt, & J. Guthrie (Eds.), *Bridging the gap between academic accounting research and professional practice* (pp. 103–109). Sydney, Australia: Institute of Chartered Accountants Australia.

ter Bogt, H. & van Helden, J. (2012). The practical relevance of management accounting research and the role of qualitative methods therein: The debate continues. *Qualitative Research in Accounting and Management*, 9(3), 265–295.

Tilt, C. (2010). The impact of academic accounting research on professional practice. In E. Evans, R. Burritt, & J. Guthrie (Eds.), *Accounting education at a crossroad in 2010* (pp. 35–40). Sydney, Australia: Institute of Chartered Accountants Australia.

Tucker, B.P. & Lowe, A.D. (2014). Practitioners are from Mars: Academics are from Venus. *Accounting, Auditing and Accountability Journal*, 27(3), 394–395.

Tucker, B.P. & Parker, L.D. (2014). In our ivory towers? The research-practice gap in management accounting. *Accounting and Business Research*, 44(2), 104–143.

Tucker, B.P. & Parker, L.D. (2019). The question of research relevance: A university management perspective. *Accounting, Auditing and Accountability Journal*, Vol. ahead-of-print. https://doi.org/10.1108/AAAJ-01-2018-3325

Unerman, J. & O'Dwyer, B. (2010). *The relevance and utility of leading accounting research*. The Association of Chartered Certified Accountants (ACCA), London, Research Report 120.

Van de Ven, A.H. & Johnson, P.E. (2006). Knowledge for theory and practice. *The Academy of Management Review*, 31(4), 802–821.

van Helden, G.J. & Northcott, D. (2010). Examining the practical relevance of public sector management accounting. *Financial Accountability and Management*, 26(2), 213–241.

Watt, I. (2015). *Review of research policy and funding arrangements*. Retrieved from: www.education.gov.au/review-research-policy-and-funding-arrangements-0

Whetton, D.A. (1989). What constitutes a theoretical contribution? *Academy of Management Review*, 14(4), 490–495.

3   The 'Bad' and the 'Ugly' of IVR

Notwithstanding the 'good' IVR can do in addressing accounting research relevance and the research-practice gap, IVR does have a precarious nature that can challenge some scholars. Undertaking IVR is not an easy thing to do. Risks and challenges accompany IVR's potential, especially if researchers are not aware of them. But forewarned is forearmed, and knowing about the possible pitfalls before undertaking an IVR study means one can be prepared for possible issues. These risks and challenges are the 'bad' and 'ugly' aspects of IVR. The bad includes the fragmented nature of IVR, the time it takes to do IVR, and the multiple researcher qualities IVR needs to perform IVR effectively. The ugly is the stigma that IVR constitutes second-rate research, given its perceived association with consulting, which has raised questions over its legitimacy. The discussion that follows reviews these perceptions rationally and offers a way forward through these criticisms.

The Bad of IVR—Risks and Challenges

Undertaking IVR is a perilous affair because it challenges social science scholars to forego "commonly held theoretical positions" with "neat models and solutions" in favour of "the new, the risky and the dangerous" (Parker, 2008, p. 912). Beginning with the bad of IVR, its fragmented and difficult nature is largely attributed to: a) the lack of a consensus definition on what IVR is; b) the time needed to undertake interventionist studies; c) the diverse skills required for a successful IVR project; and d) the reluctance of high-quality journals to publish IVR. We discuss each of these aspects next.

The Fragmented Nature of IVR

In Chapter 1, we explained that IVR has become an umbrella concept that encompasses various different interpretations of Lewin's original idea (1946, 1947). For example, action research (e.g., Wouters & Wilderom, 2008; Wouters & Roijmans, 2011), action science (Argyris et al. 1985), clinical research (e.g., Jönsson & Lukka, 2007), design science (e.g., van Aken, 2004; Andriessen, 2003), the constructive research approach (e.g., Kasanen *et al.*, 1993; Labro & Tuomela, 2003; Malmi *et al.*, 2004), and engaged scholarship (Van de Ven & Johnson, 2006).

These variations are not just limited to a definition of IVR, but also to how it should be undertaken and what it produces. For instance, Eden and Huxham (1996) state that action research could be construed as a process of consultancy involving a methodological approach with a focus on pragmatic theoretical development. With respect to how IVR should be undertaken, Eden and Huxham (1996) argue that a systematic exploration approach must be applied to action research, although they are not forthcoming about what this method should entail. Baard (2010) examined several variant frameworks for undertaking IVR used by scholars, finding that, although each variation has its merits, none exhibit the same precision, clarity, and methodical rigor as the Rothman and Thomas (1994) framework.

Some IVR variations highlight theoretical contributions as an output, whereas others emphasise practical change with little or no attention to theory. The duality of output that was key to Lewin's original intentions has been lost. Eden and Huxham (1996) argue that IVR should not choose between rigour and relevance, but rather that both must be achieved. They contend that action research should be "usable in everyday life" and there must be "an explicit concern with theory . . . formed from the characterisation or conceptualisation of the particular experience in ways which are intended to be meaningful to others" (p. 79). Hence, our emphasis on IVR and theory in Chapter 1.

Jönsson and Lukka (2007) provide a detailed review of the various interpretations of IVR, including how each differs from each other and, to some extent, from Lewin's original concept. Jönsson and Lukka (2007, p. 388) conclude that the consequence of these variations has given IVR a "fragmented nature offering the opponents a lot of weapons to undermine its scientific value". Baard (2010) also undertook a critical review of IVR, including its alternative forms, and identified the similarities and significant differences between the variations. She too concludes that the variations contribute to the fragmented notion of IVR, produces reservations about the scientific value of IVR, promotes scholarly reluctance to engage with the methodology, and accentuates the association of IVR with consulting. Baard and Dumay (2018) reflect on these issues and subsequently argue that the perceived fragmented nature of IVR is problematic in forging a future path for IVR.

So, how did this come about? As discussed in Chapter 1, Lewin integrated social science and practice in his work to change a social attitude. He underpinned IVR with governing principles that emphasise problem-solving, doing research in the field rather than in a laboratory, collaborating with the participants under study, using an iterative investigation process, and producing both practical and theoretical outputs (Peters & Robinson, 1984; Dickens & Watkins, 1999). Lewin's work on his 'type of action research' consisted of only two papers that directly addressed the idea of IVR before his unexpected passing in 1947. Accordingly, Lewin had no occasion to debate his philosophies and methodologies with other scholars, which is unfortunate because his view of social research was profoundly different from that of his peers (Peters & Robinson, 1984).

Peters and Robinson (1984) also conclude that Lewin's concept of action research was not deliberately presented as a final philosophical outcome. Consequently, his contemporaries have since produced varying interpretations of his work, with many interpretations unsupported by a unifying framework or a basis in intervention theory (Peters & Robinson, 1984; Dickens & Watkins, 1999). Lewin (1946, 1947) was always exceedingly clear in his published empirical work that, while action research was intended to solve practical problems in social systems, his approach had to address a gap between social action and social theory. Omitting theory from action research was not an option because, as Cartwright (1951) notes, using theory was important for analysing behaviour and discovering the 'general laws of social life'.

Peters and Robinson (1984) and Jönsson and Lukka (2007) state that some scholars position their interpretations close to Lewin's original notion of IVR, whereas others differ greatly. Jönsson and Lukka (2007, p. 377) state that the constructive research approach is one that "comes close to the original ideas of Lewin". However, Baard and Dumay (2018) contest this claim, finding that the founding scholars of the constructive method provide no apparent theory of practice and little or no reference to Lewin's governing principles in their approach. In our review of the literature, we find that the constructive research approach has been popular with management accounting researchers in the Finnish context. Yet, in our view, this method has too narrow a focus on management accounting to be useful outside of this specific accounting domain.

Conceived by Van de Ven and Johnson (2006), engaged scholarship is another variant of IVR aimed at reducing the gap between research and practice. It originated from a perceived need for scholars and practitioners to collaboratively produce knowledge to address problems, with the goal of generating theoretically, practically, and societally relevant research (e.g., Lukka & Suomala, 2014). As with the constructive method, we find that, although it acknowledges the importance of collaboration, problem-solving, and the duality of output, engaged scholarship is not based on Lewin's governing principles. Further, Van de Ven and Johnson (2006, p. 817) view engaged scholarship more a "mode of enquiry" rather than as "some sort of applied or action research"—perhaps in recognition that scholars have questioned the scientific contribution of the approach. We find that engaged scholarship does not recognise the need for the process of enquiry to be iterative. Also, there are questions about whether change is an integral part of the approach or whether the traditional 'fly on the wall' observations are acceptable. Lastly, there is no theory of practice which guides engaged scholarship. In our opinion, this brings the scientific contribution of engaged scholarship that Van de Ven and Johnson (2006) note into question.

Contemporary action research is process oriented. Plus, it does not generate clear theoretical contributions to scholarly knowledge. Action research has been criticised by academics for some time, so scholarly concerns about this research approach are not new (Dickens & Watkins, 1999; Eden & Huxham, 1996). However, our concerns over this variation to IVR come from a fundamental disconnect with Lewin's original premise of giving theory and practice equal emphasis—not prominence to the practical alone. Dickens and Watkins (1999) find that action research: a) produces action with little research; b) constitutes a weak research approach when focussed only on problem-solving and not theory; c) lacks the rigour associated with scientific research and, thus, can only make limited contributions to the scholarly body of knowledge; and d) does not include all the research elements outlined by Lewin. Jönsson and Lukka (2007, pp. 388–389) state that action research generates "sloppy quasi research" that is "long on action, short on research".

Clinical research emphasises practical change without any theoretical contribution. Although clinical research does stress problem-solving and change associated with interventions, its focus on patient care and treatment overshadows a need for theoretical contributions. We suggest that, given the nature of clinical research, it should not be considered as IVR in the Lewin tradition nor even as a variant.

Design science is the last in our discourse on variants of IVR. In her critical review, Baard (2010) finds design science to be extremely problematic. In Andriessen's (2007) study, the only theoretical considerations were the definition of the research problem and the intervention design. The intervention did not involve collaboration between the researcher and participants, and its design suggested a one-size-fits-all solution. Moreover, consultants were employed to design and implement the intervention for which the participants had to pay a fee. All of this is consistent with consultancy, which is not what Lewin intended for IVR. Beer (2001) argues that using consultants as intermediaries between the researcher and the social system may open the way for consultants to piggy-back self-interested recommendations onto the knowledge they are transporting. It may engender some research participant dependence on the consultants.

All these variants of IVR come together to form a fragmented picture of what IVR is and can do. This is problematic because it undermines the scientific value of IVR and its legitimacy as a research methodology. Further, it makes scholars reluctant to engage in IVR, thus limiting the relevance of accounting research and widening the research-practice gap.

Time

Achieving a duality of output can take a considerable amount of time, more often years as opposed to a year or less (e.g., Lyly-Yrjänäinen *et al.*, 2018; Campanale *et al.*, 2014; Chiucchi, 2013; Dumay, 2010; Jönsson & Lukka, 2007; Van de Ven & Johnson, 2006). Although not specific on the exact amount of time required for a valid and reliable IVR study, Jönsson and Lukka (2007) state that an interventionist researcher must develop a sound understanding of the problem and the social system, which is usually more of a medium-term proposition. Van de Ven and Johnson (2006) note that IVR should be longitudinal, which requires deep immersion in a social system, establishing familiarity and trust, and collaboration on issues as they naturally arise in the flow of a system—all this takes time (see also Jakkula *et al.*, 2006; Labro & Tuomela, 2003). As Alvesson and Deetz (2000) state, IVR can take years compared to the average of one year taken by an ethnographer.

Suomala and Lyly-Yrjänäinen (2012) highlight that IVR takes a long time because building trust and commitment between the researcher(s) and the participants takes time, and implementing an intervention can be slow-moving (see also Argyris, 1970; Fawcett *et al.*, 1994). They also claim that the more time interventionist researchers spend working in the field with the participants, the deeper the access and understanding they gain to the social system being researched. This can sometimes take more than a year alone to accomplish. Plus, they echo Jönsson and Lukka's notion that researching events as they naturally arise can prolong the lifespan of an IVR study.

As an example of a not atypical IVR study, Chiucchi's (2013) longitudinal IVR project on intellectual capital (IC) measurement and reporting system took more than five years from 2001 to 2006. She states that she could not have conducted such a rigorous examination of measuring and reporting on IC in an organisation in a shorter period of time. Additionally, IVR gave her an opportunity to understand the extent to which the case organisation benefitted from the intervention and the nature of the change that resulted. Understanding the role of intellectual capital in the firm's daily activities through meetings and the intervention took three years alone. This was followed by understanding the barriers to implementing an innovation, addressing those barriers, and completing the implementation, which took a further three years to accomplish. Campanale *et al.'s* (2014) 17-month intervention focussed on the ability of a costing system to support resource distribution and associated decision-making. However, we do not believe this period included the observations and interviews conducted to collect the initial data, and still the authors contend that 17 months was not enough time to realise the potential outcomes from the project.

By contrast, Dumay (2010) shows that an IVR project can also take a short amount of time. For example, he took only six weeks to help a university faculty redevelop its business strategy. He does, however, point out that a shorter timeframe can bring its own challenge, particularly time pressures and the need for a high level of competency in the specific skills relevant to the intervention. A project can also be considered longitudinal if the researcher follows up on an intervention. In the case of Dumay and Chiucchi (2014), the researchers were originally in the field for a short time with a strong intervention, but then followed up by observing and intervening with weaker actions as the impact of the original intervention evolved. Thus, IVR can be conducted on a continuum from a matter of weeks to many years, but shorter IVR projects tend to have stronger interventions.

Another factor in the time it takes to progress through an IVR study is the number of phases that must be completed along the way, especially as many are iterative (see Chapter 5). For instance, gaining access to a social system is applicable to all qualitative research but, in IVR, accessing a social system extends into identifying and understanding what the real-life problem is. That requires generating valid and useful information from both a social and a research perspective (Argyris, 1970). Reaching agreement on the nature of the problem also requires cooperation between the researcher(s) and the participants (Lewin, 1946, 1947; Jönsson & Lukka, 2007).

The next challenge is deciding on an intervention that is likely to address the problem. This may involve finding out whether an intervention already exists that has been used to solve a similar problem or developing a novel solution. Novel solutions typically need to be pilot-tested, which can sometimes lead to design changes and retesting, all of which extends the length of the project (Fawcett *et al.*, 1994). However, it is important to remember that interventions can cause unintended, harmful changes, so taking time as much time as is needed to get them right is crucial.

Last, just as IVR should occur along with the normal ebbs and flows of the social system functioning, those ebbs and flows cannot stop just because an intervention is occurring. For example, in Dumay (2010), the university went about its normal day-to-day operations while he and a few select staff developed the strategy, drawing on specific people when needed. Intervention design, development, and implementation should follow the natural rhythm of the organisation, but this also means that the organisation may need to allocate additional personnel and equipment if resources are repurposed away from their normal duties. However, in most cases, it is business as usual for the organisation, as change is a normal part of organisational life, and an IVR project is just one way for an organisation to implement change.

Researcher Qualities

Accounting and management scholars recognise that IVR demands multiple qualities in a researcher. Argyris (1970) refers extensively to the qualities needed to perform IVR effectively. Our interpretation of qualities is an individual's attributes, such as their perceptions, attitudes, and values, and we agree that these are important aspects for a researcher to consider when undertaking IVR. The most recent International Accounting Education Standards Board (IAESB, 2019) uses a similar term "capabilities" to describe a researcher's professional knowledge, skills, values, ethics, and attitudes, and also refer to the term "practical experience". Professional knowledge is defined as knowledge of an accounting discipline, such as auditing and assurance (IAESB, 2019). We add knowledge of research methodologies, methods, data collection, and data analysis approaches to this idea. Skills span intellectual and interpersonal expertise from problem-solving to negotiating (IAESB, 2019), and organisational skills are defined as the ability "to work effectively with or within an organisation to obtain the optimal results or outcomes from the people and resources available" (IAESB, 2019, p. 47). Practical experience incorporates a variety of workplace, managerial, and/or educational experiences (IAESB, 2019, international education standard 5).

We see researcher qualities as encompassing all these attributes, knowledge, skills, and experiences and believe they are critical to IVR given the nature of the research process, its activities, and potential outcomes. We do not discount professional values and ethics but rather categorise both of these as attributes.

The researcher qualities needed for IVR are different to those needed for other forms of research (Markides, 2007; Dumay & Baard, 2017; Dumay, 2010). Dumay (2010) emphasises that interventionist researchers require a similar set of skills to a professional manager in addition to academic research skills. Additionally, in IVR and based on our experience, researchers need the confidence to intervene, recognise that people in the emic world of practical reason may have a different worldview, and the ability to develop a rapport with those unlike themselves. To identify what researchers can learn from others, they need to be open and self-aware. Interpersonal skills focussed on communication, including listening skills, are paramount in traversing the different worldviews held by researchers and participants. Interpersonal skills are needed to develop conversations with participants that help uncover what is happening, rather than superficial interactions that result in participants only disclosing what they think the researcher wants to hear instead of the facts (Qu & Dumay, 2011, p. 256). Effective communication also requires researchers to know the language of the social system and go 'native', if required, to effectively collaborate with people. Researchers also need enough proficiencies to design and implement interventions and insights to understand the consequences of intervening actions. We exemplify the nature of these proficiencies in Chapter 11 and 12, alongside real-life examples of intervention design, development, and implementation. From our review of the IVR literature, we have compiled a summary of preferable qualities for an interventionist researcher, see Table 3.1.

Table 3.1 Researcher Qualities

Qualities	Features
Individual Attributes	Confidence and boldness Persistence Flexibility Self-awareness Trustworthiness Patience Open to learning from others Self-reflection Candour Adaptability
Knowledge	Command of the extant literature Expert knowledge (e.g., financial accounting, management accounting, auditing, organisational behaviour) Theories of practice and theories with status Culture and diversity
Skills	Ability to intervene Analytical skills Time management Data collection and analysis techniques (e.g., interview skills, coding) Interpersonal communication and listening skills Conflict management
Experience	Practical (i.e., managerial or other professional) Theoretical (i.e., educational)

Source: Baard and Dumay (2018), Dumay and Baard (2017), Chiucchi (2013), Dumay (2010), Jönsson and Lukka (2007), Markides (2007), Boog (2003), Fawcett *et al.* (1994) and Argyris (1970)

We note that in published IVR studies, accounting researchers tend to focus on interventions involving control systems (e.g., Chiucchi, 2013), costing systems (e.g., Campanale *et al.*, 2014), organisational strategies (e.g., Dumay, 2010), or supply chain management (e.g., Seal, 1999). These interventions involve organisational mechanisms, not people, so the qualities outlined in Table 3.1 are the types of skills required for these interventions.

In reflecting on researcher qualities and based on our review of the IVR empirics, we find a lack of specificity about when and how researchers should apply these qualities when undertaking IVR. This is a problematic situation, especially when considering the multifaceted nature of social systems. Hence, we integrate researcher qualities where relevant throughout this book. For example, intervening in an organisation centred on individuals working the organisation requires advanced interpersonal skills that can reach the intellectual, emotional, and behavioural aspects of the people involved (Argyris, 1970). These skills may be common to organisational behaviourists, psychologists, and experienced counsellors (Reddy, 1994), but not necessarily to accounting researchers. Similarly, intervening in a group requires its own set of highly developed skills, such as conflict management, team coordination, etc. (Argyris, 1970). We discuss this matter further in Chapter 9.

Conducting effective IVR demands a diverse repertoire of skills because the social system in which IVR occurs is complex and ambiguous, and hence challenges manifest (Dumay, 2010; Rothman & Thomas, 1994). Argyris (1970) refers to challenges in the field that interventionist researchers are likely to encounter as conditions, arguing that patience, adaptability and persistence, and interpersonal and possibly conflict management skills are required to overcome them. Suomala *et al.* (2014) also find that there are sources of tension in the field, which we infer to represent challenges in the field, requiring specific approaches by and competences from researchers (see Chapter 10). Researchers engaging in relevant research must be ambidextrous (Markides, 2007). It is critical to interventionist activities that researchers are honest and open with themselves and with other members of their research team about their competencies to undertake IVR (Argyris, 1970). It places the researcher's reputation at risk. The unintended consequences for the social system may be extremely harmful and significantly influence its survival. And, without the necessary skills to see the project through, the study is likely to fail.

Both the time and the researcher qualities needed to conduct effective IVR make this research methodology more difficult than other research traditions. But this does not mean gloom and doom for the methodology. Rather, by creating awareness of IVR's 'bad' aspects, we can prevent them from becoming problems in the first place. To start, researchers need to be realistic about how much time they have, and therefore what IVR can be accomplished in that time. For instance, with not much time, it might be better to modify an existing intervention over designing a new one. Second, planning is critical in IVR, which we discuss in Chapter 5 and 6. Third, using research teams consisting of scholars from other academic fields, other accounting disciplines, and/or with different researcher qualities can fill missing competencies in more expansive projects. Otherwise, researchers are better advised to limit their projects to those complementary to their current skill set. Notably, Van de Ven and Johnson (2006, p. 812) provide a sound argument for engaging in IVR with a mixed team of researchers and practitioners to mitigate the risks associated with time and missing researcher qualities (see Chapter 10).

Publications

Jönsson and Lukka (2007) state that with the prevailing publish or perish attitudes, it is not surprising that accounting scholars may be less inclined to engage in IVR. Scholars are required to publish regularly, even while a time-consuming IVR project is ongoing. Markides (2007) states that less experienced academics perceive both the pressure to publish and to gain tenure as scholarly responsibilities. While achieving tenure provides academic freedom to engage in relevant or useful research, it does not preclude the need to consistently publish in high-quality academic journals over limited timeframes to achieve academic rewards (Merchant, 2012). Moreover, Merchant (2012) argues for journal editors to amend their reviewing policies to accentuate useful research and for business school administrators to support the value of the useful research in their reward structures, promotion, and tenure criteria. Evidence from recently-published IVR shows promising progress in the likelihood of getting an IVR study published (ter Bogt & van Helden, 2012). Accordingly, this should motivate scholarly engagement with IVR.

The main concern with publications, beyond their acceptability in the academic discourse, is the ability of researchers to write up IVR research so that is publishable. Many journals openly encourage practice-based case studies, whereas some of the more prestigious journals might not accept case studies because of their lack of theory. But IVR demands both theoretical and practical contributions, which fulfils both demands.

There are several good publications that give advice on how to integrate case study research and theory. The two most prominent of these being Eisenhardt (1989) who outlines how to build theory from case study research, and Robert Yin's book *Case Study Research: Design and Methods*. Yin (2017) argues that theory helps to outline the research design, define the data for collections, and it mobilises researchers to generalise findings from the case study. The latter issue of generalisability is a key issue in the debate between the merits of qualitative versus quantitative research (Parker & Northcott, 2016), and one that limits the number of suitable journals interventionist researchers have as potential publication outlets. This is discussed in more detail in Chapter 13.

The Ugly of IVR—Consulting

One controversial issue relating to IVR is whether it is akin to consulting. Argyris (1970) states that researchers normally consider the act of intervening as consulting. Baard (2010) finds that scholars undertaking IVR in any form are aware of the association between IVR and consulting and, to preserve IVR's integrity and reduce scholarly reluctance to conduct IVR, they attempt to differentiate between the two. In forging a future path ahead for IVR, scholarly concerns about the association between IVR and consulting should not be ignored (Baard, 2010; Tucker & Parker, 2013; Lukka & Suomala, 2014). This persistent problem of consulting and the fragmented identity of IVR leaves scholars gridlocked on whether IVR is 'to be or not to be' on their research agendas (Baard & Dumay, 2018). So why does this association endure?

Discussed in Chapter 2, management accounting is a practice-oriented discipline where researchers conduct applied research, thus management accounting researchers and consultants share a focus on applying knowledge to solve a problem in the field. Van Helden *et al.* (2010, p. 85) defines consulting as "the process of transferring knowledge and/or skills from . . . the consultant . . . to the client". These authors also state that consultants operate in a competitive market where they provide expertise in response to market demand. In fact, some practice-oriented academics also operate consulting practices. Kaplan and colleagues referred to as 'consultant' researchers are scholars that collaborate with research participants to derive significant management accounting innovations, such as the balanced scorecard and activity-based costing (Scapens, 2008; Merchant, 2012). These innovations are extremely useful and have changed the way organisations view performance measurement; how firms translate strategy into action; and how they make hidden overheads visible. Developing and testing theories related to these innovations, however, has remained the responsibility of traditional academics (Nørreklit, 2000, 2003).

According to Kaplan (1998), the processes associated with developing management accounting innovations is "innovation action research". Kaplan (1998) argues that innovation action research relies on scholars working with case organisations to develop a theory and then examine its potential to improve organisational performance. Hence, this form of action research is focussed on creation and learning rather than testing theory (which gives us another variant of IVR conceived from yet another interpretation of Lewin's work). Kaplan (1998) is open about charging consulting fees for his work because he argues it was of value to the research participants. However, in doing so, Kaplan directly associates his variant of IVR with consulting. Jönsson and Lukka (2007, p. 382) assert that asking a research participant for consulting fees is "not a useful foundation for IVR". In our experience, there is little doubt that some management accounting scholars undertake IVR without a clear differentiation between research and consulting, thereby perpetuating the notion that interventionist researchers are consultants.

So, what is the difference between a consultant and a scholar? Van Helden *et al.* (2010) differentiates between the two based on their knowledge sources, how practice influences knowledge creation activities, and the type of knowledge they create. The source of a consultant's knowledge is experience, accumulated from previous services and solutions provided to clients, from working in teams with colleagues who share their learnings, and from professional journals. Conversely, academics source their knowledge from their teachers and mentors, from the literature, from conferences and forums where they interact with their peers, or from conducting their own research. Van Helden *et al.* (2010) define knowledge as meaningful information that is acquired through experience, interpretation, and reflection, identifying two types of knowledge: tacit

Table 3.2 Knowledge for Researchers and Consultants

Knowledge	Researchers	Consultants
Orientation	Applicable to discipline and peer groups: answering research questions	Applicable to practice: direct relevance to clients
Type	Explicit: published research results and findings	Explicit: report for a client
		Tacit: knowledge from informal contacts and client collaboration
Motives for Creating Knowledge	Discipline-driven: answering research questions and publishing research	Problem-solving demands from practice
	Academic peer groups	Exploit consulting tools and approaches
Application	Suggestive for use in practice: research implications	Knowledge is 'off-the-shelf' and made for practice

Source: Adapted from van Helden *et al.* (2010)

and explicit. Tacit knowledge is "personal, context-specific, and difficult to formalize", whereas explicit knowledge is "based on formal and systematic language" (p. 85). In Table 3.2, we identify the different types of knowledge that consultants and researchers create, along with the drivers for creating each type of knowledge. Tucker and Parker (2013) find that consultants focus on the commercial viability and value of their solutions, whereas academics are concerned with approaches to creating knowledge and their theoretical aspects (Labro & Tuomela, 2003).

Merchant (2012) states that consulting firms conduct surveys and studies to try and improve practice in the short term, but their work is unlikely to withstand scholarly scrutiny. He also asserts that organisations in need of research to help solve a problem often turn to consulting firms or think-tanks because they are 'one-stop-shops' and "speak [the] practitioners' language". Moreover, they are able to show how their results are likely to drive management practice (Merchant, 2012, p. 344).

In reflecting on this problem, Baard and Dumay (2018) state that theory is a strong point of differentiation between consulting and applied research. Lewin (1946, 1947) was unrelenting in his assertions that his form of action research must incorporate theory just as required in pure science. Consultants have no desire to develop theories or create knowledge with theoretical linkages (Labro & Tuomela, 2003; Merchant, 2012; van Helden *et al.*, 2010). Merchant (2012) argues that problem-solving research, including IVR, is still focussed on theory even though the methodology is different from traditional approaches. This differentiates researchers from consultants. Advancing theory occurs when researchers engage with practitioners in problem-solving, and where solving the problem is scrutinised in theoretical terms (e.g., Suomala *et al.*, 2014). Evidence of IVR using theory in accounting research is available in the literature. For instance, Chiucchi (2013) applied Kolb's experiential learning theory (i.e., theory of status) in her IVR study to support intervention design and to analyse and contextualise the case study results. Campanale *et al.* (2014) provide evidence of using intervention theory (i.e., theory of practice) in their research on time-driven activity-based costing in Tuscan rural hospitals. Upon reflection, convincing arguments supporting theory are a primary point of differentiation between consulting and applied accounting research, as is evident in the literature. Moreover, emphasising the role of theory, which manifests in IVR's theoretical output, differentiates consulting from IVR. The role of theory in IVR positions it as sufficiently and scientifically quite unlike consulting (see also Chapter 1).

Although we can now easily differentiate between IVR and consulting, that does not mean that interventionist researchers should stop accepting funding for their IVR research. In many countries, academics are measured on their ability to attract research funding, and research grants can come from many sources, including industry. In Australia, industry funding to perform a specific task is classified as "*Category 3: Industry and Other Research Income*". Some might still decide such research is not consulting because *bone fide* research projects require full ethics approval, whereas a consulting engagement is only subject to a service contract and any agreements relating to the intellectual property produced from the project. However, what accounting researchers must realise is that these arrangements are incredibly common in other disciplines, such as health, medicine, and engineering and especially in Europe and Scandinavia where there are fewer restrictions on engaging with industry.

In Summation

In the end, undertaking IVR can seem like a minefield for an inexperienced researcher. However, we do not want to discourage researchers from IVR because it is a valid research opportunity and one that can be extremely rewarding. IVR can provide insights that no other research can and effect real change in a way that no other research can. Our best advice is to engage with other researchers who have already gone down the IVR path. This is not dissimilar to anybody who has never before approached qualitative research. We all must start somewhere, and that somewhere was with our more experienced colleagues as either supervisors or mentors. Thus, IVR is no different than any other research approach; they all take time, practice, and understanding to get right. We also recommend you start slowly, with a small project where any unintended consequences will be minor until you learn the ropes. We certainly do not advocate undertaking huge projects on your own as a first venture, but that you should approach such huge projects in cooperation with more experienced researchers. One should always learn to walk before learning to run.

References

Alvesson, M. & Deetz, S. (2000). *Doing critical management research*. London, UK: Sage Publications.

Andriessen, D. (2007). Designing and testing an OD intervention: Reporting intellectual capital to develop organisations. *Journal of Applied Behavioural Science*, 31(8), 819–841.

Argyris, C. (1970). *Intervention theory and method: A behavioural science view*. Reading, MA: Addison-Wesley Publishing Company.

Argyris, C., Putnam, R., & Smith, D. (1985). *Action science*. San Francisco, CA: Jossey-Bass.

Baard, V.C. (2010). A critical view of interventionist research. *Qualitative Research in Accounting and Management*, 7(1), 13–45.

Baard, V.C. & Dumay, J. (2018). Interventionist research in accounting: Reflections on the good, the bad and the ugly. *Accounting and Finance*, Advance online publication. https://doi.org/10.1111/acfi.12409

Beer, M. (2001). Why management research findings are unimplementable: An action science perspective. *Reflections*, 2(3), 58–65.

Boog, B.W.M. (2003). The emancipatory character of action research, its history and the present state of the art. *Journal of Community & Applied Social Psychology*, 13, 426–438.

Campanale, C., Cinquini, L., & Tenucci, A. (2014). Time driven activity-based costing to improve transparency and decision making in healthcare. *Qualitative Research in Accounting & Management*, 11, 165–186.

Cartwright, D. (Ed.). (1951). *Field theory in social science: Selected theoretical papers by Kurt Lewin*. London, UK: Social Science Paperbacks.

Chiucchi, M.S. (2013). Intellectual capital accounting in action: Enhancing learning through interventionist research. *Journal of Intellectual Capital*, 14, 48–68.

Dickens, L. & Watkins, K. (1999). Action research: Rethinking Lewin. *Management Learning*, 30, 127–140.

Dumay, J. (2010). A critical reflective discourse of an interventionist research project. *Qualitative Research in Accounting and Management*, 7(1), 46–70.

Dumay, J. & Baard, V. (2017). An introduction to interventionist research in accounting. In Z. Hoque, L.D. Parker, M.A. Covaleski, & K. Haynes (Eds.), *The Routledge companion to qualitative accounting research methods* (pp. 265–283). New York, NY: Routledge.

Dumay, J. & Chiucchi, M.S. (2014, June 11–13). *Unlocking intellectual capital*. Paper presented at the 2014 International Forum on Knowledge Asset Dynamics (IFKAD), Matera, Italy.

Eden, C. & Huxham, C. (1996). Action research for management research. *British Journal of Management*, 7, 75–86.

Eisenhardt, K.M. (1989). Building theories from case study research. *Academy of Management Review*, 14(4), 532–549.

Fawcett, S.B., Suarez-Balcazar, Y., Balcazar, F.E., White, G.W., Paine, A.L., Blanchard, K.A., & Embree, M.G. (1994). Conducting intervention research— The design and development process. In J. Rothman & E.J. Thomas (Eds.), *Intervention research: Design and development for human service* (pp. 25–54). Binghamton, NY: Haworth Press.

International Accounting Education Standards Board (IAESB). (2019). *2019 Handbook of International Accounting Education Standards*. Retrieved from: www.iaesb.org/publications-resources/2019-handbook-international-education-standards

Jakkula, V., Lyly-Yrjänäinen, J., & Suomala, P. (2006, December). *Challenges of practically relevant management accounting research: The scope and intensity of interventionist research*. Paper presented at the 5th New Practices in Management Accounting Research Conference, Brussels.

Jönsson, S. & Lukka, K. (2007). There and back again: Doing interventionist research in management accounting. In C.S. Chapman, A.G. Hopwood, & M.S. Shields (Eds.), *Handbook of management accounting research* (Vol. 1, pp. 373–397). Oxford, UK: Elsevier.

Kaplan, R.S. (1998). Innovation action research: Creating new management theory and practice. *Journal of Management Accounting Research*, 10, 89–118.

Kasanen, E., Lukka, K., & Silonen, A. (1993). The constructive approach in management accounting research. *Journal of Management Accounting Research*, 5, 243–264.

Labro, E. & Tuomela, T. (2003). On bringing more action into management accounting research: Process considerations based on two constructive case studies. *European Accounting Review*, 12, 409–442.

Lewin, K. (1946). Action research and minority problems. *Journal of Social Issues*, 11, 34–46.

Lewin, K. (1947). Frontiers in group dynamics: ll. Channels of group life: Social planning and action research. *Human Relations*, 1(2), 143–153.

Lukka, K. & Suomala, P. (2014). Relevant interventionist research: Balancing three intellectual virtues. *Accounting and Business Research*, 44(2), 204–220.

Lyly-Yrjänäinen, J., Suomala, P., Laine, T., & Mitchell, F. (2018). *Interventionist research in management accounting: Theory contributions with societal impact*. New York, NY: Routledge.

Malmi, T., Järvinen, P., & Lillirank, P. (2004). A collaborative approach for management project cost of poor quality. *European Accounting Review*, 13(2), 293–317.

Markides, C. (2007). In search of ambidextrous professors. *Academy of Management Journal*, 50, 762–768.

Merchant, K.A. (2012). Making management accounting research more useful. *Pacific Accounting Review*, 24(3), 334–356.

Nørreklit, H. (2000). The balance on the balanced scorecard: A critical analysis of some of its assumptions. *Management Accounting Research*, 11(1), 65–88.

Nørreklit, H. (2003). The balanced scorecard: What is the score? A rhetorical analysis of the balanced scorecard. *Accounting, Organizations and Society*, 28(6), 591–619.

Parker, L.D. (2008). Interpreting interpretive accounting research. *Critical Perspectives on Accounting*, 19, 909–914.

Parker, L.D. & Northcott, D. (2016). Qualitative generalising in accounting research: Concepts and strategies. *Accounting, Auditing & Accountability Journal*, 29(6), 1100–1131.

Peters, M. & Robinson, V. (1984). The origins and status of action research. *The Journal of Applied Behavioural Science*, 20(2), 113–124.

Qu, S.Q. & Dumay, J. (2011). The qualitative research interview. *Qualitative Research in Accounting and Management*, 8(3), 238–264.

Reddy, W.B. (1994). *Intervention skills: Process consultation for small groups and teams*. Johannesburg, South Africa: Pfeiffer and Company.

Rothman, J. & Thomas, E.J. (Eds.). (1994). *Intervention research: Design and development for human service*. Binghamton, NY: Haworth Press.

Scapens, R.W. (2008). Seeking the relevance of interpretive research: A contribution to the polyphonic debate. *Critical Perspectives on Accounting*, 19, 915–919.

Seal, W., Cullen, J., Dunlop, A., Berry, T., & Ahmed, M. (1999). Enacting a European supply chain: A case study on the role of management accounting. *Management Accounting Research*, 10(3), 303–322.

Suomala, P. & Lyly-Yrjänäinen, J. (2012). *Management accounting research in practice: Lessons learnt from an interventionist approach*. New York, NY: Routledge.

Suomala, P., Lyly-Yrjänäinen, J., & Lukka, K. (2014). Battlefield around interventions: A reflective analysis of conducting interventionist research in management accounting. *Management Accounting Research*, 25, 304–314.

ter Bogt, H. & van Helden, J. (2012). The practical relevance of management accounting research and the role of qualitative methods therein: The debate continues. *Qualitative Research in Accounting and Management*, 9(3), 265–295.

Tucker, B.P. & Parker, L.D. (2013). In our ivory towers? The research-practice gap in management accounting. *Accounting and Business Research*, 44(2), 104–143. https://doi.org/10.1080/00014788.2013.798234

Van Aken, J. (2004). Management research based on the paradigm of the design sciences: The quest for fieldtested and grounded technological rules. *Journal of Management Studies*, 41(2), 219–246.

Van de Ven, A.H. & Johnson, P.E. (2006). Knowledge for theory and practice. *The Academy of Management Review*, 31(4), 802–821.

van Helden, G.J., Aardema, H., ter Bogt, H.J., & Groot, T.L.C.M. (2010). Knowledge creation for practice in public sector management accounting by consultants and academics: Preliminary findings and directions for future research. *Management Accounting Research*, 21, 83–94.

Wouters, M. & Roijmans, D. (2011). Using prototypes to induce experimentation and knowledge integration in the development of enabling accounting information. *Contemporary Accounting Research*, 28(2), 708–736.

Wouters, M. & Wilderom, C. (2008). Developing performance measurement systems as enabling formalisation: A longitudinal field study of a logistics department. *Accounting, Organizations and Society*, 33(4–5), 488–515.

Yin, R.K. (2017). *Case study research: Design and methods* (6th ed.). Thousand Oaks, CA: Sage Publications Inc.

Part 2

Methodological Foundations and Design— The Pillars of Authenticity

4 To Intervene—Integrating Philosophy and Theory

Argyris published *Intervention Theory* in 1970, probably little knowing the insights this pioneering work would impart. Closely based on the governing principles of IVR, penned by the founding father of IVR, Kurt Lewin (1946, 1947), intervention theory (IVT) derives from organisational theory, which is in turn based on a melting pot of group dynamics, inter-group relations, and organisational behaviour; psychology; cognitive science; and other behavioural sciences. Recognising and employing these foundations is critical to conducting legitimate IVR because it provides clarity on what IVR is and how to undertake it. Further, as IVR requires dual theoretical and practical output and IVT is *the* theory of IVR, IVT is the theory of practice you will be 'contributing to' in any IVR project. Jönsson and Lukka (2007) devised a philosophy of IVR for management accounting. Based on our examination of this philosophy, we find no reason why this philosophy cannot be applied to all areas of accounting IVR. It too evolves from multiple spheres, including anthropology, decision-making theory, and ethnomethodology. Alongside IVT, the philosophy establishes an integrated reliable and valid foundation for conducting contemporary IVR.

Philosophy and IVR

In this section, we accentuate some general philosophical aspects applicable to IVR, followed by our interpretation of Jönsson and Lukka's (2007) IVR philosophy.

The definitions of philosophy are diverse and subject to change given the space of time and events occurring over time (Honderich, 1995). Generally, philosophy is defined as thinking about thinking, which usually leads to forming beliefs and making claims about the world and its many components based on the knowledge we have. According to Honderich (1995), philosophy consists of three main elements: critical thinking, epistemology, and ethics. Critical thinking concerns the nature of the world we live in and our position within it—who we are as individuals, how we relate to one another, and the events in our history that change who we are. Some call this metaphysics; others a theory of existence but, given that interventionist researchers inhabit both the etic world of pure reason and the emic world of practical reason, we find this type of critical thinking to be very applicable to IVR. Moving iteratively between the two domains, generating theoretical knowledge in one and solving practical problems in the other is easier if the researcher understands who they are, which world they are in (right now), and their goals for being there. Further, critical thinking can help the transition from being a 'tourist' to an 'insider' in the emic world and moving between the objective world of knowledge and the subjective world of action.

Epistemology is the 'what' of knowledge. It concerns how knowledge is acquired, what people know, and how knowledge relates to truth, beliefs, and justifying beliefs. It is a theory of knowledge. Episteme, derived from epistemology, is an intellectual virtue that refers to scientific knowledge (Flyvbjerg, 2001). Episteme is also associated with theoretical relevance fundamental to all scholarly research, including IVR (Lukka & Suomala, 2014) (see Chapter 2). The interventionist researcher inhabits the world of pure reason and produces scientific knowledge. This knowledge is unambiguous and constitutes logical information acquired through the process of reason, which is applied to reality. Hence, the researcher uses scientific knowledge to provide rational arguments that explain why they believe an assertion to be true. For example, the researcher will ask, 'Am I justified in believing that a particular problem exists in a particular social system?' To address this question, the researcher needs to acquire or generate 'scientific' knowledge that serves as evidence to justify their beliefs. Therefore, in the context of IVR in accounting, the researcher must provide scientific or theoretical knowledge to justify intervening in a social system (i.e., the emic realm), to inform solutions to problems, and to convey the outcome of IVR to other actors in the etic world that makes sense to them (Jönsson & Lukka, 2007). We acknowledge that in the context of social science like accounting, scientific knowledge as it applies to natural sciences is not the same. Yet, interventionist researchers are compelled to generate scientific knowledge in IVR for legitimacy purposes and to achieve publication in scholarly journals (see Chapter 2 and 13).

How we morally conduct ourselves in the world could not be more relevant to IVR. From even noticing that a social problem exists, to whether we choose to watch or act once we recognise a problem exists, to the outcomes we try and engineer should we choose not to stand idly by—all are linked to our ethics. Although intervening and not intervening both have consequences, the direct 'goodness' or 'badness' that comes from intervening is usually more hard felt, which is what makes ethics so relevant to interventionist researchers (see Chapter 6). 'Goodness' values are the consequence of right actions, for example, actions that stop or alleviate anguish, solve problems, and empower and emancipate people. Conversely, 'Badness' values are the consequence of wrong actions which cause harm. Thus, ethics or moral philosophy is also referred to as the theory of value.

Closely aligned to ethics and values are the motives a researcher has for conducting IVR. Flyvbjerg (2001) draws on the work of Aristotle to align the intellectual virtue of phronesis with ethics. Flyvbjerg (2001, p. 57) interprets phronesis, as the analysis of values—"things that are good or bad for man" and states that values are a "point of departure for action"; action is central to IVR. Further, Flyvbjerg (2001) argues that phronesis is concerned with conduct and it needs consideration, judgement, choice, and experience. Our interpretation of ethics is the values an interventionist researcher holds to help them ensure that right actions are maximised and wrong actions minimised or avoided. Moreover, researchers must know the social system values to ensure ethical feasibility of their approach to intervening in the social system. Thus, phronesis is related to action but also relates to ethical wisdom and knowledge on what behaviour is appropriate in a circumstance. In other words, ethics are context-dependent (Lukka & Suomala, 2014).

The Philosophical Nature of IVR

Jönsson and Lukka (2007) did more than think about how we think about IVR; they published those thoughts as a philosophy of IVR in the context of management accounting and, despite the specificity, we believe their insights broadly apply to IVR in any accounting area (see also Baard, 2010, p. 28). We encourage readers particularly interested in the philosophy of IVR to review Jönsson and Lukka (2007). What follows here is our interpretation of their work.

Their philosophy evolved from multiple sources, including classical rationality, ethnomethodology, practice theory, decision-making, and anthropology. IVR is unique because the researcher seeks to intervene in organisations and collaboratively solve real-world problems, rather than just observing people in situ. This means that the researcher enters the social system with the intention of using a technology (i.e., an intervention) "to transform deficits into assets" (Carkhuff, 1983, p. 163). Philosophically, researchers inhabit the world of classical rationality, which centres on facts and explanation or pure reason (Wallace, 2018). Pure reason allows us to reflect on past events, consider why they occurred, and attempt to predict what events may occur in the future. Usually, this type of theorising is undertaken from the outside looking in.

However, with IVR, the researcher must enter the social system in the field to achieve a practical understanding of the problem. Here, problems do not take the shape of: 'What has happened?' and 'Will it happen again?'. More often, they take the form: 'What should I do now?' Thus, the emic realm is not concerned with pure reason but rather with action—or "practical reason" as Wallace (2018) calls it. Practical reason is concerned with matters of value and what action would be most desirable to adopt. People in social systems define their practical dilemma, deliberate on what they should do, take action, and assume responsibility for the outcomes. When researchers enter the field, they examine the problem in the practice or action context to adopt an emic viewpoint on the problem, which enables them to ask: 'Am I justified in believing what I do about a problem to be true?' Thus, in understanding the problem as it occurs in the field, interventionist researchers can adopt an ethnomethodological approach to intervening in the social system (see Jönsson & Lukka, 2007).

In entering a social system, the researcher needs to transition from outsider to insider, which requires taking on an anthropological view of living another life. Jönsson and Lukka (2007) state being an insider means that the researcher: a) has become a capable and trustworthy actor in the field of practice; b) understands the intentions of other actors in the field and communicates and acts in cooperation with them; and c) demonstrates a proficient understanding of the problem within the field of practice.

This is not to say that the researcher never holds a divergent view, quite the opposite in fact. Like a true insider, a researcher has the right and probably will hold their own different and contentious opinions about what they experience. For a researcher, becoming an insider probably does not mean asking: 'What should I do now?' But it does mean asking: 'What should a person like me do in a situation like this?' It also means access to information, the right to deliberation, and the right to take action. Jönsson and Lukka (2007) describe deliberation as developing a sound argument for how one plans to address a problem. As a researcher, however, decisions are not converted into actions through authority but rather by developing justifiable actions and then mobilising free will to support them. By justifiable, we mean that actions must be aligned with the original objectives to be addressed. In mobilising free will, we apply what we think and decide are appropriate, that is the right or wrong actions, thus "causing things to happen" (Jönsson & Lukka, 2007, p. 379). What is important to remember here is that making decisions and mobilising actions as an IVR insider means being held responsible for the consequences of those actions just like everyone else—whether intended or not.

Hence, Jönsson and Lukka's (2007) deepest and broadest insight is how the IVR philosophy allows researchers to move there and back again between the emic and etic worlds to generate solutions to problems, report results, link research findings to a theoretical framework, and, above all, accept responsibility for our actions.

Intervention Theory and IVR

IVT is a theory of practice (Sayer, 1992) that was built by Argyris (1970) from organisational theory, integrated with borrowed concepts from the behavioural sciences five decades ago, into a coherent theoretical approach to IVR that follows Lewin's original ideas and principles (Peters & Robinson, 1984; Dickens & Watkins, 1999). As a unifying theory absent from Lewin's work, IVT has potential as an umbrella theory to guide the practice of IVR (Baard & Dumay, 2018). We argue that IVT opens the 'black box' of IVR (Suomala *et al.*, 2014). Moreover, we believe that with further testing, refining, and critiquing, it has significant potential to become a contemporary theory of practice to inform the IVR landscape. To date, IVT has not seen much recognition in the accounting literature. It has only been critiqued twice since publication, and its actual use is limited to a few doctoral theses (Baard, 2010). However, IVT has been used more extensively in other domains, such as organisational development, occupational health, sociology, psychology, management information systems, and education. Recently, IVT was used in a management accounting IVR project, see Campanale *et al.* (2014).

IVT revolves around three main principles: generating valid and useful information; using free choice to make an informed decision; and developing internal commitment to the decision made. According to Argyris (1970, p. 14), these principles underpin empirical IVR, without which IVR would "lack a sense of thrust and direction". Methods and procedures derived from these principles serve to guide empirical IVR. Collectively, they constitute a valid IVR cycle for any form of intervention that a researcher may wish to embark on. In Chapter 5, we draw on the Intervention Research Framework adapted from the Rothman and Thomas (1994) Intervention Design and Development (D&D) framework to help solidify the cycle. Here, we discuss each of these three principles in more detail.

Generating Valid and Useful Information

Valid information means that the information is non-contradictory, verifiable, and relevant in that it describes the elements that define the problem. Additionally, the information must be useful as a basis for change because it, for example, begins a learning process needed to solve the problem or it establishes the host organisation's competence and effectiveness. (Different research methods and the different sorts of information they produce are discussed in further detail in Chapter 7.) Fawcett *et al.* (1994) state that the purpose of generating valid and useful information is to acquire views on: the 'what' and the 'why' of the problem; who or what within the social system the problem is affecting; the negative consequences of the problem; who should share responsibility for problem-solving; and the key features of potential interventions. Hence, with the help of the researcher, the social system itself can generate enough information to allow a meaningful analysis of the problem.

Generating valid and useful information serves three main functions. First, it allows an in-depth understanding of the organisation's characteristics and helps to develop an accurate, meaningful, and, most importantly, collaborative understanding of the problem (Lewin, 1946). As Argyris (1970) cautions, this first principle can be the most intricate because it is unlikely for there to be a clear view of what the problem is within the social system. Different people will have different views of the problem, many may not be able to accurately express their views, and some may not even be aware that a problem exists at all. This makes sense because, if those involved understood exactly what the problem was, they probably would not need a researcher. Differing views exist because people's behaviour and attitudes are influenced by their positions and associated power differentials, their group and intergroup memberships, and their personalities and values.

Given the different social values, positions, and power differentials in any social system, it is not uncommon for people to be cautious about being candid and even adeptly distort information to avoid detection that they presented a view on the problem. Here, the role of the researcher in creating a comfortable space for actors to provide valid and useful information is critical. Circumstances that can make people feel more comfortable contributing include an encouraging atmosphere, protecting the rights of all to express their views, alleviating concerns about differences of opinion, helping people clarify their views, and providing psychological safety with no undue influence or coercion. Thus, researcher qualities are important in this regard (see Chapters 3 and 9).

Second, the method of data collection should reflect a delicate balance between serving the interests of the social system and accurately conceptualising the problem. Data collection methods include, for example, informal conversations, emails, telephone calls, interviews, and workshops (e.g. Dumay, 2010; Chiucchi, 2013; Cullen *et al.*, 2013; Campanale *et al.*, 2014). Alderfer (1976) reminds us that having one's 'data' collected is not an everyday event for most people. As such, they may experience power issues, suffer morale issues, or may act differently because of the insights obtained from their data. Collecting data through focus groups can bring individuals together and sharing the information may influence how they function in their organisation. Therefore, researchers should be aware that even collecting data is likely to influence the social system, making the methods used an important consideration.

A third function related to data collection is the process of integrating the information into a meaningful pattern that conceptualises the problem. In a system of differing views, achieving congruency on the nature of the problem will usually require dialogue and negotiation. A consensual understanding of the problem conceptualises the practical task at hand and provides scope to develop provisional linkages with theory (Thomas & Rothman, 1994). This is consistent with the etic philosophical viewpoint taken by Jönsson and Lukka (2007). We see the etic aspect as important to create an intervention with "substance" and with "sound argument, reasoning and demonstration" (Neu *et al.*, 2001, p. 757). Reaching a shared viewpoint also offers preliminary insights into potential interventions that might be needed to solve the problem along with the most likely challenges to appear and exemplifies the researcher's ambidextrous qualities needed to implement a successful intervention (Markides, 2007). Markides (2007) defines ambidextrous qualities as the skills, values, and attitudes needed to produce academic research versus managerially relevant research. Both are different, but interventionist researchers need both.

Argyris (1970) argues that although collecting data and generating valid and useful information requires time, persistence, and resources, starting the process of exploring interventions serves to accurately diagnose the problem and supports the interventionist in adding to the knowledge in their field.

Making a Free and Informed Decision

This second principle of IVT is not about the researcher weighing options and executing a chosen strategy. It is about the participants of the IVR project making a free and informed choice about which of several alternative interventions they want to implement. Their choice(s) must be based on full knowledge of the concepts and possible solutions associated with each intervention, the costs and availability of human resources, and the time commitments required by the actors (Baard, 2010). With free and informed choice, the participants are less reliant on the researcher to solve their problems and more willing to implement the intervention. As Argyris (1970, p. 19) puts it, it "makes it possible [for the participants] to remain responsible for their own vocation". Argyris (1970) emphasises that freedom of choice is important for there to be sufficient willingness and motivation by those involved to work on the problem, to bring about change, to promote autonomy, and to encourage people to take responsibility for their own futures. We argue that this second principle is essential for empowering and emancipating people and for ensuring the IVR project yields outcomes with societal relevance (i.e., phronesis).

Some examples of how interventionist researchers have designed their studies to promote free and informed choice are useful here. In Campanale *et al.*'s (2014) study of effective accounting systems for rural hospitals, there were two different and very clearly-designed roles for the researchers and the participants (i.e., the financial controllers and the clinicians). The researchers had to understand the problems with the hospital's accounting system so as to propose a set of possible solutions, but they also had to be careful not to express opinions or preferences that would compromise the participants' ability to make a free and informed choice between the options. Likewise, the participants had to provide information about their problems with the current system, discuss the proposed solutions, and choose among them given their workflow, their expectations, and the merits of each choice.

Chiucchi (2013), on the other hand, had fewer clear roles and dubious free and informed choice. The project, to implement intellectual capital performance measures, included some discussions over potential interventions with the managers to help them make sense of, and solicit their engagement with, the proposals. However, despite claims that the intervention was "officially accepted", the gatekeeper and researcher played a much larger role in the design of the new system than the managers who were ultimately going to use it (Chiucchi, 2013, p. 58). Of course, no one forced the intervention on the managers, but that does not mean that the decision to implement it was as free and informed as it could have been. Notably, neither intervention was successfully implemented.

Internal Commitment

The third principle of IVT, internal commitment, follows naturally from free and informed choice. It is where a person internalises their actions and their choice of intervention and takes on a high sense of ownership for its success. Part of this ownership comes from a sense of hope that the solution will fulfil both their needs and those of the larger social system, and part comes from a sense of responsibility. Therefore, a person who has made an internal commitment is not only acting by their own free will but also with minimal dependence on others—they are emancipated. These people are far more likely to maintain a strong commitment to the intervention through its challenges; plus, they are more likely to effectively manage any implications that do occur (Argyris, 1970; Campanale *et al.*, 2014). Argyris (1970) states that committed participants more often execute decisions in a way that prevents the problem from recurring. We assert that internal commitment is a sign of positive social change, which is inclusive and distributed by an effective social system.

Overall, IVT offers a frame on how IVR is approached, where its use may yield new knowledge to justify beliefs about IVR as a legitimate methodology. Moreover, using IVT enables accounting researchers to produce research with theoretical relevance. However, Argyris (1970) clearly highlights that his form of IVT primarily focuses on the early phases of an intervention; it does not consider the total process of intervention. This is one of the reasons for introducing the Interventionist Research Framework in Chapter 5. Nevertheless, these three principles have implications for intervention activity. These are discussed next.

Implications of IVT's Theoretical Principles

Argyris (1970) outlines six implications of IVT. These implications further inform the three theoretical principles as they relate to associated intervention activities. Additionally, they provide meaning on what effective social systems are and what constitutes effective intervention activities. These implications range from the meaning of effective social systems and intervention activity, the matter of change, selecting a social system for research, the necessity for informed choice and internal commitment, and the potential for researcher and social system manipulation, to advancing knowledge and practice. They are also prime areas for theoretical advancement.

Effective Social Systems and Intervention Activity

Argyris (1970) states that effective intervention activities assist social systems to solve their problems and to function with greater effectiveness. Thus, an effective social system emerges from experiencing effective intervention activity. Understanding this first implication raises the question: 'What is an effective social system?'. The answer is any social system that successfully accomplishes its fundamental activities, which are to: a) define and achieve its objectives; b) maintain its existing patterns and boundaries; c) adapt to its outside forces and conditions; and d) tend toward a steady state which may be functional or dysfunctional (Argyris, 1970; Bruhn & Rebach, 2007). Therefore, what is 'effective' is context specific. We discuss these social system activities next.

Define and Achieve Objectives

For most individuals, groups, intergroups, and organisations, work is defined by their objectives, and their objectives usually relate to maintaining or enhancing their existence (Bruhn & Rebach, 2007). By work, we mean activities that require mental or physical effort to achieve an outcome (Robbins *et al.*, 2017). For instance, an individual may want to achieve positive self-worth or develop critical-thinking skills. A group may want to increase the quality of their output or make their processes more efficient. A non-profit organisation may want to provide food and shelter to victims of domestic violence.

Maintaining Internal Patterns and Boundaries

To achieve objectives, people need to develop and maintain patterns of relationships and processes with identified boundaries or constraints, such as laws or resource allocations (Bruhn & Rebach, 2007). However, we find the notion of boundaries and environments differs somewhat for individuals, groups, and entities. For individuals, environments can span the psychological, spiritual, socio-cultural, and/or physiological, and the patterns and processes within these environments can stretch from meanings and feelings to procedures or relationships (Bruhn & Rebach,

2007). A person's environment is their way of understanding reality and a necessary part of developing an identity, effectively managing the circumstances in which we find ourselves, and constructing ways to meet our needs and achieve our objectives. Boundaries delineate one's environment, i.e., 'the inside', from the outside (Argyris, 1970). Boundaries tend to be constructed from experiences, beliefs, choices, and a sense of responsibility. Also, they tend to be flexible to allow the maximum possibility of maintaining a stable mind, body, and behaviour.

A group's internal environment consists of individuals, group members' interrelationships and interactions, group member roles, and where each member and the group are influenced by group member actions. A group's communication and action patterns, shared understandings, norms, and relationships, both preserve their internal environment and help them adapt to the outside. Boundaries can be marked by role hierarchies, power distributions, and/or rules over rights, responsibilities, and ways of interacting, but particularly who is and who is not a member (Bruhn & Rebach, 2007).

An entity's environment extends beyond its constituent individuals and groups to include cultures (e.g., shared principles, traditions), resources, and processes (Robbins *et al.*, 2017). Most entities have relatively predictable patterns of relationships, interactions, and behaviour so as to prevent operational chaos (Bruhn & Rebach, 2007). However, the notion of boundaries for entities is more complex (Alderfer, 1976; Shapiro & Zinner, 1979; Bruhn & Rebach, 2007). Beyond simply separating in from out, for entities, boundaries stipulate what is desirable to the outside world. For example, control mechanisms promote internal coherence, act as a defence against external intrusion, and reflect 'model' behaviour by its members. Consequently, boundaries require clear definition but should also be flexible to accommodate change.

Adapting to Outside Forces and Conditions

Outside forces and conditions can influence an entity's ability to achieve its objectives (Robbins *et al.*, 2017). Forces operate on a continuum, however, from the micro to the macro, which is important because events that occur at one level influence what occurs at other levels. For instance, individual beliefs can be influenced by the mass media. Groups can be influenced by the policies and practices of the organisation they inhabit. Entities can be influenced by terrorist attacks or national legislation. According to Bruhn and Rebach (2007), adaptation refers to a social system's ability to react favourably to the outside and continue functioning regardless. Hence, social systems develop patterns of behaviours, relationships, norms, understandings, and capabilities to adapt to outside forces and conditions, and thus achieve their objectives (Argyris, 1970). Moreover, change is constant and dynamic, so adaptation needs to be continuous as well as flexible to preserve entity survival.

The Tendency Toward Steady State

The notion of a steady state generally refers to a social system's health, whereby it changes and acts by preserving a feasible interactive relationship with the external environment to preserve survival and stability (Bruhn & Rebach, 2007). Groups desiring a steady state of group membership and functioning maintain internal patterns and boundaries, so the group sustains itself as an identifiable unit. For entities, steady state is really more 'dynamic-state', where entities need to continuously adapt to external forces (Bruhn & Rebach, 2007). However, overall, maintaining a steady state involves setting objectives, establishing structures and practices, achieving stable patterns of behaviour, exercising proactive controls, solving problems, and adapting to meet external conditions.

To further understand what Argyris (1970) means by this first implication, we must now consider what makes an intervention effective. An intervention is effective based on two main aspects. First, whether the intervention helps those within a social system to increase their own competencies and learn to solve their own problem(s). Second, whether it positions those in the system to make and implement decisions at their own discretion. In both respects, the more competences within a system, the less likely it is that a problem will recur and the more likely it is that those within the system can solve their own problems autonomously. Thus, social system effectiveness relies on its competence, problem-solving, decision-making, and implementing decisions.

A social system engages in problem-solving, a process of thinking, which leads to generating a solution for the problem and requires valid information. Decision-making is also a process of thinking which requires free and informed choices constituting the basis for the decision. Implementing decisions is a process of carrying out the decision to create an effect that was intended and requires internal commitment. The way in which the researcher intervenes in the social system and helps the social system become more competent and effective relies on the researcher focusing on IVT's three principles. Therefore, the implication is that there is congruence between effective intervention activities and the activities enabling social system effectiveness.

Change: A Researcher's Main Objective?

As for the second implication, Argyris (1970) posits that generating change is not the primary objective of an interventionist. Rather, researchers should be prioritising the three theoretical principles: generating valid and useful information, ensuring informed decisions, and fostering internal commitment. The result of those three things may be change but, if change does not eventuate, that is not necessarily a bad thing, and it does not mean that the intervention was unsuccessful. Nor is change eventuating necessarily good. For example, a change may make a social system more rigid; its people may become enslaved by power differentials; tensions and internal dissonance may arise; attitudes and performance may suffer; and so on.

Moreover, Argyris (1970, p. 23) stresses that generating change is not an "adequate criterion for judging the effectiveness" of the researcher. Ultimately, it is the choice of the participants as to whether and what changes are made, not the researcher. The researcher cannot impose change on the social system because this would compromise free choice and internal commitment. Alderfer (1976) reminds us that generating valid information is a precursor to change, not a change strategy in itself. He also points out that the purpose of the first IVT principle is to develop a shared understanding of the problem so as to ascertain whether change is even required or desired by the social system.

The IVR project undertaken by Cullen *et al.* (2013) is an example of accounting research where change was an indirect outcome of the researcher's intervention. The people working in the organisation recognised the need for change during the course of the project and, accordingly, made a free and informed decision to do so. Argyris (1970) engages in a serious discussion on this second implication on pages 21 through 24, which we recommend you read for yourself . . . if for no other reason than to make your own free and informed decision.

Selecting the Social System

Number three on the implication list is that the three theoretical principles serve as some criteria for selecting the social system for research. For Argyris (1970), this touches on the question of whether IVR is going to be mutually beneficial to both the researcher and the social system. However, from a pragmatic perspective, generating valid and useful information helps researchers to know if participants are open to learning and want help to address their problem. In turn, this enables the information generated to be valid and useful and, ultimately, for any intervention to be successful. Additionally, the involvement of top managers is usually critical to an effective intervention because their power and the authority they give to gatekeepers makes a big difference in the support a researcher is given to becoming an insider. Here, the notion of ethics and moral philosophy may inform the researcher on how to manage this matter (see also Chapter 6).

Informed choice and Internal Commitment: A Necessity

Argyris (1970) argues that free and informed choice and internal commitment are necessary theoretical principles for inclusion in an IVR project regardless of the social system being researched. Without the choice of how their problem is solved, people rarely commit to being part of the solution, and therefore they are unlikely to improve the competences needed to accomplish their essential activities. Moreover, effective IVR is unlikely because the participants are likely to become dependent on the researcher to solve their problem for them, which is dangerously close to consulting.

The Potential for Manipulation

Fifth, adhering to the three theoretical principles reduces the potential for the researcher to manipulate the social system and vice versa. Argyris (1970) defines manipulation as exercising power and authority to control or pressurise for the purposes of achieving an objective. Clearly, the potential for manipulation is a two-way street. Just as researchers can want to achieve research outcomes, social systems can be in desperate need of help and want a solution at any cost. A focus on generating valid information, researchers guaranteeing freedom of choice, and participants taking responsibility for their decisions helps to ensure that ulterior motives are kept at bay, all involved feel free from coercion, and the outcomes are positive (Argyris, 1970).

Advancing Knowledge and Practice

Sixth and last, the three IVT principles combined ensure the duality of outcomes. Generating valid and useful information helps the researcher to contribute to theoretical knowledge. Creating conditions for the participants to make free and informed choices in relation to how they solve their problem and internally commit to implementing the solution may result in advancements to practice.

Interventions—Type, Focus, and Intensity

The accounting literature offers very few examples of interventions and almost no insights into whether there are different types of interventions and what each might be used for. This lack of information is problematic given the pivotal role interventions play in IVR. On the bright side, however, a lack of information is also an opportunity for a theoretical contribution. Of the few scholars that have approached the subject of intervention type, Beer (1980) and Reddy (1994) outline intervention types evident in the organisational behaviour literature. These authors identify intervention types and explain how these interventions influence individuals, groups, intergroups, and organisations. Baard (2010) offers an overview of these intervention types (see also Chapter 9).

Jönsson and Lukka (2007) developed a scheme that situated interventions along a continuum from modest to strong. Modest interventions occur when the researcher manipulates the social system to initiate some form of change, for example, introducing a new organisational procedure. Cullen *et al.* (2013) is an example of a modest intervention. In this IVR project to improve reverse logistics management processes, the intervention consisted of presentations at interactive workshops, the discussion of ideas based on participant reactions to the presentations, and the researchers contributed suggestions. Thereafter, researchers followed up with some site visits to collect data on progress (although detail thereon is limited). Conversely, strong interventions involve implementing an innovation, such as a new management control system, or redesigning jobs. Examples of strong interventions include Chiucchi's (2013) new interactive performance measurement and reporting system for intellectual capital; Campanale *et al.'s* (2014) new time-driven, activity-based costing system for use by financial controllers and clinicians in rural Italian hospitals; Dumay's (2010) strategic communications plan for the university's stakeholders; and Baard's (2010) interactive information and strategic management control system for small businesses. Overall, however, we find that this type of classification scheme offers limited insights into the nature of interventions, and is therefore not particularly useful.

What is more useful is information about the complexity of an intervention, its propensity to invoke change, its potential for far-reaching influence, and so on. Argyris (1970) describes three sorts of interventions applicable to practical problems, discussed next.

IVT—Intervention Types

Argyris's (1970) theorised intervention types are more descriptions than categories. We have termed these 'tried-and-tested', 'modified existing', and 'new' interventions, discussed next.

Tried-and-Tested Interventions

Tried-and-tested interventions rely on existing knowledge and previous experience in specific techniques that are known solutions to a problem. For example, both manufacturers and retailers commonly experience high costs associated with product returns, i.e., reverse logistics (Cullen *et al.*, 2013). Addressing these problems relies on a repertoire of theoretically developed and empirically tested interventions steeped in the body of knowledge around quality costing, supply chain management, performance measurement, and logistics management. According to Argyris (1970), tried-and-tested interventions may be beneficial when there are resource constraints that preclude a more comprehensive approach to solving the problem (e.g., Dumay, 2010). Additionally, this intervention type is appropriate when social systems need quick actions with a modest chance of success.

However, tried-and-tested interventions also have drawbacks. Each social system is heterogeneous. Even two very similar systems will each have their subtly different norms, structures and roles, lines of authority, and so forth. Consequently, homogeneous interventions may not have the same outcomes, at least not without some modifications (Wodarski, 2011). Thus, there is a risk of problems resurfacing, unintended changes, and constraining rather than freeing participants. Although one would think that this intervention type has less risk and more than a reasonable chance of working, given its origins from established bodies of knowledge, we infer that social system heterogeneity may account for why Argyris (1970) advocates for a modest probability of success.

Less experienced researchers or new researchers to IVR might find the tried-and-tested route a somewhat easier entry point into the methodology, but we advocate that all researchers proceed cautiously with this type of intervention—foremost, because the opportunities to advance theory with a 'tested' intervention are likely limited. In turn, publication may not be easy. And using an off-the-shelf, one-size-fits-all solution to a problem may not qualify as research. Whether or not it is consulting is a different and less germane story.

Modified Existing Interventions

Argyris (1970, p. 32) called our 'modified existing intervention' "the creative arrangement of existing knowledge". These interventions are implemented in a social system without testing the modifications or exploring the revised intervention's capacity for effective, practical problem-solving. This type of intervention is highly experimental in nature and comes with significant risks to the social system because it has a high probability of failure. A favourite of self-interested researchers, Jönsson and Lukka (2007, p. 392) refer to this route as the "elephant in a glass store effect", given the potential for seriously detrimental consequences when researchers choose an intervention to suit their own purposes rather than focusing on the needs of the social system.

Argyris (1970) articulates several conditions for using this intervention type. First, those in the social system must be competent. They must also have enough resources and be tolerant of experimental interventions that may not necessarily work. Also, the researcher must have an accurate perception of the intervention's potential to solve the problem. If unsuccessful, using this approach must offer some interesting contributions to the literature regarding interventions that do not work in practice and/or in different contexts. Hence, one's moral philosophy is an important consideration here. Given the risks associated with this intervention type, we posit that accounting researchers are unlikely to use them but, here again, free and informed choice is paramount.

Creating New Interventions

From too cold to too hot, we arrive at just right or, at least, perfectly appropriate. The third type of intervention is one that is developed to solve a specific problem as identified by shared consensus in the social system. This type of intervention is consistent with Thomas and Rothman's (1994) *Intervention Design and Development*, and Jönsson and Lukka's (2007) strong intervention. An example would be redesigning work processes (Lukka & Vinnari, 2017) or the interventions designed by Chiucchi (2013) and Campanale *et al.* (2014). Notably, developing a unique intervention seeks to do more than solve the problem; it also seeks to construct a conceptual model that generalises the problem and its solution(s) to some extent. This activity is extremely demanding of both the researcher and the social system. Accordingly, Argyris (1970) states that this intervention requires the amalgamation of both the researcher's qualities and the social system's resources.

Researcher(s) must have a strong sense of inner confidence and self-acceptance, be adept at model building, be prepared for intellectual challenges, and trust their own interpersonal, analytical, and conflict management skills. Accordingly, researchers should reflect and consider the extent to which they possess ambidextrous qualities as espoused by Markides (2007). Developing a unique intervention calls for researchers to be honest about their limitations and what they can or cannot accomplish. Without the trust and collaboration this type of honesty builds, an effective intervention is unlikely. Likewise, the participants must consider their limitations—the available human and financial resources—as they may need to provide additional personnel or training while the intervention occurs (Argyris, 1970). Moreover, change induced by this intervention type may directly affect individual and group social values and power, which may emancipate or de-emancipate them.

A unique intervention is a contribution, an innovation, that allows a researcher to make significant theoretical and empirical contributions on the proviso that the intervention is linked to a 'theory with status'. Plus, when all these boxes are ticked, the research is a likely candidate for publication in a high-quality journal. Researchers seeking to promote cohesion in IVR should, therefore, consider using this intervention type because it enables them to "more faithfully follow the footsteps of Lewin" (Jönsson & Lukka, 2007, p. 392). Using this type of intervention is also explicitly not consultancy. Argyris (1970) does not outline specific intervention design activities to support using this intervention type; hence, we refer to the Interventionist Research Framework in Chapter 5 for further insights.

In Summation

We do not see IVR philosophy and IVT as mutually exclusive, but rather collectively as they provide methodological foundations for IVR.

Moreover, both incorporate Lewin's governing principles of IVR. IVR's philosophy asks researchers to move between the world of pure reason and the world of practical reason—between the university and the field and from being observers to being insiders. All of this requires an understanding of competing worldviews and ambidextrous skills.

Philosophically, we gain some insights into the qualities a researcher needs to move between these worlds. IVT offers specific principles that provide greater focus on what to do once a researcher is in the field, which we would expect from a theory of practice. Ideas like using a variety of research methods to understand a problem and work toward solving it by collecting valid and useful information and mobilising free and informed choice and internal commitment, which are essential to worthy, publishable IVR that cannot be confused with consulting. In moving towards a practical view of intervention modes for use in IVR, we use the Interventionist Research Framework (IRF), which follows in Chapter 5.

References

Alderfer, C.P. (1976). Boundary relations and organizational diagnosis. In H. Meltzer & F.R. Wickert (Eds.), *Humanizing organizational behaviour*. Springfield, IL: Charles C. Thomas.

Argyris, C. (1970). *Intervention theory and method: A behavioural science view*. Reading, MA: Addison-Wesley Publishing Company.

Baard, V.C. (2010). A critical view of interventionist research. *Qualitative Research in Accounting and Management*, 7(1), 13–45.

Baard, V.C. & Dumay, J. (2018). Interventionist research in accounting: Reflections on the good, the bad and the ugly. *Accounting and Finance*, Advance online publication. https://doi.org/10.1111/acfi.12409

Beer, M. (1980). *Organization change and development: A system view*. Glenview, IL: Scott Foresman.

Bruhn, J.G. & Rebach, H.M. (2007). *Sociological practice: Intervention and social change*. New York, NY: Springer Science.

Campanale, C., Cinquini, L., & Tenucci, A. (2014). Time driven activity-based costing to improve transparency and decision making in healthcare. *Qualitative Research in Accounting & Management*, 11, 165–186.

Carkhuff, R.R. (1983). *Sources of human productivity*. Amherst, MA: Human Resource Development Press.

Chiucchi, M.S. (2013). Intellectual capital accounting in action: Enhancing learning through interventionist research. *Journal of Intellectual Capital*, 14, 48–68.

Cullen, J., Tsamenyi, M., Bernon, M., & Gorst, J. (2013). Reverse logistics in the UK retail sector: A case study of the role of management accounting in driving organisational change. *Management Accounting Research*, 24, 212–227.

Dickens, L. & Watkins, K. (1999). Action research: Rethinking Lewin. *Management Learning*, 30, 127–140.

Dumay, J. (2010). A critical reflective discourse of an interventionist research project. *Qualitative Research in Accounting and Management*, 7(1), 46–70.

Fawcett, S.B., Suarez-Balcazar, Y., Balcazar, F.E., White, G.W., Paine, A.L., Blanchard, K.A., & Embree, M.G. (1994). Conducting intervention research—The design and development process. In J. Rothman & E.J. Thomas (Eds.), *Intervention research: Design and development for human service* (pp. 25–54). Binghamton, NY: Haworth Press.

Flyvbjerg, B. (2001). *Making social science matter: Why social inquiry fails and how it can succeed again*. Cambridge, UK: Cambridge University Press.

Honderich, T. (Ed.). (1995). *The oxford companion to philosophy*. New York, NY: Oxford University Press.

Jönsson, S. & Lukka, K. (2007). There and back again: Doing interventionist research in management accounting. In C.S. Chapman, A.G. Hopwood, & M.S. Shields (Eds.), *Handbook of management accounting research* (Vol. 1, pp. 373–397). Oxford, UK: Elsevier.

Lewin, K. (1946). Action research and minority problems. *Journal of Social Issues*, 11, 34–46.

Lewin, K. (1947). Frontiers in group dynamics: ll. Channels of group life: Social planning and action research. *Human Relations*, 1(2), 143–153.

Lukka, K. & Suomala, P. (2014). Relevant interventionist research: Balancing three intellectual virtues. *Accounting and Business Research*, 44(2), 204–220.

Lukka, K. & Vinnari, E. (2017). Combining action-network theory with interventionist research: Present state and future potential. *Accounting, Auditing & Accountability Journal*, 30, 720–753.

Markides, C. (2007). In search of ambidextrous professors. *Academy of Management Journal*, 50, 762–768.

Neu, D., Cooper, D.J., & Everett, J. (2001). Critical accounting interventions. *Critical Perspectives on Accounting*, 12(6), 735–762.

Peters, M. & Robinson, V. (1984). The origins and status of action research. *The Journal of Applied Behavioural Science*, 20(2), 113–124.

Reddy, W.B. (1994). *Intervention skills: Process consultation for small groups and teams*. Johannesburg, South Africa: Pfeiffer and Company.

Robbins, S.P., Bergman, R., & Coulter, M. (2017). *Management* (8th ed.). Melbourne, Australia: Pearson Australia.

Rothman, J. & Thomas, E.J. (Eds.). (1994). *Intervention research: Design and development for human service*. Binghamton, NY: Haworth Press.

Sayer, A. (1992). *Method in social science: A realist approach*. London and New York, NY: Routledge.

Shapiro, R.L. & Zinner, J. (1979). The adolescent, the family and the group: Boundary considerations. In W.G. Lawrence (Ed.), *Exploring individual and organizational boundaries: A Tavistock open systems approach*. Chichester: Wiley Publishing.

Suomala, P., Lyly-Yrjänäinen, J., & Lukka, K. (2014). Battlefield around interventions: A reflective analysis of conducting interventionist research in management accounting. *Management Accounting Research*, 25, 304–314.

Thomas, E.J. & Rothman, J. (1994). An integrative perspective on intervention research. In J. Rothman & E.J. Thomas (Eds.), *Intervention research: Design and development for human service* (pp. 3–23). Binghamton, NY: Haworth Press.

Wallace, R.J. (2018). Practical reason. In E.N. Zalta (Ed.), *Stanford encyclopaedia of philosophy*. Retrieved from: https://plato.stanford.edu/archives/spr2018/entries/practical-reason/

Wodarski, J.S. (2011). The social work practice research conundrum. *Journal of Human Behavior in the Social Environment*, 21, 577–600.

5 An Interventionist Research Framework

As outlined in Chapter 4, IVT encompasses three main principles to guide IVR practice. The question is: How do we operationalise these principles? Thomas and Rothman's (1994) Intervention Design and Development Framework (D&D) is helpful here (Baard, 2010). The D&D Framework was originally designed to help social workers mount interventions, and so it has its origins in information science, psychology, psychiatry, sociology, education, nursing, and public health. Baard (2010) undertakes a critical review of IVR frameworks, including action research, design science, and the constructive research approach to contextualise the D&D framework. Given the challenges and ambiguity associated with the other frameworks, which we refer to the as the 'bad' and 'ugly' aspects of IVR, she recommends D&D as a practical and effective umbrella framework for conducting IVR, despite requiring some reconfigurations.

On reflection some years later, most of the frameworks Baard (2010) critiqued have not been widely used across the three broad areas of accounting IVR and the issues presented almost a decade ago still persist today. There is one useful road map to IVR, called the constructive research approach (CRA), which is popular in the Finnish context. Fashioned mostly by Kasanen *et al.* (1993) and Labro and Tuomela (2003), it consists of three broad phases with seven steps for undertaking IVR, but we find this approach too focused on management accounting research (Rautiainen *et al.*, 2017) to be broadly useful across most accounting areas. We also find that despite the merits associated with D&D, the framework needs some reconfiguration to suit an interdisciplinary/accounting context. Baard (2004) adapted the D&D framework to some extent for use in an interdisciplinary doctoral study, thereby demonstrating D&D's capacity for adaptation and use in accounting IVR. Our first modification is renaming D&D as the Interventionist Research Framework (IRF).

The chapter begins with the origins of the IRF, formerly the D&D, followed by how the IRF supports IVR for accounting. We briefly digress into the importance of clearly and explicitly explaining the methodology that frames research, especially IVR, and conclude the chapter with a description of the phases and associated activities in the IRF. Here, we also show how this framework helps to fill in the gaps of the philosophy of IVR and the principals of IVT.

The Origins of the IRF

With an integrated perspective, Thomas and Rothman (1994) contend that there are three main components to IVR: intervention knowledge development, knowledge utilisation for interventions, and intervention design and development. Each component has distinct aims, approaches, and outcomes. And each is linked to the other. See Table 5.1 for more detail. As we have adapted D&D into the IRF, we provide some background on the IRF explaining its origins from the D&D context.

Intervention Design and Development

Knowledge development and knowledge utilisation are fairly self-explanatory concepts, and we refer interested readers to Thomas and Rothman's (1994) original text for more details on these two components. However, intervention design and development require a bit more explanation. This component emerged from the dissatisfaction of human service researchers with traditional research methods—specifically, the lack of a way to intervene and fix problems (Baard, 2010). Thomas and Rothman (1994) argue that designing and developing interventions is what distinguishes IVR from other research approaches. This is because the process involves a real-world problem and reaching a corresponding practical objective rather than simply testing a hypothesis or exploring a theory. Additionally, the problem-solving process embedded in design and development activities is methodical and steeped in five paradigms and their associated procedures and techniques. The five paradigms are: a) developmental research; b) social research and development; c) behavioural community research; d) experimental social innovation; and e) model development. Table 5.2 outlines each paradigm along with its focus, objectives, and links to IVR's three components and the IVT principles.

These five paradigms inform the original six phases of D&D, with each phase having distinct objectives and activities to guide researchers in developing innovative interventions. The activities are intertwined with the pragmatisms of participants in "close intensive interaction with each other and researchers" (Thomas & Rothman, 1994, p. 13), which is consistent with Lewin's (1946) governing IVR principle of collaboration. The six phases are: a) problem analysis and project planning; b) information gathering and synthesis; c) design (intervention); d) early development and pilot testing; e) evaluation and advanced development; and f) dissemination.

Despite the potential merits associated with D&D, its use in accounting IVR has only received attention in a few doctoral theses (Baard, 2010).

Table 5.1 An Integrated Perspective on IVR

Components of Intervention Research

	Knowledge Development	Knowledge Utilisation	Design & Development
Nature	Creating or discovering knowledge, experience, and techniques to solve common problems faced by social systems Devising instrumental and practical research questions related to those problems	Applying theoretical and empirical knowledge to the field, e.g., creating customer policies for returning goods in a reverse logistics system	Systematically developing interventions to solve practical problems
Aim(s)	To contribute to developing knowledge of human behaviour in a variety of social systems and contexts To establish research findings applicable to understanding and/or solving practical problems	To transform research findings into a usable and practical form for application in the field. To apply knowledge of human behaviour to practical situations	To develop and generate practical interventions or interventive technologies to address issues, and in collaboration with the participants
Approach	Methods from social and behavioural science, i.e., surveys, interviews, focus groups, single case studies, quasi-experimentation	Processes including: selection, retrieval, appraisal, codification and synthesis of knowledge, formulating generalisations, and specifying and operationalising knowledge for application in a practical situation, e.g., meta-analysis	Systematic methodologies that involve developmental research, experimental social innovation, and model development An iterative method consisting of distinctive phases of problem analysis, intervention design, development, evaluation, and dissemination

(*Continued*)

Table 5.1 (Continued)

Components of Intervention Research

	Knowledge Development	Knowledge Utilisation	Design & Development
Outcome(s)	Knowledge about human behaviour formulated into concepts, hypotheses, theories, and empirical generalisations Practical applications	Changes in how we understand problems Practices related to social system problems D&D	Interventions to address problems, e.g., activity-based costing in service organisations, a new or modified procedure manual, training materials, surveys measuring employee satisfaction, a revised audit quality manual, a social responsibility performance management system for a charity
Linkages	Distinct research activity conducted independently of knowledge utilisation and design & development Research findings inform knowledge utilisation and design & development Conducted within Phase 1 "Problem Analysis and Project Planning"	Distinct research activity conducted independently of knowledge development and design & development Follows on from knowledge development Conducted within Phase 2 "Information Gathering and Synthesis" and Phase 3 "Design"	Distinct research activity conducted independently of knowledge utilisation and knowledge development. Directly linked to knowledge utilisation whether or not preceded by knowledge development

Source: Adapted from Thomas and Rothman (1994)

Table 5.2 Research Paradigms and IVT

Paradigm	Focus	Objectives and Links to the Framework's Phases	Links to the IVT Principles
Developmental Research	Applied research methods and empirical practice	Enables social problem assessment using applicable research methods and guides intervention planning (Phase 1)	Generating valid and useful information
		Promotes the use of effective interventions (Phase 3)	
		Evaluates intervention outcomes (Phase 5)	
		Disseminates theoretical and practical research outcomes (Phase 6)	
	Action research strategies	Enables problems identification and analysis and intervention design (Phase 1 and 3)	Free and informed choice
		Relies on social system collaboration and contribution	Internal commitment
		Develops social system commitment to the intervention	
		Enables intervention implementation and evaluation (Phase 4 and Phase 5)	
Social Research & Development	Applies a physical sciences engineering approach to intervention development	Helps with intervention design and development (Phase 3)	Free and informed choice
			Internal commitment
Behavioural Community Research	Uses concepts and methods of behaviour analysis and psychology	Supports intervention design and implementation (Phase 3 and Phase 5)	Free and informed choice
		Helps with social system change	Internal commitment

(Continued)

Table 5.2 (Continued)

Paradigm	Focus	Objectives and Links to the Framework's Phases	Links to the IVT Principles
Experimental Social Innovation	Provides a means to evaluate the intervention's ability to solve a practical problem	Enables definition of social problem (Phase 1) Creates a range of solutions or innovations to solve problems (Phase 3) May use quasi-experimentation to introduce and implement an innovation on a trial basis for a limited time, followed by intervention evaluation (Phase 5)	Generating valid and useful information Free and informed choice
Model Development	Examines how an innovation becomes standard practice when embedded within a social system	Helps to spread word of the intervention (Phase 6)	Internal commitment

Source: Adapted from Thomas and Rothman (1994), Reid (1994), Fawcett (1990, 1991), Paine *et al.* (1984), Thomas (1984), Rothman (1980) and Fairweather (1967).

We attribute this in part to the fact that the framework was originally designed for social work IVR, without specifically showing how D&D could be used in the accounting IVR context, and in part to the rare use of IVR in accounting research. As a precursor to our discourse on our adapted version of D&D, namely the Interventionist Research Framework (IRF), we discuss why and how the IRF supports future accounting IVR. Hence, we contemplate accounting as a social science and accounting research as applied field research. Both aspects inform accounting research and its relationship with IVR. Another aspect relates to an urgent need for methodological exposition when conducting IVR.

Accounting as a Social Science

This section is not intended as a primer for what accounting is, but rather it aims to show that as a social science, accounting and its associations with sociology are consistent with the interdisciplinary origins of the IRF. Further, that accounting research adopts a social-technical perspective, which infers dual outcomes for accounting research consistent with IVR.

Since the 1960s, accounting has been recognised as a social science, and the field's initial association with economics now includes other social sciences, such as sociology, psychology, and organisational behaviour and change (Baldvinsdottir *et al.*, 2010). Adopting a social science perspective, the primary intention of accounting research is to understand, explain, and potentially change or enhance the behaviours of accountants within the organisations they inhabit (Baldvinsdottir *et al.*, 2010). These behaviours include social interactions with people in organisations as well as the technical aspects of the field, for example, accounting and auditing standards, budgeting, and costing. Hence, accounting is a social-technical field that attempts to explain and understand real-world practice and behaviour through statistics, theory, and by justifying empirical findings in practical contexts. These are things accounting research and IVR have in common.

Atkinson and Shaffir (1998, p. 59) state that sociology has a long history with field research from which accounting researchers should learn and profit. Miller (2007) states that the technical dimensions of accounting are interrelated with the social dynamics of accounting. Specifically, Burchell *et al.* (1980) examine the role of accounting in organisations and society. These authors argue that pressures originating from academic inquiry and the challenges of practical action have prompted researchers to recognise and analyse the complexities of accounting in action. From a practice perspective, accounting systems provide relevant information for decision-making. They influence, shape, and potentially improve the judiciousness of the decision-making process and preserve organisational control. Further, after organisational decisions are made, they need to be justified, legitimised, and rationalised. Hence, the role of accounting precedes decision-making and provides an understanding of the action emerging from the decision-making process. Therefore, the relationship between accounting and decision-making aligns with accounting IVR's capacity to produce accounting with decision relevance.

Three areas of research have contributed to the expansion of accounting research as follows. First is 'the institutional environment of accounting', based on the work of Meyer and Rowan (1977) and the new institutional sociology (e.g., DiMaggio & Powell, 1983; Meyer & Scott, 1983). Institutionally, accounting is thought of as a mechanism providing organisations with logical concepts and approaches for managing financial resources. Here, accounting is a means to organising and monitoring organisational activities and a language for outlining organisational goals, procedures, and policies (i.e., organisational mechanisms). By this definition, accounting interventions may aim to solve problems and invoke change related to organisational mechanisms. Additionally, accounting and its practices and tools serve to legitimate the organisation both internally and externally (Miller, 2007). Thus, accounting provides a link between the organisation and its wider environment. As such, accounting researchers might examine changes in organisational accounting practices and link these changes to the dynamic demands and expectations of the external context. In turn, this may influence the legitimacy of accounting research and the sources of that legitimacy, such as societal values, ideas, and practical value (Rautiainen *et al.*, 2017). In this way, IVR provides a means of understanding and enacting organisational and social change.

Second, 'a political economy of accounting' emphasises conflicting political and economic interests in accounting within and beyond the organisation. The political economy considers how power relations are influenced by accounting and vice versa. Within organisations, power relations may change due to changes in accounting and accounting practices, and changes imposed by external political and social structures. In this context, accounting is viewed as a language and as practices that underpin the interests of groups and classes within an organisation. In the political economy, the notion of emancipation and accounting, where accounting is understood as a "social and communicative practice", function to inform and enlighten with, hopefully, the ultimate outcome of social advancement (Gallhofer & Haslam, 2003, p. 7). This is significant for accounting IVR because IVR has the potential to affect power relations and emancipate. We find the notions of power and emancipation in accounting interesting because they show that the field has emancipatory intentions that influence power relations and social system control (see Chapter 2). Additionally, accounting research may yield societally relevant research by achieving organisational liberation and empowerment, thus potentially contributing to the good of IVR (Baard & Dumay, 2018). Hence, using the IRF helps researchers decide if they want to adopt an emancipatory approach when conducting IVR because it provides a detailed conception of the IVR process prior to undertaking IVR.

Third, the ethnography of accounting is a research agenda focussed on the meanings and perceptions of accounting practices used by the people in a specific organisation. Thus, using an interpretive frame, accounting researchers seek to understand and make sense of accounting with reference to the meaning of accounting, its practices and procedures, and the change attached to accounting by actors in the field. Further, ethnography requires researchers to iteratively move from and between peripheral, active, and complete membership (Young, 1999) consistent with the 'there and back again' philosophy of IVR. Moreover, ethnography identifies researcher roles and alludes to the researcher qualities required to accomplish the demands of each role (see Chapters 3, 9, and 10).

These three accounting research agendas represent the extent to which accounting research draws on and contributes to sociological research, thus establishing a relationship between sociology and IVR and positioning the IRF to support future accounting IVR.

Accounting as Applied Research

Accounting research is generally envisaged as an applied research genre because it focuses on the technologies and technical practices used by accounting practitioners. Hence, accounting research should ultimately provide new insights for practice (Guthrie *et al.*, 2011; Ittner & Larcker, 2002). Applied accounting research aims to find a solution to a contemporary individual, organisational, or social problem (Richardson, 2004). To understand how the IRF may support future accounting IVR, we reflect on the meaning and characteristics of applied accounting research.

Richardson (2004) provides commentary on exploring the difference between applied and positivistic perspectives that supports our views on this matter. First, Richardson (2004) notes that applied accounting research is consistent with Boyer (1996), who promoted the inclusion of "scholarship of engagement" within the scope of scholarship. Richardson (2004, p. 158) argues that applied accounting research is an example of this form of scholarship because it exemplifies and requires "engagement between university stakeholders and academics, and results in research that guides stakeholders' advancement of their own interests and/or increases their capacity to cope with reality". From this quote, we infer that: a) the applied nature of accounting research means researchers engage real-life practitioners with a view to helping them solve their own problems (emancipate and empower); and b) doing accounting IVR is a way for scholars to achieve research impact critical for career prospects and institutional funding (see Chapter 2).

Second, like IVR, applied accounting research adopts a pragmatic approach, whereby it helps people understand the world in which they live and work. It provides organisations with a means to acquire actions and other technologies to help them manage their reality, which is also consistent with the ethnographic accounting research agenda. The ultimate outcome of pragmatic research is that the research findings should make a difference to an organisation. This notion extends to the fact that people are active participants in the research process; pragmatism is ethnocentric because it is anchored in the context and needs of the organisation.

Third, there is a juxtaposition between substantive significance and statistical significance. Argyris (1970) argues that behavioural significance in IVR is more important than statistical significance. Positivist research uses statistical significance to provide an explanation of phenomena using causal variables derived from a theoretical framework. However, on its own, statistical significance cannot explain the prevalence of a phenomenon or be used to intervene in a social system because both the researchers and the participants must understand a situation before they can confidently act to effect a change. Statistical significance provides reassurance that research outcomes do not happen by chance but does not provide an in-depth understanding of the situation, required for action. For research to be applied, it must focus on both theory and practice.

Four, Richardson (2004) argues that the intention of applied research is to intervene in practice. Thus, any intervention is likely to have an impact, successful or otherwise, and so applied researchers must accept responsibility for the consequences of that impact. In part, this speaks to our argument about the need for ambidexterity in an interventionist researcher. In Chapter 2, we advised that intervening in an organisation can have unintended, and possibly harmful, consequences; hence, researchers must be honest and critical of their own competencies and exercise ethical judgement. Ethics is a fundamental, but multi-faceted, tenet in applied research that spans the ethical treatment of research participants, the relationship between the university and the community, and how research findings are used (more on this in Chapter 6). Yet the applied nature of accounting research is consistent with IVR, and the IRF positions researchers well to conduct authentic, legitimate, and ethical IVR.

Field Research in Accounting

Field research reveals real-world phenomena achieved by active involvement with an organisation (Merchant & Van der Stede, 2006; Ahrens & Dent, 1998; Thomas & Rothman, 1994) and spans case studies, clinical and qualitative research (Merchant & Van der Stede, 2006), action research, action science, and design science (Jönsson & Lukka, 2007). These qualitative traditions have addressed complex problems using interdisciplinary approaches and stimulated researcher engagement with the minutiae of life in social systems (Parker, 2014). Each approach to field research differs based on whether the researchers are trying to understand a social system by observing its people as objective outsiders or as insiders or both. Thus, the degree of researcher involvement is the primary differentiator between field research approaches (Young, 1999). Young (1999) observes a continuum of field researcher roles, moving from observation through interaction, participation (sociology), investigative participation (existential sociology), peripheral membership, and active membership to complete membership (ethnomethodology). Accounting IVR may require researchers to move along this entire continuum as they progress through the IVR process.

Ahrens and Dent (1998) state that field research provides a rich literature that deepens our understanding of the relevant phenomena within a research context. Here, the term 'rich' refers to making understandable the actions and motivations of highly competent individuals who regularly mobilise accounting in their everyday working lives (Ahrens & Dent, 1998). Thus, field researchers learn about the world and accounting from the perspective of its people and from within the research context (Atkinson & Shaffir, 1998). To attain this richness, field researchers need to supplement the observations of actors with other qualitative research techniques, including interviews and document analysis. In accounting research, field research involves the study of relevant social-technical aspects of accounting in a natural setting, enabling theory building, testing, and refining existing theory, and generating research findings applicable to the social system context. Field studies, therefore, move beyond advancing theory to creating usable knowledge that focusses on the problems practitioners have.

Research shows that field research is frequently used in management accounting (e.g., Jönsson & Lukka, 2007; Merchant & Van der Stede, 2006; Ahrens & Dent, 1998). But, according to Merchant and Van der Stede (2006), there is scope for field researchers to adopt this approach to test theories and make substantive contributions to knowledge creation in other areas of accounting research as well, such as sustainability accounting, accounting education, accounting and auditing, standard-setting, corporate reporting, corporate governance, and public sector and non-profit accounting. By this, we are not suggesting that accounting researchers outside of management accounting are not engaged in field research, nor are we asserting that field research is the only way to contribute to knowledge development. Extending field research in multiple accounting interest areas offers possibilities to move beyond identifying and explaining the existence of some phenomena to acquiring a deep understanding of why the phenomena exist in the first place (Merchant & Van der Stede, 2006). Deriving these deep understandings may create usable knowledge that can help to solve real-world problems through interdisciplinary collaborations.

As mentioned in Chapter 1, Jönsson and Lukka (2007) view IVR as field experimentation, where the researcher is immersed in the organisation under study. When the researcher becomes an insider and collaborates with or 'acts together' with the participants, field research starts to become IVR. The degree of immersion of the researcher in the organisation moves beyond observing and interacting with the participants to adopting multiple membership roles along the continuum advocated by Young (1999). Jönsson and Lukka (2007) also view IVR as a form of field research because IVR moves beyond creating usable knowledge; it also aims to solve real-world problems. Thus, the IVR process is embodied in the IRF.

In summary, field research is a possibility in many areas of accounting, especially since management accounting has already set the precedent, and IVR is an extension of field research. Thus, accounting researchers can adopt the IRF to extend their field research to IVR.

Qualitative Accounting Research and Methodological Exposition

So, is the IRF just another 'do-it-yourself' checklist for IVR? Several disappointing rejections have taught us that submissions to high-quality academic journals are not favourably received or considered for publication when they present a 'how-to' on accomplishing IVR. However, evidence from the literature points towards the need for a methodical step-by-step guide to conducting IVR (Baard, 2010; Parker, 2014).

Parker (2014) states that qualitative research helps researchers access the 'black box' of social system cultures, behaviours, processes, practices, routines, and complexity, while Suomala *et al.* (2014, p. 305) say it is a "black box needing careful opening". Additionally, qualitative research mobilises interdisciplinary approaches to manage complex problems that are not generalisable in nature. Yet Parker (2014) also argues that qualitative methodologies must be explained in far more granular detail than positivist approaches. This is because, in lieu of statistical testing, the methodology used is one of the sources of a study's reliability, validity, and legitimacy (see Chapter 8).

Parker (2014, p. 24) criticises qualitative researchers for paying "brief cursory lip service" to the methodologies and methods employed when sufficient explanations of the approaches taken have not been provided. He argues that qualitative researchers must: articulate their approach, the version of the methodology used, justify why it is appropriate for the study, explicate the key concepts and principles underlying the research approach, and acknowledge its strengths and limitations. It is unequivocally the qualitative researchers' responsibility to instil confidence in the reader over the principles, concepts, and the 'how-to' of the methodology chosen for the study (Parker, 2014). In the same way as an emerging and mainly qualitative research methodology, IVR researchers need to instil confidence in the accounting research community over the principles, concepts, and the 'how-to' of IVR. Because the IRF is underpinned by theoretical principles and clearly defined activities, it can both instil this confidence and help accounting researchers open the black box of a social system.

Given the scepticism of accounting researchers toward IVR and the scholarly reluctance to use it, interventionist researchers need to present methodological transparency on how IVR is accomplished even more so than other qualitative researchers in the field. Using the IRF may provide interventionist researchers with the confidence and fortitude to undertake this alternative research form.

The Interventionist Research Framework (IRF)

The IRF, as shown in Figure 5.1, is an integrated model consisting of six phases. Each phase is performed sequentially, but iteratively, as there is potential to go back to earlier phases as new information arises that brings opportunities or difficulties (Thomas & Rothman, 1994). Also, IVR usually occurs alongside a social system's normal activities. There-fore, researchers may find that some phases merge, overlap, or are not needed. This 'there and back again' nature of the IRF is both flexible and consistent with Lewin's governing principle.

In each of the six phases, there are critical objectives that the researcher must meet and research activities that must be performed (Thomas & Rothman, 1994; Fawcett *et al.*, 1994). These objectives and activities have been refined based on our experience of conducting IVR following the D&D. That said, each research context is different, and researchers need to exercise some latitude in which objectives and activities are relevant to their IVR project and how best to undertake that work. Details on each of the phases follow.

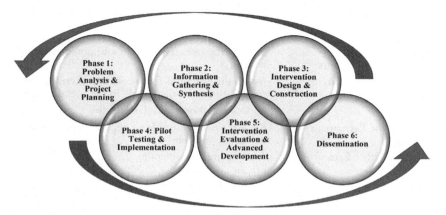

Figure 5.1 The Interventionist Research Framework (IRF)

Phase 1—Problem Analysis and Project Planning

Phase 1 consists of five critical objectives, based on one of Lewin's IVR principles—collaboration (Fawcett *et al.*, 1994), which researchers can use to secure commitment to the research study and its processes. Phase 1 involves knowledge development with respect to identifying and understanding the nature of the research/practical problem, see Table 5.3.

The first step is to identify the social system that has a problem to be solved, for example, a non-profit organisation, a hospital, a group of retailers—any individual, group, or organisation. For example, Campanale *et al.* (2014) observed that European public hospitals were experiencing budgetary and cost control problems. So, their research domain was rural public hospitals in Tuscany, and their social system was a large public teaching hospital. The participants were mostly clinicians and administrators. Identifying and selecting organisations is also contingent on the problems being of current or emerging interest to the participants and the researchers (see Chapter 9). Research that aims to solve a problem of interest is more likely to attract participants. In other words, it is better to approach an organisation asking, 'What can I do for you?' than 'What can you do for me?'.

Second is gaining entry to and cooperation from the social system (see Chapter 9). Fawcett *et al.* (1994) advise that identifying and having conversations with organisational informants is critical in this phase because informants can introduce researchers to the organisational 'gatekeepers' and they can lead to research participants. Campanale *et al.* (2014) identified the hospital's top management as the gatekeepers. These were the people that had the power to allocate the personnel and other resources required for a successful intervention. Thus, they were pivotal in

Table 5.3 Phase 1—Problem Analysis and Project Planning

Critical Objectives	Activities
Identify and Enlist Research Participants	Identify the research domain and potential social system(s)
Assess the Feasibility of the Setting	Assess the potential for accessing, entering, and cooperating with the people in the social system
	Initiate collaborative relationships
Identify the Participants' Concerns	Review the literature for a general orientation on the issues/problem
Analyse Those Concerns	Analyse main problem(s)
	Identify theory/develop a theoretical framework relevant to the problem
Set Goals and Objectives	Plan the IVR project

Source: Adapted from Thomas and Rothman (1994) and Fawcett *et al.* (1994)

promoting organisational change. Informants may also clarify an organisation's customs and help researchers understand how to articulate the benefits of their research to the social organisation. Further, informants may provide initial ideas on what the problem is, why the problem is a problem, and who is affected by the problem. Although not always the case, our experience of informants is that they are usually people with whom one has an existing professional relationship or comes by way of recommendation from an academic colleague.

We find that working with organisational informants is fundamental to establishing collaborations with the organisation. By way of informal conservations about a problem of interest, we gain insights on the issues that prevail. Collaborative relationships form and emerge by asking people to help identify and understand the nature of the problem, plan the research project, and implement interventions. In turn, collaboration creates a sense of ownership and internal commitment to the research process and solving the problem consistent with IVT. Currently, the literature is not forthcoming in providing clear accounts on how researchers select and gain entry to social systems (see Chapter 9). We know that, in any field research, access to research participants is challenging and can take a long time without any guarantees of successful entry.

Third is identifying concerns of the participants. Our interpretation of 'concerns' refers to issues evident in an organisation. In part, conducting a literature review on the nature of the problem and organisations that are affected by the problem is a useful starting point, i.e., begin with the etic. This knowledge helps to develop the initial links between the problem and theory. Consistent with knowledge utilisation, Jansen (2018) considered how literature reviews could amalgamate knowledge that contributes to solving specific practical problems with the ways in which this knowledge can be applied. A literature review may also reveal interventions that have been used to solve similar problems. For instance, Campanale *et al.* (2014) found that European public hospitals relied on traditional accounting systems, which were not able to provide detailed and insightful cost and resource management information to support their operations in the face of increasing budget constraints and pressure to control costs. From a literature review, they found that time-driven, activity-based costing might be a solution.

Fawcett *et al.* (1994) found that researchers should avoid imposing etic views of a problem and how to solve it on the social system. Researchers should also understand the problem from a social system's perspective and the extent and significance of the problem to those affected by it. Again, this is critical to mobilising collaboration between the researcher and the organisation and for the participants to commit to their chosen solution. Reviewing the professional literature may also be useful for finding this emic perspective. To some extent, researchers can merge this phase with the information gathering phase, employing qualitative data collection approaches, such as interviews or focus groups, to better understand the nature of the problem from an organisation's perspective.

The fourth objective is to analyse the participants' concerns. Fawcett *et al.* (1994) recommend considering the questions listed in Table 5.4. Beer (1980) states that the process of diagnosing the problem itself can be an intervention because it can create awareness of the problem, which may stimulate a change in the social system. Therefore, the method of data collection is an important consideration in IVR. Additionally, the method selected should reflect a delicate balance between serving the interests of the researcher and encouraging organisational involvement in the process of IVR. Thomas and Rothman (1994) indicate that there is no specific research technique in IVR for this—a view that is consistent

Table 5.4 Problem Analysis

Critical Aspects of Problem Analysis	Questions
• Structuring the problem in the context of the social system • The behaviour of the participants	• How is the problem defined in terms of the divergence between the ideal and the actual conditions in the social system? (see Chapter 10) • Whose behaviour initiates the problem? • Whose behaviour sustains the problem?
• Exploring why the problem manifests • Discovering whether an intervention has already been applied and, if so, why it was not successful	• For whom or what does the current conditions/situation present a problem? • What are the adverse consequences of the problem for those affected? • Who or what benefits from the adverse consequences of the problem? • How does the social system and/or its people benefit from the current problem?
• The role of the immediate and broader social system context in solving the current problem	• Who shares responsibility for solving the problem? • Who or what behaviours must change to support problem resolution? • What social system conditions/situation must change to support problem resolution? • What degree of change is necessary for problem resolution?
• Intervention research goals	• At what level or levels in the social system should the problem be dealt with? (i.e., individual, group, entity) • Is problem resolution, technically, financially, socially, and politically feasible at the identified level(s)?

Source: Adapted from Fawcett *et al.* (1994)

with Argyris (1970). In our experience, a variety of rigorous and organic approaches, including surveys, interviews, and focus groups, for instance, can be used (see Chapter 7) But, ultimately, which technique to use is up to the researcher and depends on the nature of the project.

The last objective, setting intervention goals and objectives, directly relates to the IVR project (Fawcett *et al.*, 1994). This is the point at which researchers should strategise and plan their IVR projects (see Chapter 6). Further, because the IRF outlines phases of objectives and activities that can also be interpreted as milestones, research tasks can be designed around these steps to create a detailed plan of how the research study ideally should proceed. Fawcett *et al.* (1994) contend that the broader goals aimed at the outcomes desired from intervention efforts also need to be established here. In thinking about the desired outcomes, researchers can try to anticipate whether any changes in individual behaviour, group interactions, and/or organisational mechanisms are likely to contribute to achieving those broader research goals.

Phase 2—Information Gathering and Synthesis

This phase, where researchers gather and synthesise information, may overlap or merge with Phase 1. Therefore, part of Phase 1 and all of Phase 2 are consistent with generating valid and useful information, the first IVT principle. As shown in Table 5.5, Phase 2 involves using existing knowledge sources to understand what other scholars and professionals have done to enhance our understanding of the problem and interventions used to address the problem. From this base, we then generate new knowledge of our own.

Fawcett *et al.* (1994, p. 31) suggest that Phase 2 should be referred to as "not reinventing the wheel". It is important to know what other

Table 5.5 Phase 2—Information Gathering and Synthesis

Critical Objectives	Activities
Draw on Existing Information Sources	Identify existing sources of information, e.g., the academic and professional literature; empirical data
Acquire Knowledge From the Field	Become an insider in the social system
	Conduct original research, e.g., descriptive surveys, interviews, forums, focus groups, observations, etc.
	Analyse and synthesise the data collected
Identify Successful/ Unsuccessful Past Interventions	Identify the functional elements of these interventions and how they are relevant to the diagnosed problem
	Consider implementation strategies

Source: Adapted from Thomas and Rothman (1994) and Fawcett *et al.* (1994)

scholars, regardless of discipline, have discovered in relation to the same or a similar problem, if anything at all. The first useful knowledge source is archival knowledge and published empirical research. Given the scarcity of IVR in the accounting literature, we recommend that researchers extend their review beyond accounting to include other social sciences where IVR is prevalent, e.g., social work, public health, psychology, nursing, dementia, and organisational development (see Baard, 2010). Consistent with Boyer (1996), accounting scholars can then to contribute to the "scholarship of discovery" by generating new knowledge and to the "scholarship of integration" by crafting theoretical relationships between different fields. The professional literature is another source of knowledge on whether and how organisations may have addressed similar problems in the past.

New knowledge is acquired by conducting original empirical research, using interviews, observations, focus groups, etc. with participants who are currently experiencing or who have experienced similar problems. Table 5.4 contains some example questions that could be asked during an interview to elicit a detailed account of the problem.

To generate a body of knowledge about their social system, Campanale et al. (2014) conducted semi-structured interviews with 16 different public-sector hospitals, including the hospital under study. The interviews were designed to increase their understanding of how the current accounting systems were failing these users—for example, the inability to directly allocate fixed costs. Campanale and colleagues took an etic approach and just listened to the respondent's answers. However, the questions they asked were designed to stimulate thinking and awareness of the issues under consideration, which means these interviews could be construed as a low-intensity intervention. To support the synthesis of the information gathered, the participants were divided into two groups. The 'follow-up group' consisted of all 27 interviewees, and 'restricted group' consisted of just the interviewees from the hospital under study.

The last objective in this phase, acquiring knowledge on past relevant interventions, can reveal a range of potential solutions to a problem and how interventions have been implemented. More often, though, it inspires ideas for new interventions.

Phase 3—Intervention Design and Construction

We cover the intricacies of creating interventions in more detail in Chapter 11; this section merely introduces the general objectives and activities to be undertaken in this phase of the framework. The original D&D Framework calls Phase 3 'Intervention Design and Development'. To avoid confusion with the original D&D framework, we renamed Phase 3 'Intervention Design and Construction'. The intervention is the essence of the IRF and reflects Lewin's principle of solving a problem. Despite the centrality of intervention design to IVR, not much has been published on this subject in the literature. Intervention philosophy offers no guidance. Jönsson and Lukka (2007) discuss strong and modest intervention types but do not explain how to design one. Argyris (1970) theorises about three different types of interventions but does not translate his theories into practice. And Kasanen *et al.'s* (1993) market-test method (i.e., weak, semi-strong, and strong) helps to ascertain an intervention's ability to solve a problem but does not outline how to create an intervention. So, how do we systematically and deliberately design and construct accounting interventions for real-world contexts?

Following Baard (2004) and Baard (2010), we therefore put forward two critical objectives and a series of intervention design activities (see Table 5.6).

The first critical objective is to form a design team so that the researcher and the participants can collaborate. Identifying people who might be good for this team begins in Phase 1, but here is where the team is formalised. Thomas and Rothman (1994) argue that collaboration is critical because creating an intervention must explicitly and sensitively embrace the realities of the participants to provide a meaningful intervention capable of solving real problems. Doing so also promotes the development of free and informed choice for the participants, and their internal commitment to adopting the intervention, consistent with IVT's second and third principles. An intervention's ability to solve problems also informs the reliability and validity of IVR (see Chapter 8).

Table 5.6 Phase 3—Intervention Design and Construction

Critical Objectives	Activities
Form the Design Team	Choose the researchers and participants who will help to design the interventions
	Involve this design team in all facets of the intervention design
Conceive Interventions That Might Solve the Problem	Construct design objectives consistent with problem analysis and diagnosis
	Identify design problems
	Establish intervention requirements
	Design intervention concept(s)
	Generate and select solution alternatives
	Formulate an intervention model
	Construct intervention prototype(s)
	Test the prototype(s) in controlled conditions.

Source: Adapted from Thomas (1984), Thomas and Rothman (1994), Fawcett *et al.* (1994) and Mullen (1994)

Further, Thomas and Rothman (1994) state that intervention design and development must occur within assimilated contexts, that is using both researcher's (etic) and the participants' (emic) perspectives. The notion of an assimilated context is important because intervention design may also "emerge from a complex mixture of political considerations, the personal influence of key stakeholders, economic constraints, and the availability of necessary program staff and technology", (Mullen, 1994, p. 164). This means that people, the political climate, and the availability of resources will influence intervention design, and thus should be considered.

The second critical objective is to begin constructing interventions. Here, Mullen (1994) argues that problem identification and analysis is central to intervention design. Although it is not unusual to develop an intervention and then refine it as problems arise, the thinking in human services is that one should follow a problem-solving model when designing interventions. Problem-centred intervention design means researchers should first diagnose and analyse the problem, as outlined in Phase 1 (Mullen, 1994). In reflecting on the limited literature on accounting IVR, the researchers seem to have done the right thing and identified a problem before finding a solution (e.g., Campanale *et al.*, 2014; Chiucchi, 2013; Cullen *et al.*, 2013; Seal *et al.*, 1999). Hence, in accounting IVR, we recommend scholars apply a problem-solving model to intervention design. More information on this is outlined in Chapter 11.

In adapting the original D&D Framework to the accounting context, we moved intervention development from Phase 4 to Phase 3 because, in social work, interventions are mostly oriented toward individuals and small groups, whereas accounting interventions are more likely to operate at the organisational level. This extra complexity tends to require thinking further ahead into the details of intervention implementation as part of the design.

Phase 4—Pilot Testing and Implementation

The original D&D Framework calls Phase 4 "Early Development and Pilot-Testing". We call it 'Pilot Testing and Implementation' because pilot testing can also be used to test the implementation method that researchers intend to use in their IVR project. The critical objectives and activities of this phase appear in Table 5.7.

IVR in real-world contexts is risky and conducting a pilot test of the intervention can help to mitigate that risk. It helps researchers determine whether an intervention is feasible, suitable, and potentially able to achieve what it was designed to achieve. Chapter 12 outlines a theoretical approach to implementing interventions, along with some insights into pilot testing through two different interventions—one successful, the other not.

Table 5.7 Phase 4—Pilot Testing and Implementation

Critical Objectives	Activities
Conduct a Pilot Test	Develop a plan for trial use in a pilot test
	Establish a procedure for pilot testing
	Select a site for the pilot test
	Conduct the pilot test
	Review the results using appropriate research techniques
Trial the Implementation Procedure	Design and develop the implementation procedures
	Trial the implementation techniques as part of the pilot test
Refine the Intervention Design and Implementation Procedures	Identify and address any design problems that arise
	Refine the intervention (if required)
	Refine the implementation procedures (if required)
Implementation	Choose an appropriate implementation methodology
	Formulate an implementation plan
	Implement the intervention
	Monitor the implementation

Source: Adapted from Thomas and Rothman (1994), Fawcett *et al.* (1994) and Rothman and Tumblin (1994)

Phase 5—Intervention Evaluation and Advanced Development

Evaluating an intervention means understanding the effects and effectiveness of the intervention—in other words, whether it works in practice (Thomas, 1994). Integral to intervention evaluation is ascertaining whether it can continue to deliver ongoing benefits in its current form or whether further development will be required in the short-to-medium term (Thomas, 1994). Table 5.8 lists the two critical objectives and associated activities in this phase.

First, critically appraising an intervention depends on having clearly defined objectives (Thomas, 1994). In planning for intervention evaluation, Thomas (1994) states that researchers must know what aspects of the intervention they want to evaluate, for example, simplicity and ease of use, capacity for problem-solving, compatibility with the organisational context, and so on. He also recommends not evaluating an intervention too early. Assessing an under-developed intervention may undermine the participants' confidence in the researcher(s) and, therefore, the ability of the intervention to solve the problem. The intervention may be rejected too early in the IVR process or, worse still, the organisation may abandon the IVR project entirely. However, when the time for evaluation does

Table 5.8 Phase 5—Intervention Evaluation & Advanced Development

Critical Objectives	Activities
Critically appraise intervention outcomes and effectiveness	Plan intervention evaluation
	Specify the evaluation objective and what intervention aspects will be evaluated
	Select intervention evaluation methods
	Collect and analyse data on intervention effectiveness
	Identify intervention features for refinement or advanced developmental work
Advanced intervention development	Determine time, effort, and other resource requirements for refinement/advanced developments
	Implement refinements/advanced modifications

Source: Adapted from Thomas and Rothman (1994), Fawcett *et al.* (1994) and Thomas (1994).

come, researchers should also consider applying the most intensive evaluation they possibly can, given the available time, resources, and participant willingness.

Descriptive surveys, interviews, and focus groups are all good evaluation techniques, which benefit IVR projects in several ways. Beyond generating insights to help further improve an intervention, these techniques help researchers to generate theoretical findings. Involving the participants in the evaluation process can help to identify problems with the intervention at a deeper level, gather suggestions about what might help to fix those problems, and strengthen collaborations. In this regard, choosing evaluation techniques carefully is important because good collaborations also strengthen the participants' commitment to the intervention and IVR process (Baard, 2004).

Advanced intervention development, that is, further development in the medium-to-long term, is contingent upon many factors—for instance, the urgency and severity of the organisational problem, the nature of the intervention, the quality and extensiveness of early development and pilot testing, time and resource constraints, the extent to which the intervention interferes with ongoing organisational functioning, and the organisation's tolerance for a long IVR process. There are no prescriptions governing intervention evaluation and advanced development. Accounting scholars should decide for themselves the extent to which they implement Phase 5 in their IVR project.

Phase 6—Intervention Dissemination

Three themes characterise the process of implementing an intervention (Baard, 2004, 2010): the commercial appeal of an intervention (or not, as the case is in accounting); disseminating results; and the impacts of reporting on IVR's practical outcomes (see Table 5.9).

Table 5.9 Phase 6—Intervention Dissemination

Critical Objectives	Activities
Disseminate Theoretical Outputs	Identify an appropriate academic journal
	Publish academic findings
	Prepare and publish a professional IVR report
	Use published IVR to support doctoral education

In social work, interventions are viewed through a commercial lens. Thomas and Rothman (1994) discuss branding, writing guidelines for an intervention's use, working out a price for the 'product', identifying markets and ways to create demand, and how to provide ongoing support for those who adopt the intervention. Notoriously underfunded, these measures may be necessary in the human services sector. However, monetising interventions is probably not appropriate in accounting if for no other reason than it associates IVR with consulting. Any intellectual property arising out of an intervention can always be handled by a university commercialisation team in the same way as any other innovation.

With IVR, there are two sets of outcomes—theoretical and practical. Channels for disseminating theoretical results include publishing papers in reputable academic journals and introducing IVR into undergraduate and higher education programs (more in Chapter 13). Similarly, practical outcomes can be published in professional journals or incorporated in the professional accreditation programs. We recommend reading Corrigan *et al.*'s (1994) discussion on communicating the practical outputs of research, and Rooney (1994) for theoretical outputs. Additionally, Jönsson and Lukka's (2007) philosophical insights on post-intervention analysis are helpful when publishing IVR to an academic audience.

There is scant empirical evidence within accounting IVR on the impacts of reporting one's solutions to real-life problems. Learnings from clinical psychology, social work, psychiatry, and other health sciences have little relevance to accounting because the nature of the interventions is very different. Thus, there is a great opportunity for future research to advance theory on this topic.

In Summation

Accounting is a diverse field of research. Rooted in the social sciences, most of its disciplines are applied, and both quantitative and qualitative methodologies are commonplace. Thus, accounting research shares some common ground with IVR. The IRF is a flexible, viable, and legitimate umbrella framework that can be adapted to and used for accounting IVR across all of accounting areas. It embraces all of Lewin's governing IVR principles and explicitly operationalises Argyris's (1970) theoretical principles of IVT. As a result, the IRF provides a cohesive and consistent guide to approaching IVR. Its benefits include:

- The potential to produce practical, theoretical and societally relevant accounting research;
- Precision and clarity on the IVR process;
- Explicit phases, critical objectives, and activities that offer a universal approach to IVR with enough flexibility to adapt the framework to diverse projects; and
- Unambiguous methodological transparency.

Thus, there is significant merit in following the IRF when conducting accounting IVR; it is so much more than a 'do-it-yourself' checklist.

References

Ahrens, T. & Dent, J.F. (1998). Accounting and organizations: Realising the richness of field research. *Journal of Management Accounting Research*, 10, 1–39.

Argyris, C. (1970). *Intervention theory and method: A behavioural science view*. Reading, MA: Addison-Wesley Publishing Company.

Atkinson, A.A. & Shaffir, W. (1998). Standards for field research in management accounting. *Journal of Management Accounting Research*, 10, 41–68.

Baard, V.C. (2004). *The design and implementation of an IT consulting system in South African small businesses*. (Doctor of Technologiae), Central University of Technology, Bloemfontein, South Africa.

Baard, V.C. (2010). A critical view of interventionist research. *Qualitative Research in Accounting and Management*, 7(1), 13–45.

Baard, V.C. & Dumay, J. (2018). Interventionist research in accounting: Reflections on the good, the bad and the ugly. *Accounting and Finance*, Advance online publication. https://doi.org/10.1111/acfi.12409

Baldvinsdottir, G.F., Mitchell, F., & Nörreklit, H. (2010). Issues in the relationship between theory and practice in management accounting. *Management Accounting Research*, 21, 79–82.

Beer, M. (1980). *Organization change and development: A system view*. Glenview, IL: Scott Foresman.

Boyer, E.L. (1996). The scholarship of engagement. *Journal of Public Service and Outreach*, 1(1), 11–20.

Burchell, S., Clubb, C., Hopwood, A., Hughes, J., & Nahapiet, J. (1980). The roles of accounting in organisations and society. *Accounting, Organizations and Society*, 5(1), 5–27.

Campanale, C., Cinquini, L., & Tenucci, A. (2014). Time driven activity-based costing to improve transparency and decision making in healthcare. *Qualitative Research in Accounting & Management*, 11, 165–186.

Chiucchi, M.S. (2013). Intellectual capital accounting in action: Enhancing learning through interventionist research. *Journal of Intellectual Capital*, 14, 48–68.

Corrigan, P.W., Mackain, S.J., & Liberman, R.P. (1994). Skill training modules: A strategy for dissemination and utilisation of a rehabilitation innovation. In J. Rothman & E.J. Thomas (Eds.), *Intervention research: Design and development for human service* (pp. 317–352). Binghamton, NY: Haworth Press.

Cullen, J., Tsamenyi, M., Bernon, M., & Gorst, J. (2013). Reverse logistics in the UK retail sector: A case study of the role of management accounting in driving organisational change. *Management Accounting Research*, 24, 212–227.

DiMaggio, P.J. & Powell, W.W. (1983). The iron cage revisited: Institutional isomorphism and collective rationality in organizational fields. *American Sociological Review*, 48, 147–160.

Fairweather, G. (1967). *Methods for experimental social innovation*. New York, NY: John Wiley and Sons.

Fawcett, S.B. (1990). Some emerging standards for community research and action. In P. Tolan, D. Keys, F. Chertok, & L.E. Jason (Eds.), *Researching community psychology: Integrating theories and methodologies* (pp. 64–75). Washington, DC: American Psychological Association.

Fawcett, S.B. (1991). Some values guiding community research and action. *Journal of Applied Behaviour Analysis*, 24, 621–636.

Fawcett, S.B., Suarez-Balcazar, Y., Balcazar, F.E., White, G.W., Paine, A.L., Blanchard, K.A., & Embree, M.G. (1994). Conducting intervention research— The design and development process. In J. Rothman & E.J. Thomas (Eds.), *Intervention research: Design and development for human service* (pp. 25–54). Binghamton, NY: Haworth Press.

Gallhofer, S. & Haslam, J. (2003). *Accounting and Emancipation*. London, UK: Routledge.

Guthrie, J., Burritt, R., & Evans, E. (2011). The relationship between academic accounting research and professional practice. In E. Evans, R. Burritt, & J. Guthrie (Eds.), *Bridging the gap between academic accounting research and professional practice* (pp. 9–20). Sydney, Australia: Institute of Chartered Accountants Australia.

Ittner, C. & Larcker, D. (2002). Empirical managerial accounting research: Are we just describing management consulting practice? *European Accounting Review*, 11(4), 787–794.

Jansen, E.P. (2018). Bridging the gap between theory and practice in management accounting: Reviewing the literature to shape interventions. *Accounting, Auditing and Accountability Journal*, 31(5), 1486–1509.

Jönsson, S. & Lukka, K. (2007). There and back again: Doing interventionist research in management accounting. In C.S. Chapman, A.G. Hopwood, & M.S. Shields (Eds.), *Handbook of management accounting research* (Vol. 1, pp. 373–397). Oxford, UK: Elsevier.

Kasanen, E., Lukka, K., & Silonen, A. (1993). The constructive approach in management accounting research. *Journal of Management Accounting Research*, 5, 243–264.

Labro, E. & Tuomela, T. (2003). On bringing more action into management accounting research: Process considerations based on two constructive case studies. *European Accounting Review*, 12, 409–442.

Lewin, K. (1946). Action research and minority problems. *Journal of Social Issues*, 11, 34–46.

Merchant, K.A. & Van der Stede, W.A. (2006). Field-based research in accounting: Accomplishments and prospects. *Behavioural Research in Accounting*, 18(1), 117–134.

Meyer, J.W. & Rowan, B. (1977). Institutionalised organisations: Formal structure as myth and ceremony. *Journal of Sociology*, 83(2), 340–363.

Meyer, J.W. & Scott, W.R. (1983). *Organizational environments: Ritual and rationality*. London, UK: Sage Publications.

Miller, P. (2007). Management accounting and sociology. In C.S. Chapman, A.G. Hopwood, & M.S. Shields (Eds.), *Handbook of management accounting research* (Vol. 1, pp. 285–295). Oxford, UK: Elsevier.

Mullen, E.J. (1994). Design of social intervention. In J. Rothman & E.J. Thomas (Eds.), *Intervention research: Design and development for human service* (pp. 163–193). Binghamton, NY: Haworth Press.

Paine, S.C., Bellamy, G.T., & Wilcox, B. (1984). *Human services that work: From innovation to standard practice*. Baltimore, MD: Paul H. Brookes Publishing Company.

Parker, L.D. (2014). Qualitative perspectives: Through a methodological lens. *Qualitative Research in Accounting & Management*, 11, 13–28.

Rautiainen, A., Sippola, K., & Mättö, T. (2017). Perspectives on relevance: The relevance test in the constructive research approach. *Management Accounting Research*, 34, 19–29.

Reid, W.J. (1994). Field testing and data gathering on innovative practice interventions in early development. In J. Rothman & E.J. Thomas (Eds.), *Intervention research: Design and development for human service* (pp. 245–264). Binghamton, NY: Haworth Press.

Richardson, A.J. (2004). Applied research in accounting: A commentary. *Canadian Accounting Perspectives*, 3(2), 149–168.

Rooney, R.H. (1994). Disseminating intervention research in academic settings: A view from social work. In J. Rothman & E.J. Thomas (Eds.), *Intervention research: Design and development for human service* (pp. 353–367). Binghamton, NY: Haworth Press.

Rothman, J. (1980). *Social R&D: Research and development in the human services*. Englewood Cliffs, NJ: Prentice-Hall.

Rothman, J. & Thomas, E.J. (Eds.). (1994). *Intervention research: Design and development for human service*. Binghamton, NY: Haworth Press.

Rothman, J. & Tumblin, A. (1994). Pilot testing and early development of a model of case management intervention. In J. Rothman & E.J. Thomas (Eds.), *Intervention research: Design and development for human service* (pp. 215–233). Binghamton, NY: Haworth Press.

Seal, W., Cullen, J., Dunlop, A., Berry, T., & Ahmed, M. (1999). Enacting a European supply chain: A case study on the role of management accounting. *Management Accounting Research*, 10(3), 303–322.

Suomala, P., Lyly-Yrjänäinen, J., & Lukka, K. (2014). Battlefield around interventions: A reflective analysis of conducting interventionist research in management accounting. *Management Accounting Research*, 25, 304–314.

Thomas, E.J. (1984). *Designing interventions for the helping professions*. Beverley Hills, CA: Sage Publications.

Thomas, E.J. (1994). Evaluation, advanced development and the unilateral family therapy experiment. In J. Rothman & E.J. Thomas (Eds.), *Intervention research: Design and development for human service* (pp. 267–295). Binghamton, NY: Haworth Press.

Thomas, E.J. & Rothman, J. (1994). An integrative perspective on intervention research. In J. Rothman & E.J. Thomas (Eds.), *Intervention research: Design and development for human service* (pp. 3–23). Binghamton, NY: Haworth Press.

Young, S.M. (1999). Field research methods in management accounting. *Accounting Horizons*, 13(1), 76–84.

6 Planning and Protecting Your IVR Project

The nature of the Interventionist Research Framework (IRF) enables researchers to use the framework as a tool for planning an IVR project that will support conducting legitimate IVR. All the chapters following Chapter 6 are related to specific IRF phases and the work required for each phase. In each subsequent chapter, we have embedded IVR project planning in our discourse. Hence, in this chapter, our discussion on IVR project planning centres on ethical, budgetary, and intellectual property matters.

Ethical Considerations for IVR

IVR projects involve human research participants, and therefore ethical considerations throughout the research process relating to research participants are critical. We view ethical considerations as paramount to research because they reflect the fundamental principles that guide accounting scholars on how to undertake IVR, and their actions when undertaking IVR and any other form of research. However, the ethical considerations in different countries vary. Hence, we advise you to check with your university on the ethical requirements before embarking on an IVR project.

Most countries provide specific ethical principles, standards, and guidelines for conducting research. For example, in the United States of America (USA), there is the National Institutes of Health (NIH) that outlines seven primary principles guiding ethical research (www.nih.gov/health-information/nih-clinical-research-trials-you/guiding-principles-ethical-research). In the United Kingdom (UK), the Economic and Social Research Council, belonging to the United Kingdom Research and Innovation (UKRI) organisation, presents a comprehensive framework on research ethics. The framework enables researchers to consider multiple ethical issues for the duration of a research project and offers helpful guidance on a range of research conduct and governance matters (https://esrc.ukri.org/funding/guidance-for-applicants/research-ethics/). In Australia, the 'National Statement of Ethical Conduct in Human Research' recently updated in 2018, developed by the National Health and Medical Research Council, the Australian Research Council and Universities Australia, guides all research undertaken by Australian scholars involving people (www.nhmrc.gov.au/about-us/publications/national-statement-ethical-conduct-human-research-2007-updated-2018#block-views-block-file-attachments-content-block-1).

The Australian national statement on ethical conduct states that ethical research involving people extends beyond doing the right thing and includes researchers conducting themselves in the right spirit and with respect and concern for human beings (NHMRC, 2018). Most ethical guidelines embrace numerous ethical issues, such as risk; informed and voluntary consent; participant recruitment; participant coercion and pressure; confidentiality; research involving vulnerable populations; protecting identifiable participant information; providing payment and reimbursements to participants;, data collection, use, and management; and communicating research findings (NHMRC, 2018). Although all these issues are important, there are three main ethical considerations given the central theme of IVR in this book on which we focus our discourse. They include IVR project risk, being an ethical IVR researcher, and constructing an IVR ethics application.

IVR Project Risk

Customary accounting research may carry little risk, but there is always the possibility that things go wrong, and a little risk evolves into moderate and serious risk, despite prudent intentions and careful planning and research practice. Accounting IVR may carry little risk, but it can also be subject to greater risk given the nature of the research approach. Thus, IVR scholars need to exercise extreme care and diligence. In accounting IVR, research participants enter into a relationship with researchers whom they might not necessarily know particularly well and whom they will need to trust. We have discussed ways to build trust in Chapters 10 and 12 and elsewhere in this book.

The NHMRC (2018) acknowledges that relationships between participants and researchers may develop due to the duration and nature of the research. Specifically, that methodologies such as IVR involve "degrees of collaboration that blur the lines between researcher and participants (e.g., co-researchers in action research)" (NHMRC, 2018, p. 25). Thus, researchers may influence research participants and vice versa. Hence, you should anticipate relationship building, and where appropriate, the relationships may require modification or discontinuing the research (NHMRC, 2018). In Chapter 10, we address the issue of researcher and research participant marginality that may occur in IVR to help create awareness of mitigating the risks associated with relationships that develop during the IVR project.

Table 6.1 Accounting IVR Risk to Participants

Form of Risk	Features
Inconvenience (Low Risk)	Participating in a survey. Expending time participating in research.
Discomfort (Less Serious than Harm)	Anxiety induced by participating in an interview or focus group or being observed.
Psychological Harm	Feelings of worthlessness, distress, guilt, anger, or fear related to disclosure of identifiable, sensitive, or embarrassing documents and information.
Devaluation of Personal Worth (Harm)	Humiliation, manipulation, or treated disrespectfully or unjustly.
Social Harm	Damage to social networks or relationships with others
	Discrimination in access to benefits, services, or employment.
	Social stigmatisation.
Economic Harm	The imposition of direct or indirect costs on participants.
Legal Harm	Discovery and prosecution of criminal conduct.

Source: Adapted from NHMRC (2018)

Within IVR, collaboration between researchers and research participants is paramount. Scholars intervene in the everyday lives of participants with the potential for participants to foster change based on the intervention; this all carries risk. The NHMRC (2018, p. 12) defines risk as "potential for harm, discomfort or inconvenience", involves the likelihood that risk will occur, and "the severity of the harm including its consequences." To create researcher awareness of the various forms of risk, we outline a range of potential risks that may manifest in accounting IVR in Table 6.1.

Accounting interventionist researchers are responsible for managing risks associated with their IVR projects. Identifying risks includes anticipating participant perception of the risks, evaluating the probability and severity of project risks, assessing how to minimise risks, and justifying the risks in the context of the overall potential beneficial outcomes of the project.

An Ethical Interventionist Researcher

Accounting interventionist researchers are subject to their country's national ethical guidelines and their professional codes, rules, and policies relating to ethical behaviour, as mandated by professional associations. We acknowledge that professional association's ethical principles

Table 6.2 Ethical Principles for Professionals

Principle	Features
Integrity	Apply honesty, fair dealing, and truthfulness in all professional and business relationships.
Objectivity	Do not allow bias, conflict of interest, undue influence to compromise judgements.
Professional Competence and Due Care	Sustain professional knowledge and skill and other capabilities to ensure competence service delivery Due care implies acting diligently and incorporating responsibility.
Confidentiality	To respect the confidentiality of information of others acquired through professional relationships.
Professional Behaviour	Comply with the regulatory and statutory framework and avoid discrediting conduct.

Source: Adapted from APES (2018)

and standards may differ, and that these differences may prevail in different countries across the globe. Australian accounting professionals are expected to comply with and observe the code of ethics outlined by the Accounting Professional and Ethical Standards Board (APES), see Table 6.2. All these principles are equally applicable to conducting research and closely align with the principles of conducting ethical research.

While all the standards apply to interventionist researchers, in our view, the principles relating to competence and responsibility are particularly important principles underpinning the conduct of ethical research. Throughout this book, we observe the matter of researcher qualities and how the qualities required for IVR are different from non-interventionist qualitative research. Competence refers to knowledge, skills, experience, and training—is the researcher qualified to do what they are proposing to do in their research project? Thus, competence is an integral component of researcher qualities for maintaining the quality and integrity of their research; assessing and managing research risk; selecting and recruiting the intervention team and research participants; upholding standards in the field, including ethical considerations across all IVR work; and being aware of and honest about one's limitations when embarking on IVR (Bruhn & Rebach, 2007; Gitlin & Czaja, 2016). We find that competence is important for intervening given the diverse nature of social systems where specific competences are required for intervening in these social systems and for designing, constructing, and implementing interventions aimed at a specific social system (see Chapter 11).

Responsibility corresponds to accountability because researchers conducting quality and ethical IVR are accountable for the processes and outcomes of the IVR project (Bruhn & Rebach, 2007). Responsibility coincides with due care, and you must treat the research team members and research participants with due care, including assessing and managing risk and adopting an ethically sound approach to doing IVR. Moreover, competence is a value that is strongly correlated with responsibility because researchers are responsible for knowing what they are doing. Responsibility means accepting the limits of your capabilities and knowing when to say—"I cannot do this"—and either withdrawing from IVR work or referring to another scholar who "can do this." Bruhn and Rebach (2007) argue that responsibility obligates researchers to follow up on research participants' progress as participants move through the IVR activities to ascertain their levels of commitment to the project, discover any problems or unintended and harmful effects, or beneficial outcomes resulting from the intervention. Researchers also need to learn how effective they were in their conduct of IVR and in the intervention design and implementation that mobilises research participants to bring about change in organisations.

Accountability serves as the moral evaluation of the intervention concerning research participant values, the sustainability of participants' integrity despite change emerging from the intervention, and the climate of the collaborative partnership where participants also need to demonstrate accountability and researchers retain their reputation. Researchers are responsible and accountable for sharing the IVR experience. Doing so enhances scholarly knowledge in their field and potentially beyond and the practical knowledge of practitioners, managers, and other professionals.

The IVR Research Ethics Application

This section aims to show how developing a considered ethics application can support IVR project planning and integrate ethical issues across the IVR process supported by the IRF. One of us, Vicki Baard, has been an active member of two university ethics committees as a reviewer of ethics applications from diverse business and management disciplines. We do not argue against the fact that constructing an ethics application is a sometimes frustrating and time-consuming process that demands considerable effort and attention. Generally, it can be an intimidating and stressful experience. Our personal belief is that at each stage of the research process, researchers must carefully identify, examine, and address ethical issues from the beginning because, "Ethics is not an appendage added onto a [intervention] study once it has been designed and is ready to be implemented" (O'Mathúna, 2012 p. 85).

In my (Vicki Baard's) experience, I have encountered ethics applications where researchers addressed ethical concerns only after they received detailed feedback. Sometimes the projects described in the applications were so under-developed that the entire application was an ethical bomb waiting to explode. Sometimes masters and doctoral students submitted applications too early in the research process because they were worried about the time it would take for the review and approval process. Alternatively, students wrote up their project proposal to suit the ethics application form rather than outlining the research they want to do. Other applications contained methodological concerns that would negatively impact on research instruments and data collection methods, which in turn potentially exposed research participants to inconvenience, discomfort, and harm. O'Mathúna (2012) states that intervention studies with flawed methodologies and methods are an ethical concern because they can waste time and resources and elevate project risk. Additional issues related to the prevalence of significant spelling and grammatical errors, ambiguously drafted participant information letters, and poorly drafted consent forms demonstrating a disagreeable degree of respect for the participants, especially given the commitment and time desired from participants. As an ethics application reviewer (Vicki Baard speaking here), observing all these issues, leads me to question the researcher's capabilities to undertake research, whether the research is likely to be beneficial to anyone, and the overall quality of the research process, including outcomes and outputs. So how do we move forward on the intimidating task of completing ethics applications? How do we use ethics applications to outline ethical issues, evaluate the quality and integrity of the project, and use it to support project planning?

Table 6.3 shows how the IRF phases potentially align with the ethical elements outlined by the Australian National Statement of Ethical Conduct in Human Research. Additionally, we outline the ethical research issues associated with each phase and ethical element that researchers should consider. Thus, Table 6.3 also demonstrates how the basics of an IVR project align with ethical requirements, and the way in which we plan for and execute our research influences our ethical approach to research, and vice versa. Using the IRF phases enables researchers to estimate a timeline required for the research, including a contingency for unexpected delays, which supports planning and budgetary considerations. We recognise that our international audience may have their country and institution specific ethical guidelines, which may differ from the Australian interpretation. However, the point we make here is that carefully thinking about the ethical research issues and aligning them with all the essential IVR research objectives and activities enables researchers to develop a high-quality research proposal, to plan for their IVR project, and construct an ethics application that can enhance the probability of a successful IVR project.

Table 6.3 IRF and Alignment with the NHMRC Guidelines

IRF *(see Chapter 5)*	NHMRC Guidelines	Ethical Research Issues to Consider
Phase 1: Problem Analysis & Project Planning	Element 1: Research Scope, Aims, Themes, Questions & Methods (p. 26).	Why is conducting this research important?
		What are the aims of this research?
		What is the research question(s) that this project intends to explore?
		What are the benefits of exploring the research question(s)—does the research contribute to knowledge or understanding, enhanced social or individual wellbeing, or researcher capabilities?
		To whom or what are the benefits likely to flow?
		How will the research methodology, methods, and design achieve research aims and address the research question?
		What measures are you taking to assure the reliability and validity of data collection and analysis, results, and overall generalisability?
	Element 2: Recruitment (p. 28).	This element relates to the recruitment strategy (see also Chapter 9).
		Who are the potential participants?
		How will participants be identified and recruited?
		What is the justification for adopting the identified recruitment strategy?
		What is the impact of any existing relationships between researchers and potential participants on the recruitment strategy?
		How will the recruitment strategy be developed to incorporate obtaining informed and voluntary participant consent?
		What are the risks of the identified recruitment strategy for potential participants or the viability of the project?

Element 3: Consent (p. 30).	What strategies will this research use for obtaining participant consent? For example, orally, in writing, returning a survey, registering interest in participating, expressing interest via social media, consultation, or negotiation?
	To what extent does the project, the participants, or the context warrant multiple strategies for obtaining consent?
	What information about your project will be forwarded to potential participants to obtain consent?
	How can a participant opt-out of their consent they have already provided?
Phase 2: Information Gathering & Synthesis	
Element 4: Collection, Use, and Management of Data (p. 32).	What data or information does the project require to achieve its aims and address the research questions?
	How will data be collected or accessed, and how will information be generated using the data?
	How will the data or information be used and analysed, and by whom?
	Will the data or information be disclosed or shared, and, if so, with whom?
	How will data or information be stored, for how long will it be stored, and how will you dispose of it when the project is over?
	What are the actual and potential risks associated with data or information collection, utilisation, and management, and how will these risks be minimised? What is the probability and severity of any harm that may result (see Table 6.1)?
	How will data or information collection and management comply with country or institution specific ethical principles?
Phase 3: Intervention Design and Construction	
Element 5: Communication of Research Findings or Results to Participants (p. 38).	To what extent could the research results and findings be significant for the current or future welfare or wellbeing of participants or other research stakeholders?

(Continued)

Table 6.3 (Continued)

IRF *(see Chapter 5)*	NHMRC Guidelines	Ethical Research Issues to Consider
Phase 4: Pilot Testing & Implementation	(Please note that Element 5 may apply across multiple IRF phases, including Phase 1, relating to problem diagnosis.)	To what extent could the research generate findings or results relevant to participants? How are potential research participants in the research notified in advance of the relevance and significance of the findings to them and others? Will the consent of participants be obtained to enable any planned or necessary disclosure of findings or results?
Phase 5: Intervention Evaluation & Advanced Development		How will the results and findings be communicated to research participants and by whom? How will the results and findings, if applicable, be disclosed to third parties or the wider public?
Phase 6: Dissemination	Element 6: Dissemination of Research Outputs and Outcomes (p. 40).	How will the research outputs or outcomes be reported, published, or otherwise disseminated? Will the researchers offer research participants a timely and suitable summary of the research outputs or outcomes? (See also Chapter 13 on using non-technical language to communicate research output.) How will the planned dissemination of research outputs or outcomes contribute to knowledge development (i.e., theoretical advancement) and social system practices (practical knowledge advancement and societally relevant knowledge)?

Source: Adapted from NHMRC (2018)

When the research project is complete, researchers have ongoing responsibilities related to the ethical aspects of their research. These responsibilities include:

- Complying with relevant policies for research data or information to be retained for a specified period of time.
- The arrangements concerning the individual, organisational, and community intellectual property and copyright inherent in the research outputs—this is particularly important for IVR concerning the intervention design and development.
- A strategy or plan to contact or monitor research participants concerning sustained use of the intervention and potential change emanating from the intervention.

Overall, in our experience, applying a considered approach to the ethics application also informs the planning of your research project and positions researchers for a productive and successful research experience. Researchers can always expect questions and comments from ethics application reviewers. The purpose of these comments is not only to address the ethical requirements of research but also to support good quality research and to help researchers with their projects. We advocate that researchers use these comments and questions as they would an academic journal reviewer's response to a journal article submission in a high-quality and reputable journal.

Developing an IVR Budget

In this section, we discuss some issues that IVR scholars should consider when developing and managing the budget for their IVR project. Like all forms of research, IVR costs money to undertake, and it may have some hidden costs. Hence, we offer some resources that an interventionist researcher can use to develop budgets, especially when you need to make a funding application to your university, an external body, or even the research partner (social system) where the research takes place. Moreover, we use the IRF to outline some of the items that might incur some costs in developing IVR research.

Funding Your IVR Project

In writing this section, we recognise that people reading this book may include a diverse community of accounting scholars and scholars from other management and business-oriented disciplines. Therefore, our intention is not to offer budgetary prescriptions or provide a tutorial on budgeting, rather to offer what we think are essential considerations when thinking about or constructing a budget for your IVR project.

Generally, there are three main sources of funding. First, scholarly research funding that you may accumulate through achieving publications or an annual modest research amount received by each scholar from your department or faculty/school within your Higher Education Institution (HEI) to use exclusively for research purposes. Although it is unlikely that you will need to submit a formal budget when using your internal institutional research funds, we find that developing a budget, in any event, is useful to support your IVR project initiative and associated activities. Second, your HEI might offer internal competitive grant schemes specifically aimed at its institutional scholars. Third, outside funding institutions such as professional associations, government agencies, private and public organisations, and communities, may also offer competitive grant schemes. Hence, you should include persuasive grant writing skills in your suite of researcher qualities because conducting IVR may require financial support for each phase in the overall IVR process (see Chapter 3).

We find that the primary aim of any grant application is to convince the reviewers of the funding agency to grant funding to your IVR project to support project objectives, the nature of the intervention and its implementation, and to help deliver the project outputs/outcomes serving the interest of social systems represented by the funding agency. Moreover, your grant application should ensure that the project you are seeking funding for is consistent with the funding agency's vision, mission, strategic outlook, and general purview of interest. Thus, constructing a detailed and sensible budget is a highly important component of any grant application.

We find little or no consensus in the accounting IVR literature on specific strategies and practices on grant writing to facilitate accounting IVR. In reflecting on grant writing, we acknowledge the diverse nature of our scholarly audience and their potential IVR projects. Additionally, HEI's normally provide extensive scholarly support in writing grant applications, as attracting external funding is important for these institutions. Hence, we provide some resources on grant writing and developing a project budget that we have found helpful and used in our IVR projects; see Table 6.4.

The Costs of Your IVR Project

Developing and justifying a budget for your IVR project takes time and careful thought. Additionally, it includes an in-depth understanding of the nature of your IVR project and its needs and appreciating an institution's or organisation's motive for offering to fund a research project. Ideally, achieving congruence between the two positions the project for potential success.

Table 6.4 Grant Writing Resources

Grant Writing Source	Features
Gitlin and Czaja (2016)—Chapter 23	Outlines general grant writing tips.
	Identifies unique IVR grant writing challenges.
UKRI Economic and Social Research Council https://esrc.ukri.org/funding/guidance-for-applicants/how-to-write-a-good-research-grant-proposal/	Provides a research funding guide.
	Presents advice on writing a good grant proposal.
	It offers insights on research ethics.
	Considers research impact, innovation, intellectual assets, and property consistent with IVR.
	Exemplifies budgetary considerations when writing a grant proposal.
The United States, National Institutes of Health (NIH) https://grants.nih.gov/grants/how-to-apply-application-guide/format-and-write/write-your-application.htm	Provides extensive advice on writing a grant application.
	Developing your project budget.
Probono Australia https://probonoaustralia.com.au/news/2012/11/top-10-tips-for-grant-writing/	Offers general grant writing tips.
	Note that Fund Assist was developed by the National Centre for Education and Training on Addiction. However, the information and tools provided are sufficiently generic for use by any scholar writing a grant application.
Fund Assist http://fundassist.flinders.edu.au/introduction	
The Guardian www.theguardian.com/higher-education-network/blog/2013/apr/19/tips-successful-research-grant-funding	
Community Grants Hub www.communitygrants.gov.au/information-applicants/strong-evidence	Provides extensive and helpful support for developing grant applications.

Each funding provider has specific rules about allowable and non-allowable budgetary items. Allowable budgetary items, also referred to as direct costs, might include costs for participant recruitment; data collection and associated travel costs; data capture and analysis; and intervention design and construction including relevant supplies and equipment. Indirect costs may be related to a university or other HEI's administrative costs associated with helping scholars to complete the grant application process, addressing any potential legal issues relating to grant funding contracts, and other support costs associated with general and financial administrative oversight of funded research projects. For instance, some

HEI's require anywhere from 10% to 20% of the overall funding awarded to cover administrative costs. We find that funding providers may only allow you to include a specific percentage in the overall budget, for these administrative costs.

Moreover, each provider has clear procedures for budget development related to allowable salary or wage, on-cost rates for research staff, travel, and accommodation specifications (e.g., flying economy class), non-allowable costs (e.g., travel, supplies, equipment), and any in-kind mandatory or non-mandatory contributions. For instance, one of us (Vicki Baard) has been successful in receiving internal university and external funding provider competitive grants, wherein both instances, budgetary items for teaching relief were non-allowable as per the funding agency rules (see also Chapter 11). Our last point here is that rules and procedures of funding agencies serve as a guide on what you can or cannot accomplish in your IVR project. Further, funding agencies normally specify the maximum funding allowed for a specific project, which enables scholars to evaluate whether the nature and cost of their proposed IVR activities meet or exceed the funding limit. The evaluation means that scholars must either modify their IVR project to meet the funding constraints outlined by the rules and procedures or find an alternative or complementary funding to complete the project. Anecdotally, in our experience, we find that all these funding constraints can help temper our idealistic IVR project to the realities and economics of doing real-world IVR.

In the context of accounting IVR, we find that it is essential to think about and construct your budget at the same time that you are developing your research proposal and as a part of your IVR project planning. When developing your IVR project budget, it is essential to adopt a prudent and realistic approach such that you do not under or over estimate your financial needs. Further, reviewers from the funding providers will spot a greedy, over-zealous researcher from a distance, and anecdotal evidence abounds on grant applications that have been mercilessly rejected mainly due to disagreeable budgets. In Chapters 11, 9, and 10, centred on intervention design and construction, recruiting the intervention team, and selecting and recruiting participants, we refer to budgetary requirements to support these activities. Moreover, these chapters provide insights into the diverse needs of IVR projects that are likely to influence your project budget. When constructing your budget, we find that using the IRF (Chapter 5) and project management tools (Chapter 12) is particularly beneficial. Using project management tools, we find it useful to align your specific project milestones associated with each IVR phase and to show the budgeted cost associated with each phase's IVR activities. This helps in identifying the potential costs for each phase and it will also help you monitor and manage the project funding regardless of its source. Table 6.5 outlines the IRF phases and associated budgetary items and costs.

Table 6.5 IVR Phases and Potential Costs

Possible Budgetary Expenditure	Recruiting Participants	Grant Application Writing	Research Assistant	Office Supplies and Equipment	Co-investigator(s)	Copyeditor/Proofreader	Access to External Data	Access to Software	Transportation	Accommodation	Internal Data Collection	Transcription Services	Professional Services	Contingency	Graphic designer	Conference fees
Phase 1: Problem Analysis & Project Planning	x	x	x	x	x	x	x	x	x	x	x	x	x	x	x	
Phase 2: Information Gathering & Synthesis			x	x	x		x	x			x		x	x	x	
Phase 3: Intervention Design and Construction			x	x	x		x	x			x		x	x	x	
Phase 4: Pilot Testing & Implementation			x	x	x		x	x	x		x		x	x	x	
Phase 5: Intervention Evaluation & Advanced Development			x	x	x		x	x	x		x		x	x	x	
Phase 6: Dissemination		x			x	x	x	x	x	x		x	x	x	x	x

Developing and Protecting Intellectual Property

An often-neglected question asked at the beginning of an IVR project is: "What are the intellectual property issues for scholarly contemplation concerning their intervention and the intellectual property of their research participants emanating from the IVR project?" This question is often difficult to answer, because sometimes at the beginning of any research project, you may not be aware of any potential intellectual property (IP). After all, the discovery is still undiscovered. As Serenko and Dumay (2017, p. 330) outline, serendipity plays a major role in the academic research process "especially from the perspective of discovering new and interesting phenomena". From an IVR perspective, this could be very important because you will often be working with companies or organisations who profit from solving the problem you are solving. Therefore, under the right circumstances, you could discover and even later commercialise valuable intellectual property. Thus, you, your university, and the organisation (social system) would have an interest in understanding what that IP was and who owns the rights to the IP.

In Phase 1 of the IRF, you need to plan how to manage any IP issues that come up as part of your research protocol in conjunction with your university and research site. The main question is, how do you consider the

IP and assess who may have rights to it? You also need to make sure that the organisation that you are working with is aware that you will be using the information you gather to develop and disseminate conference papers, academic articles, and even external dissemination to other managers and accounting professionals. There would be nothing worse than reaching the end of an IVR project and not having your research participants be aware of these outputs and then try to prevent you from having it, especially academic articles published because they do not want to see their competitors being made aware of commercially sensitive information.

Your university, as does ours, will probably have a division within its research administration function that looks after intellectual property and commercialisation issues. In our university, we have the Office of Commercialisation and Innovation which helps identify, evaluate, and commercialise the university's IP. Fortunately, they offer excellent advice on how your research might develop IP. We have reproduced a document called the "Impact Canvas", published by the Macquarie University Office of Commercialisation and Innovation, which consists of a guideline and form that you can use as a checklist to develop an idea of how IP impacts your IVR project in Appendix 1 to this chapter. Our university has created this form and released it with a Creative Commons license so that you can use it and distribute it to your colleagues freely. We highly recommend you undertake this process in conjunction with your university and its IP and commercialisation administrators. By making sure that IP is taken care of from the onset of the IVR project, it can potentially save you a lot of time and frustration at the end. It is also advisable to update the research protocol document and the checklist as the project moves through its phases up until the last phase of dissemination, because if the IP issues are not taken care of, dissemination may be impossible or fraught with problems.

In Summation

To finalise this chapter, we want to reiterate that ethical, budgetary, and intellectual property matters are essential, but often overlooked, elements of your IVR project. Ethical considerations are very important and if not completed correctly, can jeopardise the outcomes, especially in the dissemination phase. Having an appropriate budget will allow you to complete the research on time with adequate resources. Last, by making sure you consider IP issues and deal with them at the beginning of the IVR project, you will prevent any arguments and potential legal issues. Most importantly, making sure that ethical, budgetary, and intellectual property matters are part of your research protocol and plan is essential.

References

Accounting Professional and Ethical Standards Board (APES). (2018). *APES 110 code of ethics for professional accountants (including independence standards).*

Retrieved from: www.apesb.org.au/uploads/standards/apesb_standards/ 23072019020747_APES_110_Restructured_Code_Nov_2018.pdf

Bruhn, J.G. & Rebach, H.M. (2007). *Sociological practice: Intervention and social change*. New York, NY: Springer Science.

Gitlin, L.N. & Czaja, S.J. (2016). *Behaviourial intervention research: Designing, evaluating, and implementing*. New York, NY: Springer Publishing Company LLC.

National Health and Medical Research Council (NHMRC). (2018). *National statement on ethical conduct in human research*. Retrieved from: www.nhmrc. gov.au/about-us/publications/national-statement-ethical-conduct-human-research-2007-updated-2018#block-views-block-file-attachments-content-block-1

O'Mathúna, D.P. (2012). Ethical considerations in designing intervention studies. In B.M. Melnyk & D. Morrison_Beedy (Eds.), *Intervention research: Design, conduction, analyzing and funding* (pp. 75–89). New York, NY: Springer Publishing Company.

Serenko, A. & Dumay, J. (2017). Citation classics published in knowledge management journals: Part III: Author survey. *Journal of Knowledge Management*, 21(2), 330–354. doi:10.1108/JKM-07-2016-0300

Appendix 1

"Impact Canvas", Macquarie University Office of Commercialisation and Innovation https://staff.mq.edu.au/research/commercialisation

7 Methods for Collecting, Storing, and Analysing IVR Data

Our intention is this chapter is not centred on debating the merits of qualitative versus quantitative research methods. This debate has received attention in several forms over the years and continues to do so as found most recently in a special issue of the *Accounting and Finance* journal (de Villiers *et al.*, 2019). Rather, we demonstrate that each of the methods can produce different types of information related to various IVR activities, such as selecting research participants, problem diagnosis, identifying potential interventions, revealing intervention design requirements, and intervention evaluation. Although accounting IVR mostly uses case studies, the disciplines of psychology, social work, and other allied human and social sciences where IVR originated also use experimental methods. Therefore, in this chapter we show that there are potential opportunities to employ different research methods to support effective IVR (see Baard, 2010). The idea of considering both approaches is also from intervention theory, which takes a non-prescriptive stance and provides arguments for and against different research approaches (see Argyris, 1970), similarly with IVR in social work (Thomas & Rothman, 1994). In writing this chapter, we also aim to encourage those researchers to engage in the research approach that is most relevant and useful for answering the research question of the IVR project.

Mechanistic and Organic Research Methods in IVR

The idea of discussing mechanistic (quantitative) and organic (qualitative) research approaches originated from Argyris (1970). He debates how using rigorous and organic research tools can be used in IVR to increase the chances of generating valid and useful information about organisational problems, harnessing participants' free and informed decision-making related to all aspects of intervention, and promoting participants' internal commitment to the IVR project. Here, rigorous or systematic tools include the use of surveys or questionnaires, whereas organic tools refer, for example, to interviews, observations of organisational life, focus groups, and document analysis. Using rigorous research approaches and tools is likely to facilitate an objective and valid problem diagnosis and analysis to obtain a general sense of the nature of the problem. Additionally, quantitative approaches help researchers to collect data that logically links to concepts forming a theoretical framework, establish statistical significance about the effectiveness of the intervention and any associated change produced, and enables researchers to generate theoretically relevant IVR. Following Argyris (1970), statistical significance in IVR means that there is a high probability that the outcomes or outputs of intervening did not happen by chance.

Conversely using rigorous research can be limiting as there is little or no room for: exploring and understanding how and why organisational actors' actions occur as they do; understanding how and why the problem manifests in a specific context; accessing actor experiences of the problem; and exploring approaches to developing reliable and valid interventions. Unintended consequences could arise from only using mechanistic approaches. For instance, surveys designed by researchers generally satisfy their needs, helps researchers to retain power and expertise, while keeping a distance from the research participants. Consequently, it may create dependent and even submissive roles for research participants providing them with little responsibility and low feelings of essentiality in the IVR project (Argyris, 1970). Hence, mechanistic approaches may potentially polarise the researcher and the research participants, resulting in the research participants feeling 'excluded' from the research process. The researcher and the research participants remain in the etic realm and emic realms respectively, with little instrumentation to bring the two together to collaborate. Thus, people in organisations have little scope to develop confidence and trust in researchers, exercise free choice, develop their commitment to the intervention and the research project, and serve as catalysts for organisational and social change; this might seriously compromise the overall IVR project (e.g., Chiucchi & Dumay, 2015). Moreover, one would potentially generate statistical significance, but what about behavioural significance, which is integral to IVR?

Only using organic approaches might mean that information generated is too subjective, yet this provides an opportunity for achieving a rich or deep understanding of the issues that prevail. Using organic approaches supports getting organisations and people working in them to be committed to the process because researchers are using a more inclusive approach to generating information, for example, through interviews rather than a 'cold, impersonal survey'. Baard (2010) offers a detailed view on the differences between adopting purely mechanistic or organic research. However, it is important to note that organic approaches increase the probability that research participants will help provide useful and valid information because the power between the researcher and the participants is equalised. Additionally, participants' involvement and participation in the IVR work is encouraged, thus mobilising collaboration with researchers. In turn, collaboration promotes exercising free choice and being committed to the project and positioning participants to drive beneficial change after the researcher leaves the research site. Using organic approaches is also a way in which behavioural significance doing IVR could be ascertained. Baard (2010, p. 36) states that behavioural significance occurs "when an event (e.g. intervention implementation) results in a difference in the behaviour and the values of the participant system and constitutes a significant departure from the steady-state prevalent prior to intervention implementation." Hence, behavioural significance becomes more meaningful than statistical significance when evaluating an intervention's influence on an organisation and how people feel about how the intervention has influenced their everyday lives.

Consequently, researchers should think about delicately balancing the approach adopted with continuously generating information and analysis during the IVR process. In our view, researchers should also view mechanistic and organic research approaches on a continuum, where you can decide for yourselves in the context of your accounting IVR project what and how much of each approach is relevant and helpful to your research. We do not want polarisation that might come from adopting only mechanistic research approaches, as all approaches have their place. This said, organic approaches are used more in IVR, as we demonstrate in this chapter (see Baard, 2010, p. 20).

IVR Methods and the Relationship With Case Study Research

IVR is an umbrella methodology incorporating many research methods. IVR has its origins in case study research and draws upon all the normal tools of case study research, such as interviews, documents, and observation. Yin (2017) classifies case study research as a method, as do many other commentators on qualitative research. However, researchers should not only use these methods as advocated by Yin. Instead, researchers must think about collecting data as an approach to conducting IVR as a specific methodology. Therefore, the choice of research methods in an IVR project should be not be entirely developed from a 'case study' perspective. The choice of method should be purposeful and structured to the IVR project being undertaken, and specifically linked to solving the IVR project's problem.

More importantly, the first thing we must consider is the question or problem under investigation in Phase 1 (Problem Analysis & Project Planning). Thus, the process of collecting and analysing data continues throughout all phases of the IVR project, with the emphasis on collecting data being at the beginning of the project and the analysis being more intensive towards the end of the project; as if they were two ends of a continuum as shown in Figure 7.1.

Phase 1: Problem Analysis & Project Planning

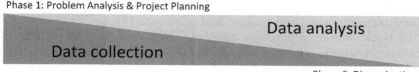

Phase 6: Dissemination

Figure 7.1 The Data Collection and Analysis Continuum in IVR

Figure 7.1 might seem like an oversimplification because there will undeniably be times within an IVR project where you will have intense periods of data collection and analysis. However, you first need to gather that data, and towards the end of the IVR project, during the dissemination phase, the analysis is largely done.

The need to gather data and to be flexible is indicative of the pragmatic approach to conducting research. It does not matter what the research method is, so long as it helps answer the research question, or in the case of IVR, helps resolve the problem at hand as Gray and Milne (2015, p. 56) aptly state:

> This is, of course, entirely consistent with a pragmatic approach to research methodology, mixed methods design and pluralism. Which method(s) is selected depends on the problem at hand, and which is likely to deliver the outcomes that work, while understanding fully that what works is likely to be contingent and temporary. This problem choice/focus, call for constant experimentation.

The experimentation with different methods of data collection and analysis is consistent with IVR that relies on experimentation with interventions. Thus, it leads naturally to assume that each experiment may require different data collection methods and different modes of analysis. The interventionist researcher is also a catalyst for change as part of that experimentation process, and therefore is consistently gathering and analysing data, which Dumay (2010, p. 61) refers to as a "catalytical" process within IVR (see Chapter 12).

Additionally, one must also think if the type of data you are collecting uses the appropriate research methods for that data. According to Yin (2017), six common data types are essential to case study research, including documentation, archival records, interviews, direct observation, participant-observation, and physical artefacts. However, when we think about IVR, we will probably think about these data sources differently because most case study research generally observes rather than participates in the field. Although, Yin (2017) does consider direct and participant observations as separate methods, which are part and parcel of IVR, and an interventionist will use participant observations more often than in a normal case study research project. So, it is worthwhile for us to explore how to collect, store, and analyse data relating to IVR.

A large volume of literature addresses these methods and their data collection, storage, and analysis, so what we present in this chapter is just a brief overview. The interventionist researcher should study them more closely when they choose a specific method for collecting and analysing data. Our advice is to follow advice given by Parker and Roffey (1997) and return to the "methodological drawing board" before embarking on the data collection and analysis journey. Planning how you gather and analyse data beforehand is just as, if not more important than, planning how to implement an IVR project. Subsequently, gathering and analysing data will also have a profound effect on how you disseminate the results from your study. Additionally, developing reliability, validity, and generalisation in your case study research is also essential. While we mention the important issues of reliability, validity, and generalisations in this chapter, researchers should refer to Chapter 8 for an in-depth discussion on managing these issues constructively in your IVR project.

Data Sources, Analytical Methods, and Tools

In this section, we will take you through our understanding of the main data sources, analytical methods, and tools that you might use in IVR. Research databases and new technology encompassing new automated analytical tools are providing interventionist researchers, including other qualitative and quantitative researchers, with new ways of thinking and analysing data that generate new and interesting insights (see also Chapter 8). Thus, what we expect is that as interventionist researchers become more skilled and familiar with these new data sources, analytical methods, and tools, they will change the face of analysis.

Mechanistic tools are useful when the researcher has significant amounts of data to analyse, and the analysis of this data will help provide insights into answering the research question and solving the organisation's problem. However, organic tools whereby the researcher is involved with people and collects the data through human interaction, and then uses the human mind to process and analyse the data, is an organic form of data collection. But these days, software is becoming more powerful and can analyse mountains of text mechanically from the organic collection process. However, there is no one right answer as to which method should be used, because as we outlined above, choosing the method that best suits answering the research question should be the litmus test.

Table 7.1 lists the key data sources, collection methods, and analytical tools for accounting based IVR using Yin's (2017) original classifications, plus elaborations from our experience as quantitative, qualitative, and interventionist researchers. The table is by no means comprehensive as there is a plethora of different sources, collection methods, and data storage and analytical tools. As we discuss in Chapter 8, the heart of any IVR project should be the research database, and it is now possible to use computer-aided qualitative data analysis software (CAQDAS) to store and analyse all data collected in the IVR project. We even advocate that most quantitative data and analysis outputs from other sources should be stored in the research database so that there is one comprehensive place for all data and results. For example, there might be a need to analyse quantitative data stored in spreadsheets using statistical software. Whereas it is not possible to use CAQDAS to perform complex statistical analyses, it is possible to store the data and the outputs of the analysis in the CAQDAS database.

The different data sources have different purposes and are more suited to being collected and analysed during different phases of the Interventionist Research Framework (IRF) using different research methods and tools. Thus, during the discussion of data sources, research methods, and analysis, we will also outline the most appropriate phase during the IVR project. We remind the reader of the IRF phases to make references to Table 7.1 easier:

- Phase 1: Problem Analysis & Project Planning
- Phase 2: Information Gathering & Synthesis
- Phase 3: Intervention Design and Development
- Phase 4: Pilot Testing & Implementation
- Phase 5: Intervention Evaluation & Advanced Development
- Phase 6: Dissemination

Internal Documentation

Internal documents are most useful at the beginning of an IVR project, where you begin to develop an idea of what the problem is and the data required to support your initial planning. While these documents are useful, you must also recognise that you are now dealing with sensitive information from the research site (i.e., social system). Gaining access to this information as an academic, in many jurisdictions, will require you to have ethical approval, which includes permission from the organisation to collect such data (see Chapter 6). Thus, you must also set up your research database with the appropriate usernames and passwords for storing the data and keeping it secure.

Another key issue is backing up your data from your computer to another location. You should always have an exact duplicate of your database in another location. These days with cloud backup services such as Microsoft OneDrive and DropBox, you can seamlessly backup to the cloud provided you have a good internet connection, which is more common now than 10 years ago. However, sensitive data might have special

Table 7.1 Data Sources, Collection Methods, and Analytical tools for Accounting IVR

Data Sources	Collection methods	Data Collection, Storage, and Analytical tools	Phases
Internal Documentation • Letters, memoranda, e-mails, and other personal documents, such as diaries, calendars, and notes • Agendas, announcements, minutes of meetings, and other written reports of events • Administrative documents, such as proposals, progress reports • Budgets and other management accounting reports • Financial statements and other detailed accounting information • Annual, corporate social responsibility, social and environmental, corporate governance, and other organisational reports	• Directly sourced from the organisation and IVR participants • Electronic resource planning (ERP) systems • Customer relationship management systems • Accounting information systems	• Computer-based office suite productivity and management software • CAQDAS • Text analysis software	1, 2, & 3
External Documentation • Formal studies or evaluations related to the case that you are studying • News clippings and other articles appearing in the mass media or community newspapers • Publicly available information, such as Census and other statistical data	• Sourced from academic and professional journals • Sourced from printed documents, the internet, or news media databases • Made available by federal, state, and local governments	• CAQDAS • Text analysis software • Reference management software • Statistical analysis software tools	1,2,3, & 6
Surveys and Interviews • Electronic surveys • Manual/computer-based surveys • Structured, semi-structured, and unstructured interviews	• Use external web-based software to survey participants • Paper/computer • Voice recordings	• Survey Monkey • Text analysis software • CAQDAS	2, 3, 4, & 5

Direct Observation Data collected while observing the activities of participants inside the research site (social system).	Field notes, documents, pictures, videos or recording made from observing • Meetings • Cafes and cafeterias • Work being undertaken • Training sessions	• CAQDAS • Text analysis software	1, 4, & 5
Participant Observation Data collected while working with the participants inside the research site (social system) to solve the problem identified in the IVR project	Field notes, documents, pictures, videos, or recordings made from the implementation process.	• CAQDAS • Text analysis software	4 & 5
Physical Artefacts Observations about objects that are an integral part of finding a solution to or the output of completing the IVR project	Field notes, documents, pictures, videos, or recordings made from the interaction with physical objects implementation process • Printed research project report • Computer printouts • Management accounting reports	• CAQDAS • Text analysis software	1, 4, & 5

Sources: Adapted from Yin (2017)

security requirements that prevents backing up to the cloud, and a secure drive on a university server might be needed, as was the case for one of our doctoral students recently. Make sure the back up of your IVR project database is attended to in your protocol document and your budget.

These days most documents that we use in IVR are available in PDF format and thus easily attached to a CAQDAS software system that is also our research database. However, you may find that you collect a lot of paper documents, and we would suggest that these documents are scanned into PDF format and then included in your research database as it will make analysing the documents much easier. We also recommend that once you have scanned the documents, you return these to the source, or securely destroy if they are no longer required so that non-authorised persons cannot accidentally access them. Thus, tying in your data collection methods with developing your research database helps build reliability and security for your data.

Analysing documents and other text-based data is one of the biggest challenges of both qualitative and IVR. Many papers about qualitative research analysis are available to interventionist researchers, with the most common being content analysis, which Krippendorff (2013) espouses as a methodology in its own right and not just a research method. One problem with many research methods, including content analysis, is that there are probably just as many approaches to analysing text-based data as there are academic papers recommending it as a methodology, which has led to some controversy about its usefulness and contribution (Dumay & Cai, 2014, 2015; Goebel, 2015; Guthrie, 2014). Even Krippendorff (2013), the author of the only real methodology book on content analysis, identifies that few content analysis studies ever follow his methodology properly.

To ensure that researchers follow methodologies and methods properly, we advocate that you should always review the original methodology, rather than relying on interpretations found in published papers, as the guideline for the method that you use to collect and analyse your data. As indicated in the beginning of this chapter, going back to the "methodological drawing board" is essential, not just for text analysis but for all analysis (Dumay, 2014). For example, a common way of analysing text data in qualitative research is the use of grounded theory (Glaser & Strauss, 1967; Strauss & Corbin, 1990). However, since the original paper by Glaser and Strauss (1967), even the original proponents no longer see eye to eye on how to use grounded theory, and thus it has diverged into separate paths (Strauss & Corbin, 1990). In response to this divergence, and the need to understand how grounded theory can be applied in qualitative accounting research, Parker and Roffey (1997) return to the "methodological drawing board" to give researchers insights on how to apply it. By doing so, Parker and Roffey (1997) allow accounting researchers to understand the origins of grounded theory as an analytical method and to achieve high-quality outcomes.

Computer-Based Office Suite Productivity and
Management Software

Most workplaces have some form of computer-based office suite productivity and management software installed on their computers. In accounting, the most commonly used electronic document is a spreadsheet. Similarly, there are mountains of documents produced using word processing and presentation software, and data that users store in databases, and reports made using desktop publishing software. Regardless of whether you use a PC or Apple-based computers, computer-based office suite productivity and management software is ubiquitous. Thus, many of the documents that you receive from organisations will be in these electronic formats.

Another important tool is email client programs that allow people to create, send, receive, and store emails. For many people these days, emails are the lifeblood of communication and our primary source of information in the IVR project. However, emails are even more sensitive than documents normally sourced from an organisation. Therefore, interventionist researchers should take extreme care in storing and using emails within your IVR project. We recommend that you review carefully emails that you use in the project that may breach any sensitivity arrangements or ethical concerns with your research participants.

The most common computer-based productivity and management software in use today is the Microsoft Office 2016, or Office 365 Suite of programs. In most organisations, and even in our university, we have little choice of what software to use because it is dictated to us by the organisation. For example, all computers in our university use office 365 and programs such as Word, Outlook, Excel are frequently used to communicate information internally and externally. However, in competition, there are many other forms of software available to perform the same tasks, and this can be problematic in exchanging and recording data (https://en.wikipedia.org/wiki/List_of_office_suites). Wikipedia is used here because it is the best summary resource we could find. However, these days even though documents are created on different software platforms, they are often interchangeable, and can still be easily stored in a research database and CAQDAS programs.

CAQDAS

While grounded theory and its coding techniques are useful, we must also be aware of the technology available to implement. There is no doubt that the power of computing has greatly increased since Glaser and Strauss (1967) wrote their first paper of grounded theory, and since Krippendorf (1980) published his first book on content analysis. The advances in technology enable CAQDAS programs to become essential tools for use in IVR because they serve as the database and they perform organic and mechanistic data analysis tasks. For example, our university provides us with free access to NVivo for our research. We can use NVivo to manually code documents based on our reading and open and axial coding, as recommended by Parker and Roffey (1997). Additionally, we could also use some of the automated text analysis features found in NVivo to mechanically create word counts and word tree reports. Tools like NVivo and other CAQDAS programs are constantly developing and assisting researchers with the ability to analyse greater and greater volumes of data that were not available when many of the data analysis techniques in common use today were first devised.

Other Text Analysis Tools

In response to the amounts of text-based data, many other software programs are now available to help researchers collect, store and analyse data. Unlike CAQDAS programs that can serve as the research database and analysis tools, these software programs are more likely to be useful as alternative data analysis tools. For example, another program our university provides a free license to is a text analysis software program called Leximancer that helps to develop different insights into text that is not possible with NVivo (see https://info.leximancer.com/). Leximancer is designed as a data analysis tool and really cannot be used as a complete research database effectively. Thus, we might take the output from Leximancer and store these files in NVivo if we wanted to archive the outputs. However, an advantage of using tools such as Leximancer and even NVivo, is that you can specifically record the data and processes in the analysis, so that another researcher can repeat it and achieve the same results, thus building reliability and validity into your IVR project and its outcomes.

External Documentation

In Yin's (2017) book, he combines internal and external documents and classifies them as "Documentation". However, we make the distinction between internal and external documentation because in IVR the internal documentation is used more at the beginning of a project, whereas external documentation is more likely relevant towards the middle and end of the project. External documentation is extremely important in IVR in the triangulation process, whereby different data sources combine to build construct validity, which we discuss in more detail in Chapter 8. Also, because external documents are from outside the organisation, they are not subject to the same kinds of data security measures needed for internal documentation. However, like internal documents, researchers should treat them in much the same way as internal documents with regards to data storage and analysis.

The main differentiation of internal versus external documents used in IVR is the format and source. In Table 7.1, we identify three different parts of external data, but these are prime examples rather than an exhaustive list. Because the interventionist researcher is an academic, many of the theories that researchers use in an IVR project are available in academic journal articles and texts. Like internal documents, these days most of these articles are available in PDF format and can easily be stored in our research database using CAQDAS programs. Data sourced from printed documents, the internet, or news media databases and governments are also normally available or can be converted to office and PDF documents and likewise included in the database using CAQDAS programs, and this data can be similarly stored and analysed using CAQDAS and text analysis software. However, we recommend two additional storage and analysis tools, bibliometric software databases and statistical analysis software tools, which we discuss next.

Reference Management Software

Considering that the interventionist researcher needs to understand different theories and disseminate the research, they must also understand how to use reference management software to organise the papers they use. The software is useful because it allows researchers to store the attributes of published articles, news reports, websites, pictures, diagrams, and many other sources of data that are part of an IVR project. Even though the main purpose is to store academic articles and their attributes, any computer-based data can be stored. Additionally, a reference management software database has functionality that can also double as the IVR project's research database, but its main limitation is that it is not capable of detailed analysis like CAQDAS. Thus, reference management software use is best for managing data that you later cite in the dissemination stage. Therefore, when an IVR project reaches the dissemination phase, the data and data sources stored in the reference management software's database can easily be inserted into the text as citations and a reference list automatically appears at the end of the document.

There are many reference management software packages available to choose from (see https://en.wikipedia.org/wiki/Reference_management_software). At our university, we are given free licenses for Endnote and Refworks, with Endnote being the package that is most popular with our researchers and students. However, not all people are fortunate enough to have free access to these programs and choose another package called Mendeley. Mendeley also has researcher social network functionality and can be downloaded for free (www.mendeley.com/newsfeed). We do not advocate using one package over another. The interventionist researcher should understand which program their colleagues are using and endeavour to use the same software to allow for easier exchange of data. However, data interchange is relatively easy because the software uses standardised bibliometric files to exchange data, and most support extensible mark-up language (XML) data exchange.

The data exchange functionality also extends from the reference management software to CAQDAS. For example, a researcher can export an XML file from Endnote and import the data, including PDF and other file format copies of the data, into an NVivo file. This functionality allows for the easier gathering of data in the reference management software first, and when complete, become part of the IVR database where further analysis and integration of data can take place using CAQDAS.

Statistical Analysis Software Tools

There are also many statistical analysis software tools for the interventionist researcher to choose and use. These tools are most important when trying to make sense of large pools of numerical data that you might get from external databases, such as the bureau of statistics and other government sources. Unlike quantitative researchers in accounting who often analyse large pools of accounting data based on external databases, this would be uncommon in an IVR project, and thus we will not dwell on the processes concerned with analysing market data. However, we are more likely to use statistical packages for summarising and categorising large volumes of data, then performing regression analyses.

One example of statistical analysis software is in helping develop the reliability needed for other analytical methods such as content analysis. In content analysis, Krippendorff (2013) has developed a measure called Krippendorf's alpha to judge the reliability of a manual content analysis performed by individual coders. Arguably, many researchers use measures such as the percentage of agreement or even Cronbach's alpha to judge the reliability of the content analysis. However, Krippendorf's alpha has been specifically developed to judge intercoder reliability, whereas the former two methods, and other methods not mentioned here, have not (Hayes & Krippendorff, 2007). The code for calculating Krippendorf's alpha is in Hayes and Krippendorff (2007) for SPSS and SAS software packages and links to macros for other software packages such as R, Matlab, and Python can be found at https://en.wikipedia.org/wiki/Krippendorff%27s_alpha#A_computational_example.

Like text analysis software, researchers can also develop output from statistical analysis software that can be stored in the research database using CAQDAS. For example, outputs from statistical analysis software include documents with tables and graphs that can come in a variety of outputs such as spreadsheets, text documents, and PDF files. These data formats are compatible with CAQDAS, and thus the researcher can easily incorporate them into the database. We cannot emphasise enough how important it is to have one location for all data and outputs, especially variations of outputs for use during the dissemination process.

Surveys and Interviews

Surveys and interviews are common data sources for an IVR project, the latter being the most common. Surveys are a good tool to use, especially in the early phases of an IVR project as the researcher attempts to understand the context and the problem. In these stages, it is important to get the input of the participants into understanding the problem and then developing the proposed solution or outcome. For example, in the research project by Dumay (2010), at the Sydney Conservatorium of Music, he used an online survey to gather information about the academic and professional staff views on the then-current strategy before deciding on how to develop a new strategy, which was the eventual outcome of the IVR project. He then followed this up with interviews with key staff who assisted in the development of the eventual strategy document.

Conducting Surveys

To conduct the surveys, Dumay (2010) used a proprietary survey software package. However, most interventionist researchers do not have access to such programs. A common survey instrument is SurveyMonkey (see www.surveymonkey.co.uk/) that offers a relatively easy-to-use and low-cost platform for conducting surveys. At our university, we can also use a survey platform on a secure server in our university. You will find that most universities already subscribe to a professional survey system, which they may make available to researchers conducting IVR and other research projects. The output from survey software can be in the form of spreadsheets or database tables, which can be easily analysed using office software, statistical analysis tools, and CAQDAS. Again, before conducting surveys, please take into consideration the ethical requirements of your university.

Conducting Interviews

Interviews are a key data source for any IVR project and are a central method for collecting data for IVR (Dumay, 2009). Therefore, a lot of care and attention needs to be paid to collecting interview data because if interviews do not follow interview guidelines, one could end up with biased information (Qu & Dumay, 2011), resulting in an unworkable solution and even a failed project. However, in IVR, the interviewer is not like a normal interviewer in case study research because of their direct involvement in the organisation. Thus, the interviewer is not an observer but can be one of the natives that may lead the participants to feel less inclined to cooperate, thus rendering the intervention process ineffective (Baard, 2010; Dumay & Baard, 2017).

According to Alvesson (2003), there are three ways of looking at interviews being the neopositivist, localist, and romanticist perspectives on the use of the research interview. When reflecting on interview methods, Qu and Dumay (2011, pp. 239–240) argue "that the neopositivist view (studying facts) corresponds more to structured interviews, the romanticist view (focusing on meaning) to unstructured interviews, and the localist perspective (social construction of situated accounts) to semi-structured interviews, with overlap at the boundaries". As a result, Qu and Dumay (2011, p. 238) "adopt a localist perspective towards interviews and argue that the localist approach opens up alternative understanding of the interview process and the accounts produced provide additional insights". The Qu and Dumay (2011) insights are useful because they highlight the importance of a researcher developing appropriate skills to conduct interviews using the localist perspective. Thus, developing interviewing skills is important for interventionist researchers so that they recognise how to get the best and unbiased responses from the participants.

Another issue to consider is how to conduct interviews that are not face-to-face. In IVR as with most research, we use face-to-face interviews, but these days there is no guarantee that the person you need an interview from and work with during an intervention is situated close enough for face-to-face interviews to occur. As Tucker and Parker (2018, p. 1490) outline:

> advances in communications technology have to an extent, mitigated the 'tyranny of distance' by enhancing the accessibility of researchers to interviewees as data sources previously prohibited for reasons relating to both time and expense. In an increasingly global research community, researchers now have the option of using telephone as well as videoconferencing mediums in addition to traditional face-to-face means through which to collect data.

For example, one of us (John Dumay) in a current IVR project, is working with a company which has branches across Australia, and thus the participants could be in one of several different locations spread across the country. While his research is still in the formative stages and he is not yet conducting interviews, the current intervention requires him to deal with people using different modes of communication, including telephone, Skype, Microsoft teams, and GoToMeeting platforms. Thus, when it gets to the point of interviewing, he will need to be cognisant of Tucker and Parker's (2018, p. 1507) findings that advocate "evidence collected in the current study is consistent with the premise underlying [information richness theory] insofar as the recognition that different communication media are perceived to differ in the amount of information they are able to convey". It appears that face-to-face interviews are still the primary choice of researchers despite the multiple modes available to them, and thus care and consideration of the potential inadequacies of other modes of interview need considering.

Once the interview mode is decided, then the researcher needs to decide on how they are going to record the interview data. The most common way to record interview data is via a voice recording and then having the recording transcribed into text to import into the research database. It is important to note here that not all people will agree to be interviewed. In our experience, while it is rare, you need to prepare for a person who objects to being interviewed. Thus, having your notepad handy, along with your interview protocol, is essential during an interview. The unwillingness of some participants also highlights the ethical dimensions of interviewing because you are using other people's words as evidence. In most instances, those people will want to remain anonymous, and this may also be a requirement of any ethical approval from your university. In general, you should never identify the participants of an interview unless they explicitly give permission. Even then, some journals are even reluctant to publish a publicly available text that can be attributable to a specific person, and thus having interviewees remain anonymous seems to be the rule; having an identified person is a rare exception. The next issue you will have with interview data is converting it from the voice recording to text. Traditionally, researchers have had to make use of transcribing services to convert their recordings to text, which involved a human being listening and speed typing, and this could be a reasonably expensive exercise for a project depending on how many recordings the researcher is making. However, these days there are services on the web that use voice recognition software with varying levels of success. Even some of the CAQDAS software vendors are offering transcription services and other value-added benefits so that interview data can be easily stored in both text and voice format and formatted for easier analysis (see NVivo Transcription at www.qsrin-ternational.com/nvivo/nvivo-products/transcription). Additionally, other voice recognition software such as Dragon NaturallySpeaking also allows you to import voice files for recognition, thus taking a lot of time and expense out of interview transcripts. However, regardless of the tool that you use for transcribing data, the eventual success of the transcription is highly dependent on the quality of the voice recording, so you must test the environment in which you are going to conduct interviews to ensure high-quality recordings.

Once you have your recordings transcribed and stored in your research database and CAQDAS software, the analysis process is the same as for any other form of text. Thus, we point you to the previous discussion about analysing text using CAQDAS and other text analysis software. However, the main format that text analysis takes for interview data is content analysis. As such, we highly advise you to read Krippendorff

(2013) and Parker and Roffey (1997) as these are two very informative texts that will help you go back to the methodological drawing board before embarking on text analysis.

Direct and Participant Observation

In Table 7.1, we separate observations into direct and participant because while similar, these methods achieve two separate purposes. Direct observation, which is more related to case study research, is the process of gathering data while observing activities of participants inside the research site (social system). However, participant-observation is more related to IVR because it is data collected while working with the participants inside the research site (i.e., social system) to solve the problem identified in the IVR project.

Collecting data for non-interventionist case study research tends to focus on interviews, documents, with some direct observation (Jönsson & Lukka, 2006; Yin, 2017). However, in IVR, the researcher relies heavily on their involvement in the process under investigation, their observations of the participants, and the outcomes of the research (intervention) process that allows the researcher to collect more "subtle and significant data", and put academic theory into action (Jönsson & Lukka, 2006, p. 7). Detailed field notes that the researcher needs to write during direct and participant observations are also useful in the dissemination phase because recording detailed accounts of the change process increases "the level of recollection when writing up the results of the research" (Dumay, 2009, p. 499). Done successfully, the outcomes of any analysis will result in thick descriptions of the IVR project and result in dissemination in academic articles and project reports that can be generalised to other organisational settings (see Lukka & Kasanen, 1995; Parker & Northcott, 2016; Yin, 2017).

The main downfall of collecting data from direct and participant observation is the time needed to write up the field notes, which is the main method for recording what you observe. Also, because direct participation is the mainstay of IVR, all the associated dangers of having an inexperienced or unskilled researcher in the field apply, as we have discussed elsewhere in Chapters 3 and 10. Similarly, as with interviews and documents, storing and analysing the field notes should be done in conjunction with ensuring they are part of the research database so that you can analyse the data using CAQDAS and other text analysis software packages.

In Summation

In this chapter, we have presented a high-level review of the methods you can use to collect, store, and analyse data in IVR. In the introduction to this chapter, we explain that research can be mechanistic or organic, with organic research collection and analysis methods the more common realm in IVR. However, as we see from Table 7.1, some mechanistic research methods and analytical tools are useful. The difference between mechanistic and organic methods and analysis is considerably different than the debate between qualitative and quantitative research because, in IVR, we can use both forms of data. However, due to technology and internet growth, we have access to more and more data based on text, and hence we need text-based databases to store and analyse this data.

As we outline in our discussion, the use of CAQDAS programs is essential for creating a research database and for analysing data. However, while CAQDAS was originally designed for manual coding, computers have become much faster and are now capable of analysing large amounts of text using pre-programmed logarithms, and now CAQDAS programs include more mechanistic analysis tools. Specific text analysis programs, such as Leximancer, supplement and complement CAQDAS analysis by allowing researchers to input and automatically analyse significant amounts of text-based data. Thus, while there may be organic approaches to collecting the data, we can use both organic and mechanistic methods for data collection and analysis and develop insights that might not have been possible before.

References

Alvesson, M. (2003). Beyond neopositivists, romantics and localists: A reflective approach to interviews in organizational research. *Academy of Management Review*, 28(1), 13–33.

Argyris, C. (1970). *Intervention theory and method: A behavioural science view*. Reading, MA: Addison-Wesley Publishing Company.

Baard, V.C. (2010). A critical review of interventionist research. *Qualitative Research in Accounting & Management*, 7(1), 13–45.

Chiucchi, M.S. & Dumay, J. (2015). Unlocking intellectual capital. *Journal of Intellectual Capital*, 16(2), 305–330.

de Villiers, C., Dumay, J., & Maroun, W. (2019). Qualitative accounting research: Dispelling myths and developing a new research agenda. *Accounting & Finance*, 59(3), 1459–1487. doi:10.1111/acfi.12487

Dumay, J. (2009). Reflective discourse about intellectual capital: Research and practice. *Journal of Intellectual Capital*, 10(4), 489–503. Retrieved from: www.emeraldinsight.com/10.1108/14691930910996607

Dumay, J. (2010). A critical reflective discourse of an interventionist research project. *Qualitative Research in Accounting and Management*, 7(1), 46–70.

Dumay, J. (2014). Reflections on interdisciplinary accounting research: The state of the art of intellectual capital. *Accounting, Auditing & Accountability Journal*, 27(8), 1257–1264.

Dumay, J. & Baard, V.C. (2017). An introduction to interventionist research in accounting. In Z. Hoque, L.D. Parker, M. Covaleski, & K. Haynes (Eds.), *The Routledge companion to qualitative accounting research methods* (pp. 265–283). Oxfordshire, UK: Routledge and Taylor and Francis.

Dumay, J. & Cai, L. (2014). A review and critique of content analysis as a methodology for inquiring into IC disclosure. *Journal of Intellectual Capital*, 15(2), 264–290. doi:10.1108/JIC-01-2014-0010

Dumay, J. & Cai, L. (2015). Using content analysis as a research methodology for investigating intellectual capital disclosure: A critique. *Journal of Intellectual Capital*, 16(1), 121–155. doi:10.1108/JIC-04-2014-0043

Glaser, B. & Strauss, A. (1967). *The discovery of grounded theory: Strategies of qualitative research*. London: Wiedenfeld and Nicholson.

Goebel, V. (2015). Is the literature on content analysis of intellectual capital reporting heading towards a dead end? *Journal of Intellectual Capital*, 16(3), 681–699.

Gray, R. & Milne, M.J. (2015). It's not what you do, it's the way that you do it? Of method and madness. *Critical Perspectives on Accounting*, 32, 51–66.

Guthrie, J. (2014). In defence of disclosure studies and the use of content analysis: A research note. *Journal of Intellectual Capital*, 15(2), 291–292.

Hayes, A.F. & Krippendorff, K. (2007). Answering the call for a standard reliability measure for coding data. *Communication Methods and Measures*, 1(1), 77–89. doi:10.1080/19312450709336664

Jönsson, S. & Lukka, K. (2006). *Doing interventionist research in management accounting*. Gothenburg Research Institute, Gothenburg.

Krippendorff, K. (1980). *Content analysis: An introduction to its methodology*. London, UK: Sage Publications.

Krippendorff, K. (2013). *Content analysis: An introduction to its methodology* (3rd ed.). Los Angeles: Sage.

Lukka, K. & Kasanen, E. (1995). The problem of generalizability: Anecdotes and evidence in accounting research. *Accounting, Auditing & Accountability Journal*, 8(5), 71–90.

Parker, L.D. & Northcott, D. (2016). Qualitative generalising in accounting research: Concepts and strategies. *Accounting, Auditing & Accountability Journal*, 29(6), 1100–1131. doi:10.1108/aaaj-04-2015-2026

Parker, L.D. & Roffey, B.H. (1997). Methodological themes: Back to the drawing board: Revisiting grounded theory and the everyday accountant's and manager's reality. *Accounting, Auditing & Accountability Journal*, 10(2), 212–247. Retrieved from: www.emeraldinsight.com/10.1108/09513579710166730

Qu, S.Q. & Dumay, J. (2011). The qualitative research interview. *Qualitative Research in Accounting & Management*, 8(3), 238–264. Retrieved from: http://dx.doi.org/10.1108/11766091111162070

Strauss, A. & Corbin, J. (1990). Grounded theory research: Procedures, canons, and evaluative criteria. *Qualitative Sociology*, 13(1), 3–21.

Thomas, E.J. & Rothman, J. (1994). An integrative perspective on intervention research. In J. Rothman & E.J. Thomas (Eds.), *Intervention research: Design and development for human service* (pp. 3–23). Binghamton, NY: Haworth Press.

Tucker, B.P. & Parker, L.D. (2018). Researcher perceptions and choices of interview media: The case of accounting research. *Accounting & Finance*, 59(3), 1489–1517. doi:10.1111/acfi.12393

Yin, R.K. (2017). *Case study research: Design and methods* (6th ed.). Thousand Oaks, CA: Sage Publications Inc.

8 IVR Reliability, Validity, and Generalisations

For any research methodology to be legitimate, it must have reliability and validity, and IVR is no different. Much is written about reliability and validity in positivist and interpretive research, but the same cannot be said for IVR (Baard, 2010). McKinnon (1988) reports that reliability and validity issues are frequently omitted or muted from the results of field research. Further, she asserts that reliability and validity issues are paramount with this kind of research: "Failure to attend to these issues in the conduct of the study prejudices attainment of the researcher's faith in the results . . . [and] the dissemination and communication of the research, restricting the audience who will read and accept the results" (McKinnon, 1988, p. 35).

Given the scholarly scepticism about IVR as previously discussed, we recommend researchers take extra care to address reliability and validity in their IVR studies and to be explicit about these issues when writing articles. Therefore, in this chapter, we discuss the meaning of reliability and validity in accounting IVR and consider generalisations from IVR projects. Some lessons learned from case study research follow, which may help to forge a new path ahead for interventionist researchers in stimulating thought and action on this critical issue.

Reliability, Validity, and Generalisation in IVR

Four elements underpin IVR's legitimacy: reliability, validity, theory, and the intervention (Baard, 2010). As a kind of qualitative 'field experimentation' (Jönsson & Lukka, 2007), IVR goes beyond standard case study observations to intervene, seek change, and empower the experiment's participants. IVR is therefore more complex and, consequently, reliability and validity issues receive greater scrutiny from scholars. But, just because something is more complex or more difficult, does not mean it should be compromised (McKinnon, 1988, p. 35).

Reliability and validity are often fused in qualitative research because they are difficult concepts to distinguish, especially in field research (Baard, 2010; Ahrens & Chapman, 2006). According to McKinnon

(1988), reliability and validity are different in that they are specific to research methods and instruments. Golafshani (2003) agrees that qualitative researchers must consider reliability in research design, data analysis, and in appraising the standard of their research, citing the terms credibility, dependability, and applicability/transferability as essential quality criteria. She also notes that an inquiry audit is a measure of dependability, which can be used to examine the research process and outcomes.

Yin (2017) states that a valid study has appropriately collected and interpreted data that are accurate reflections of a real-world setting. Broadly speaking, validity consists of internal and external validity, which are contingent on the aims and processes of research methodologies, research methods, and the research project itself. Internal validity relates to how research findings are consistent with reality. External validity is defined as the extent to which research findings can be reproduced in other contexts and is viewed as a foundation for generalisation (Davila & Oyon, 2008). Davila and Oyon (2008) contend that external validity is achieved through an audit of the research process, and that validity enhances the plausibility and trustworthiness of qualitative research. From this, they conclude that trustworthiness emanates from a researcher's ability to persuade other scholars that their research findings are worthy of attention. Golafshani (2003) argues reliability and validity in qualitative research are conceptualised as trustworthiness and quality, and that reliability fosters validity.

Two further issues emerge from our understanding of validity. First, both reliability and validity refer to auditing the research process. In IVR, the research process would be, say, the Interventionist Research Framework (IRF) in all its phases. These phases comprise methodical steps; thus, it is possible to critically assess and verify each objective and activity via an audit. For this very reason, the IRF makes a good choice for conveying reliability and validity. Also, despite the subjective nature of IVR, the IRF is an objective methodology because any accounting researcher can apply the framework to their IVR project. Moreover, it is aligned with Intervention Theory (IVT) and so reinforces IVR's legitimacy.

Second, validity promotes generalisation. Parker and Northcott (2016) view validity in qualitative research as the credibility of the evidence or data collected and assessed, along with the inferences drawn. Further, they contend that credibility associated with research quality and trustworthiness are substitutes for validity as the foundation for qualitative generalising. They describe two forms of qualitative generalisation: theoretical and natural. Aimed at accounting scholars, theoretical generalisation generalises "social processes across different settings and developing theoretical insights (. . . about form and meaning of social phenomena)" (p. 1119). Naturalistic generalisation "is a democratising approach to knowledge generation requiring researchers, their subjects and their readers to induce experiential-based, tacitly accumulated knowledge about institutional, organisational and accounting contexts and processes" (p. 1119). Naturalistic generalisation is aimed at transferring practice findings and insights to similar cases in other settings and mobilising discussions among social systems influenced by the research. We find these two notions of generalisation particularly helpful to IVR's reliability and validity. By using the IRF, researchers can generalise theories and, therefore, produce theoretically relevant research consistent with IVR's duality of output. Likewise, researchers can generalise practice to address the research-practice gap.

The final consideration for reliability and validity concerns the intervention. The validity of an intervention is contingent upon its design, construction, and type. The IRF outlines steps to execute intervention design and construction, one of which is pilot-testing and another is a structured approach to implementation. These too offer reliability and validity to support the project's results. Pilot tests provide a safety net for catching detail and surety in the methods used.

Lessons Learned From Case Study Research

Case study research is also deemed a methodology when it draws together multiple methods to attain reliable and valid results. It is one of the most misunderstood and misquoted methodologies known to social science researchers because many researchers consider it a method, not a methodology. Throughout this book, we have sometimes referred to a case study as a method, but what we present here is a methodological approach because of concerns with reliability, validity, and qualitative generalisations. One could be forgiven for this error, considering that even the most popular book about case study research by Yin (2017) uses the term *methods* in its title. However, as Guthrie *et al.* (2004, p. 417) outline:

> Methods are the means whereby one collects and analyses data. Methodology refers to the philosophical issues which underlie those methods. The terms, thus, mean very different things—but [researchers and] journals vary in the extent to which they are exercised by that difference.

Understanding the relationship between IVR and case study research as a methodology is necessary because it impacts on how we use different methods for designing, implementing, and disseminating IVR. Like IVR, case study research has its own epistemology that depends on the approach taken. It also suffers from the same fragmentation and misunderstandings as IVR (Dumay & Baard, 2017). Thus, Yin's (2017) procedural emphasis on developing reliability, validity, and generalisations mean it is often regarded as a positivist methodology. We argue that the case study is not a positivist methodology, especially IVR-based case studies, because the evidence we collect relies on collating circumstantial evidence to come to our conclusions and qualitative generalisations.

As Massaro *et al.* (2019, p. 46) outline, a major issue is that researchers can apply the "case study methodology to multiple ontologies" being positivist, constructivist, and critical realist (see also Tsang, 2014). Thus, the interventionist researcher has at least three different ontologies to choose from when undertaking IVR, and each ontology has a different approach to reliability, validity, and generalisations. For example, case studies using a positivistic approach may emphasise external validity over internal and construct validity (Gibbert *et al.*, 2008). However, in keeping with IVT and the methodological argument, we advocate an approach based on the IRF, aligning true IVR more towards a qualitative approach akin to Yin's case study methodology.

There is no doubt that if you apply Yin's (2017) methodology meticulously and follow some of his recommendations, such as developing hypotheses or propositions or testing a theory, you are, arguably, following a positivist methodology, that is, the scientific method (Shanks, 2002). However, in IVR, it is virtually impossible to be called a positivist due to one simple fact: the researcher is fully immersed in the research project, and therefore is not an idle observer (Lincoln & Guba, 1994). IVR is quite the opposite because it relies on the researcher's active participation. Plus, the methods for developing reliability, validity, and generalisations are distinctly different from those employed by positivists. Some methods used in IVR have positivist links, as Argyris (1970) advocates, because sometimes the researcher is confronted with mountains of data requiring statistical analysis. However, if the data and its subsequent analysis are part of the overall case study data, then we are using mixed methods. Also, quantitative data analysis forms part of the triangulation of data sources (Yin, 2017). Then, the case study is far from being positivist because it does not conform with the epistemology of positivist research.

In Dumay and Baard (2017), we note that IVR projects mostly have the features of single case studies because IVR necessitates researchers to work with individual social system contexts solving individual problems. As such, IVR fits with Yin's (2017, p. 2) definition of a case study, being research that "investigates a contemporary phenomenon (the "case") in depth and within its real-world context". IVR is similar because it involves a single case or multiple related cases that have the potential to lead to theoretical generalisations. Therefore, it can be argued that the main difference between case study research and IVR is that the researcher does not observe managers dealing with problems, rather they help solve real-world problems (Dumay & Baard, 2017).

Because of the links between case study research and theory, we advocate borrowing epistemologies for developing reliability, validity, and generalisations from Yin (2017) and other qualitative researchers. Table 8.1 outlines different methods for developing reliability, validity,

Table 8.1 Qualitative Attributes and the IRF

Attribute	Methods of Developing the Attribute	Relevant Phases of the IRF
Reliability	• Research protocol • Research database	• Phase 1 (plus iterations) • Phase 2
Construct Validity	• Use multiple sources of evidence • Establish chains of evidence • Participants review case evidence and results	• Phase 2, 3, 4, 5, & 6 • All six phases • Phases 1, 4, 5, & 6
External Validity	• Use social theory to analyse the data and explain the results	• Phases 1, 3, 4, 5, & 6
Theoretical Generalisation	• Develop theoretical insights that extend beyond the boundaries of the original study	• Phase 6
Naturalistic Generalisation	• Transfer the findings and insights to analogous cases in other settings	• Phase 6

Source: Adapted from Yin (2017), Parker and Northcott (2016), Dumay (2010), Dumay and Baard (2017) and Baard and Dumay (2018)

and generalisation, along with the relevant phases of the IRF. Note, though, that this is only a guide, not a fixed prescription.

Reliability

Developing a Research Protocol

The purpose of a research protocol is to increase reliability, but developing a good research protocol for an IVR project requires planning from the outset. The basics are to record all the steps involved in all research phases from design to dissemination. As Yin (2017, p. 46) states, "without such documentation you could not even repeat your own work—which is another way of dealing with reliability". A research protocol is essential for developing future IVR projects because, without records of successful and unsuccessful IVR projects, how will researchers learn from the experiences of others? Additionally, you will have something to fall back on to help reliably guide future projects. Table 8.2 outlines our suggestions on some essential research protocol elements. But, again, there are no strict rules on developing a protocol, so you can include anything else you feel is necessary.

Another reason having a research protocol is important is that new participants or research assistants may come and go throughout the IVR project. When a new person joins, they will not have the same knowledge

Table 8.2 Suggested Elements and Content for a Research Protocol

Protocol Element	Content
What is the problem requiring a possible intervention?	A brief problem statement with some reasoning on why IVR is a potential solution.
What is known?	Once you establish the potential for an IVR project, you need to record what is known about the problem, including facts, circumstances, and context. It is important to list all available qualitative data, quantitative data, and other resources for a potential IVR project.
Thoughts about the proposal?	What level of intervention might be necessary? As IVR is conducted using different intervention modes, it is important to establish the intervention mode needed.
The motivation for the project?	As IVR is a process with managerial and academic outcomes, it is important to list the likely benefits for each party. Conducting IVR with a bias towards solving the management problem or the academic output is unbalanced. Ensure that you establish the desired outcomes so that each party is aware of what the other needs to get out of the project.
Methodology and methods?	Because IVR is a methodology, you need to start to think about the different research and analytical methods needed for the project from the beginning. This is essential for identifying the different skill sets needed plus the human, physical, and monetary resources required for the project.
Analytical framework?	Before starting the project, think about the theory or theories that will be useful for framing the experiments and interventions. IVR is more conducive to using social theory.
Dissemination?	Consider how you are going to disseminate the results of the IVR project. Dissemination is often neglected in the initial planning stages but is essential because dissemination requires human, physical, and monetary resources. Remember that disseminating the project results through journals and conferences, both academic and professional, can be difficult.

as the chief investigator but reviewing the research protocol is a quick and easy way to bring them up to speed. A research protocol also helps with dissemination (see Chapter 13) because the sources of information used to inform the intervention provide an initial framework to begin the dissemination process because you should identify potential target journals that might publish IVR articles.

As a last point, we recommend writing the research protocol at the very beginning of a project. However, research is an iterative process, and change as the project develops is inevitable. These changes should be recorded in the research protocol, so it provides a complete picture of the IVR project and, therefore, reliability.

Developing a Research Database

Compared to even a decade ago, the amount of data we can use in our research is staggering. While having a rich and seemingly endless source of data may seem advantageous, it does raise the problem of having so much data that it becomes unwieldy to manage. A research database is a way to organise and analyse the data, so this does not become a problem.

Yin (2017, p. 131) defines a research database as a repository, distinct from the final case study report, which holds case study notes, documents, field materials, and preliminary narratives on the data. Today, software, such as Atlas.ti, MAXQDA, or NVivo, is without question the best approach to storing, organising, and analysing IVR data. Packages are available in both online and desktop versions, and any can help store and analyse text, audio, video, graphics webpages, and social network sources.

Functionality is one factor that should play into your choice. For example, is the data analysis process manual or automatic? Each has its pros and cons, so which will add reliability to your project? It is also wise to consider which programs, if any, might be provided by your university and which programs your fellow colleagues and collaborators use to reduce compatibility issues. At some point in any IVR project, you will need to share data with the participants, the members of the design team, assistant researchers, and so on. So, compatibility is not an issue to be taken lightly. Moreover, making the entire data collection and analysis process available to all team members increases the reliability of the research project (Yin, 2017).

Validity

Establishing the validity of research results is an essential part of any research project, including IVR. In case study research, Yin (2017, p. 24) identifies three types of validity: construct, internal, and external. Internal validity relates to causal relationships and is assessed according to whether a researcher has sufficient evidence to infer a causal relationship as opposed to a spurious relationship. Internal validity is not particularly relevant to qualitative research.

However, construct and external validity require a different type of reasoning, which is more conducive to IVR. When conducting IVR, one pieces multiple sources of quantitative and qualitative data together, much like a jigsaw puzzle, to reach conclusions based on evidence. The researcher acts like the great detective, Sherlock Holmes, piecing together circumstantial evidence to develop an explanation that is plausible and robust. This is known as abductive reasoning, whereby you develop the most likely explanation for what you observe based on the evidence available. However, there may be doubts about the conclusion, so using methods that build construct and external validity reinforce your conclusions.

Construct Validity

According to Yin (2017, p. 24), construct validity "relates to identifying the correct measures for the concepts under research". To achieve construct validity, Yin (2017) recommends three strategies: use multiple sources of evidence, establish chains of evidence, and have participants review case evidence and results. We next describe these three strategies and give examples from IVR projects.

First, using multiple sources of evidence is almost a given in IVR. Because we interact with human beings and observe their behaviours, we are presented with rich amounts of qualitative and quantitative data about the organisation. Arguably, we always have too much data, and the main challenge is to sort through them to try to understand what is relevant and what is not. Some of the common data sources in IVR are interview recordings and transcripts, financial and management accounting reports, strategic plans, and internal and external websites. Ideally, researchers should collate and store these sources in a research database so that the evidence can be easily retrieved and analysed.

The problem with using single sources of evidence is that they are incomplete. For example, analysing the annual report of a company yields high-level financial data and management commentary to understand the business model. It can also provide information about social and environmental impact. However, accounting researchers recognise that information produced by an organisation is often biased and presented with a high-level of abstraction. When it is publicly available, it may even be a façade that obscures the true inner workings of the enterprise (Cho *et al.* 2015). However, in IVR, we want to become part of the everyday processes, which requires inside information. Therefore, while publicly available documentation is a valid source, it can, and probably should, be supplemented with other data, such as interviews, field notes, and internal documents.

An interventionist researcher seeks a complete picture, which is only possible using as many available data sources as realistically possible. As with any case study project, the interventionist researcher has limited access to the amount and type of data available, especially sensitive information. Like any employee, not everyone in every organisation has full access to all organisational data and may even find data that was not intentionally made available to them. In this case, the researcher needs to return any sensitive data and ensure that it will not be used or otherwise disseminated; researchers must only use data intentionally provided for the IVR project. Access to limited data represents a potentially incomplete picture of the project and limits developing solutions to organisational problems and drawing conclusions.

Yin (2017) states that case study researchers can triangulate many sources of evidence to overcome any deficiencies in one particular source of data. Massaro *et al.* (2019, pp. 54–55) highlight that "triangulation is the most-used validation technique". But the problem with triangulation (and other validation techniques), is that many "authors do not cite any methodological contribution when describing the specific tests applied [and] do not cite anyone to explain how they triangulated or coded their data". Thus, triangulation often appears in form, but not in substance.

Considering IVR uses evidence to solve problems, the researcher and the participants risk developing invalid solutions if the evidence used has no substance—not exactly the outcome we are looking for in a successful IVR project. Yin (2017, p. 127) calls this "converging lines of inquiry", whereby researchers use different sources of data concurrently to arrive at their conclusions. Thus, multiple sources of evidence need to be aligned when developing arguments, analysing data, and presenting findings. So how can you accomplish this in practice? The following is a two-fold technique that Dumay teaches his doctoral students.

First, one must rely on the case study research database to organise and classify data sources. Table 8.3 that follows is an excerpt from a thesis showing how the student applied specific codes to interview data and field observations (Jamaluddin, 2015). The codes are extremely useful because, in most databases, data is automatically sorted in alphabetical order, which does not allow you to categorise databases on titles. Therefore, if one were to use H for the headquarters interviewees, you could easily arrange the texts by using the H1 code as a prefix, even in a folder stored on your computer. These codes are easily transferable to a case

Table 8.3 Example of Coding Sources for a Case Study Research Database

Interviewee	Organisation	Functional Responsibility	Interview Date	Interview Code	Fieldnote Code
H1	HQ—strategy	Director, Planning & Resourcing	26 Mar 12	H1–1	
H2	HQ—strategy	Director, Performance & Accountability	26 Mar 12	H2–1	
A1	Academy A	Manager, Strategic Planning	30 July 12	A1–1	
			16 Oct 13	A1–2	FN-5
		Director, Strategic Planning & Performance	16 Oct 14	A1–3	FN-17
			2 Dec 14	A1–4	FN-24

study database, such as NVivo. There you can identify sources and nodes and, because the two will appear in alphabetical order, they will be easy to find and sort.

More importantly, these codes are useful in triangulating findings with data by developing what are called alignment tables that present the results alongside the different data sources. From an accounting perspective, one can think of this as a ledger for recording evidence of transactions. Table 8.4 provides an example of an alignment table produced by the same student. Note how the student aligns their arguments with the data sources, which is extremely useful when writing up and disseminating results. We will build on using these tables for writing up and disseminating data in Chapter 13.

Second, using chains of evidence builds on using multiple sources of evidence and the data triangulation process as outlined above. Linking different phases of the IVR project is the ultimate 'chain of evidence' that is desired. Thus, it surpasses a mere data triangulation exercise to show clear links between the problem, the research protocol, the case study database, the citations to specific sources of evidence (triangulation), and

Table 8.4 Summary of Analysis with Data Sources

Argument	Data Sources			
	Interviews	*Documents*	*External Publications*	*Websites*
The management accounting at OZ Academy is based on the existing management control system the budgeting and reporting process	• A4–1 • A3–1 • C1–2 • A1–1	• FS-5	• Guthrie and Clayton (2010) • Misko and Wynes (2009a) • IPART (2013) • Misko and Wynes (2009b)	• Education • STB • OZ Academy • Regional Academy A
The VET reform, system reform, and governance reform that are still currently taking place continually change the way OZ Academy is managing its operations	• H3–1 • A6–1	• FS-6 • MS-1 • MS-2	• Koutsogeorgopoulou (2009) • Misko and Wynes (2009a) • Guthrie and Clayton (2010) • State Auditor's General Report 2011 • Education's Annual Report 2012	• Education • STBs • OZ Academy

the eventual report. Building chains of evidence requires the researcher to align all the phases of an IVR project.

As we outlined at the beginning of the chapter, the interventionist researcher acts like the great detective, Sherlock Holmes, piecing together circumstantial evidence to develop an explanation that is plausible and robust. Yin (2017, p. 134) holds the same view arguing that "as with forensics evidence, the process should be tight enough that evidence presented in 'court'—the case study report—is assuredly the same evidence that was collected from the case study site during the data collection process". Developing a chain of evidence shows the real value of a case study database, which is to ensure that "no original evidence should have been lost, through carelessness or bias, and therefore fail[s] to receive appropriate attention in considering the findings in a case study" (Yin, 2017, p. 135). Demonstrating evidentiary chains throughout the research project will build construct validity, the likely strength and success of the intervention, and allow for the dissemination of convincing project outcomes.

Third, have participants review case evidence and results. Callon (1986, p. 201) states that:

> The observer must consider that the repertoire of categories that he uses, the entities that are mobilised, and the relationships between these are all topics for actors' discussions. Instead of imposing a pre-established grid of analysis upon these, the observer follows the actors to identify the manner in which these define and associ-ate the different elements by which they build and explain their world.

This quote is important for IVR when considering how researchers develop their evidence and disseminate results. As with many different types of qualitative research, the results are not derived from statistical generalisations, so they are open to interpretation and potential bias from the researcher's personal point of view. Facione (2020, p. 22) calls these research biases a "dominance structure":

> In a nutshell this theory suggests that when we settle on a particu-lar option which is good enough, we tend to elevate its merits and diminish its flaws relative to the other options. We raise it up in our minds until it becomes for us the dominant option. In this way, as our decision takes shape, we gain confidence in our choice and we feel justified in dismissing the other options, even though the objective distance between any of them and our dominant option may not be very great at all. But we become invested in our dominant option to the extent that we are able to put the other possibilities aside and act on the basis of our choice.

Unfortunately, research bias comes too naturally to us all. Hence, as interventionist researchers, we must put in processes in place to avoid research bias from occurring. Yin (2017, p. 240) recommends having the case study report reviewed "not just by peers (as would be done for any research manuscript) but also by the informants and participant in the case". For example, Chiucchi and Dumay (2015, p. 310) sent the results of their IVR project to their main participant and gatekeeper "who read and corroborated our findings. He confirmed that our story is a true and fair account of what happened". Thus, attaining feedback from key individuals supports developing construct validity in IVR projects.

While following Yin's (2017) advice helps the researcher to add construct validity from a case study perspective, interventionist researchers can go one step further by including participant feedback throughout the project from Phases 4, 5, and 6. For example, in Dumay (2010), the intervention was to develop a new strategy for the Sydney Conservatorium of Music crafted by both the professional and academic staff. Those staff reviewed the strategy document as it evolved and incorporated their feedback into the final document that was sent to the university at the close of the project. What this shows is that, in IVR, researchers can continually draw on feedback from participants to build construct validity.

External Validity

Using social theory to analyse data and explain results helps develop external validity. As we are mainly dealing with qualitative research case studies and IVR, and not positivist research, it is likely that social theories will help us develop outcomes that we can learn lessons from, rather than applying hard rules. We cite Latour (1986, p. 264) in support of our argument that what we are concerned with is how things work, not what rules research develops:

> It also follows that the nature of society is negotiable, a practical and revisable matter (performative), and not something that can be determined once and for all by the sociologist who attempts to stand outside it (ostensive). The sociologist should, accordingly, seek to analyse the way in which people are associated together, and should, in particular, pay attention to the material and extra somatic resources (including inscriptions) that offer ways of linking people that may last longer than any given interaction.

The distinction between performative outcomes over ostensive ones is a key distinguishing factor of IVR because each intervention is essentially unique and will always achieve different outcomes; no social system can ever be identical. Thus, to explore these outcomes, we now turn to what generalisations are and the differences between naturalistic and qualitative generalisations.

Generalisations

The following quote by Yin (2017, p. 37) highlights one of the most misunderstood issues in accounting research, namely generalisation:

> Besides making it easier to design your case study, having some theory or theoretical propositions will later play a critical role in helping you to generalize the lessons learned from your case study. This role of theory has been characterized throughout this book as analytic generalization and has been contrasted with another way of generalizing the results from empirical studies, known as statistical generalization. Understanding the distinction between these two types of generalization may be your most notable accomplishment in doing case study research.

Often qualitative accounting researchers insert an apology in their limitations section for not being quantitative (positivist) researchers, and thus not being able to generalise the findings (de Villiers *et al.*, 2019). However, nothing can be further from the truth if one truly understands the difference between qualitative and quantitative generalisations. We must realise that, inevitably in IVR, we use qualitative methods to gather and analyse data as our main source of evidence. We are not saying that the results from numerical or statistical analysis should not be used as evidence. However, in IVR, the researcher has a one-on-one relationship with the research site and, moreover, the researcher immerses themselves in the project with participants. Thus, the research and data collected align with an ethnography.

In an IVR case study, the researchers should not consider an individual unit of analysis in the same way that units of analysis are represented in quantitative positivist studies. An IVR research site is not a single case within a larger population. It is a unique case developed to solve a unique problem. It is not possible to make a statistical generalisation from a single unit of study, and trying to do so would be absurd, so we need to remove any thought of statistical generalisation as a primary outcome for IVR. What IVR can do, and can do very well, is to make qualitative generalisations (Parker & Northcott, 2016). We identified two categories of qualitative generalisation previously in this chapter. We next discuss both generalisations and use the research by Chiucchi and Dumay (2015) and Dumay (2010) as examples.

Theoretical Generalisations

As the name states, theoretical generalising is to provide persuasive findings to those interested in developing theory (Parker & Northcott, 2016). The findings of an IVR project are likely to be based on thick descriptions about the intervention that form a convincing and valid argument to support the claims made. Here, chains of evidence and abductive reasoning are vital to constructing a sound argument. The evidence must be so tight that almost no other explanation is possible.

Chiucchi and Dumay (2015) deliver theoretical generalisations in their intervention to create an IC report for an Italian public utility company. They used actor-network theory (ANT) to frame their analysis, justifying the link to IVR as follows (p. 308):

> Since we are interested in exploring the process of introducing the IC concept and its subsequent journey inside an organisation, it is fundamental to follow the actors experimenting with IC and to understand where they focus their attention, on accounting or on managing. For this reason, we use ANT to analyse data and discuss findings and more specifically the four translation moments identified by Callon (1986): problematisation, interessement, enrolment and mobilisation. Additionally, ANT is useful for longitudinal studies following actors over time.
>
> (Bukh & Kjærgaard Jensen, 2008, p. 148)

The aspects of translation are particularly adept to developing the thick description required for theoretical generalisation. They also relate to phases in the IRF. For example, translation requires the researcher to discover the "obligatory passage point" (Callon, 1986, pp. 205–206) that the participants must pass through to resolve a problem, which, in this case, was the IVR project to produce an IC report. In passing through that point, different participants can address their own problems and their reason for participating, helping them achieve their personal goals (Chiucchi & Dumay, 2015). Also, in the second phase of their project, Chiucchi and Dumay (2015) identify why some people left and other people joined the IVR project. Hence, ANT extended the analysis beyond just the outcomes of the IVR project to the participants and the depth of their involvement.

More importantly, Chiucchi and Dumay (2015, p. 327) produced theoretical generalisations of ANT in their reflections on both the expected and unexpected theoretical outcomes: our research shows how the translation process is continual and not staged. The network formed during Phase 1 did not collapse as we might expect after achieving the initial aim of producing the IC report. Rather, IC continued to survive but in a state of flux since the associations among the actors, developed during Phase 1, changed. Some actors built a direct and strong association with IC, and IC played a pivotal role in building associations between human actors, such as Dr Couch and Ms Scholar, while other actors disassociated.

Thus, Chiucchi's and Dumay (2015) research not only contributes to how convincing arguments and theoretical generalisations can be made using ANT but also has practical outcomes for the participants.

Naturalistic Generalisations

Naturalistic generalisation does not oppose theoretical generalisation, rather it complements it. Chiucchi and Dumay's (2015) intervention was based on two experiments with producing an IC report. The study was longitudinal with the purpose of trying to understand if either or both reports helped to articulate public value. Dumay *et al.* (2015, p. 277) argue that longitudinal studies are important because "most public sector entities do not have the same short-term myopic financial pressures of publicly listed companies, they have the opportunity to implement IC-based management and strategic practices". Thus, Chiucchi and Dumay (2015) contend that IC is not an ostensive concept, but is part of an arrangement of knowledge management that people use to achieve outcomes in specific contexts (Mouritsen, 2006). It is the rich descriptions of knowledge that articles like Chiucchi and Dumay (2015) provide that allow readers to immerse themselves in a story about practice and then transport the lessons they learned to other contexts. This is what can make a difference to our understanding of IC and public value creation.

In Summation

Latour's (1986) distinction between the ostensive and performative is a mainstay in IC research that has long sought to understand practice over time (Guthrie *et al.*, 2012; Mouritsen, 2006). IVR is a journey that takes time; it is not a collection of individual data points that can be analysed in aggregate. Moreover, it is a road that can never be travelled again—a unique sample, not a sample of one. However, in the accounting literature, there are still too many articles that apologise for not generalising. These articles open up criticisms from the uninformed that IVR is not serious research because, if a finding is open to interpretation, it cannot be proven as reliable or valid. Those claims equate to saying that experience cannot be relied upon, cannot be validated, and cannot be generalised to other circumstances; only quantifiable facts can. If that were true, we would not need job interviews—anyone could do any job. We would not need references, as our experience could never be validated. And we would stay in the same job forever because we could not generalise our experience to another role.

For the interventionist researcher, reliability, validity, and generalisation are about presenting a complete picture of a situation, assembling evidence that leads to a conclusion (or conclusions), and logically removing the possibilities for how those findings came to be until only plausible explanations remain. The different phases of the IRF guide researchers through this process by recommending tools such as a research protocol and research databases. It is entirely possible to conduct IVR without these. However, your ability to generalise a reliable and valid outcome will increase if you consider techniques for instilling these qualities in your research from the very beginning and keep them up to date through all phases of the IVR project. Also, as Massaro *et al.* (2019, p. 54) outline, case study research is often not transparent as a methodology, because "techniques strongly supported by Yin, such as a case study protocol" are rarely reported. Thus, interventionist researchers need to be aware of such criticisms and ensure that their IVR projects use these tools to ensure reliability, validity, and the ability to make qualitative generalisations.

References

Ahrens, T. & Chapman, C.S. (2006). Doing qualitative field research in management accounting: Positioning data to contribute to theory. *Accounting, Organizations and Society*, 31, 819–841.

Argyris, C. (1970). *Intervention theory and method: A behavioural science view*. Reading, MA: Addison-Wesley Publishing Company.

Baard, V.C. (2010). A critical review of interventionist research. *Qualitative Research in Accounting & Management*, 7(1), 13–45.

Baard, V.C. & Dumay, J. (2018). Interventionist research in accounting: Reflections on the good, the bad and the ugly. *Accounting & Finance*. doi:10.1111/acfi.12409

Bukh, P.N. & Kjærgaard Jensen, I. (2008). Intellectual capital statements in the Danish utility sector: Materialisation and enactment. *Journal of Human Resource Costing & Accounting*, 12(3), 148–178. doi:10.1108/14013380810919831

Callon, M. (1986). Some elements of a sociology of translation: Domestication of the scallops and the fishermen of St Brieuc Bay. In J. Law (Ed.), *Power, action and belief: A new sociology of knowledge?* (pp. 196–233). London: Routledge & Kegan Paul.

Chiucchi, M.S. & Dumay, J. (2015). Unlocking intellectual capital. *Journal of Intellectual Capital*, 16(2), 305–330.

Cho, C.H., Laine, M., Roberts, R.W., & Rodrigue, M. (2015). Organized hypocrisy, organizational façades, and sustainability reporting. *Accounting, Organizations and Society*, 40, 78–94. http://dx.doi.org/10.1016/j.aos.2014.12.003

Davila, T. & Oyon, D. (2008). Cross-paradigm collaboration and the advancement of management accounting knowledge. *Critical Perspectives on Accounting*, 19, 887–893.

de Villiers, C., Dumay, J., & Maroun, W. (2019). Qualitative accounting research: Dispelling myths and developing a new research agenda. *Accounting & Finance*, 59(3), 1459–1487. doi:10.1111/acfi.12487

Dumay, J. (2010). A critical reflective discourse of an interventionist research project. *Qualitative Research in Accounting and Management*, 7(1), 46–70.

Dumay, J. & Baard, V.C. (2017). An introduction to interventionist research in accounting. In Z. Hoque, L.D. Parker, M. Covaleski, & K. Haynes (Eds.), *The Routledge companion to qualitative accounting research methods* (pp. 265–283). Oxfordshire, UK: Routledge and Taylor and Francis.

Dumay, J., Guthrie, J., & Puntillo, P. (2015). IC and public sector: A structured literature review. *Journal of Intellectual Capital*, 16(2), 267–284. doi:10.1108/JIC-02-2015-0014

Facione, P.A. (2020). Critical thinking: What it is and why it counts [Essay]. *Insight Assessment*. Retrieved from: www.insightassessment.com/Resources/Importance-of-Critical-Thinking/Critical-Thinking-What-It-Is-and-Why-It-Counts/Critical-Thinking-What-It-Is-and-Why-It-Counts-PDF

Gibbert, M., Ruigrok, W., & Wicki, B. (2008). What passes as a rigorous case study? *Strategic Management Journal*, 29(13), 1465–1474.

Golafshani, N. (2003). Understanding reliability and validity in qualitative research. *The Qualitative Report*, 8(4), 597–607.

Guthrie, H., & Clayton, B. (2010). *Building Capability in Vocational Education and Training Providers: The TAFE Cut*, National Centre for Vocational Education Research (NCVER), Adelaide.

Guthrie, J., Parker, L., & Gray, R. (2004). Requirements and understandings for publishing academic research: An insider view. In C. Humphrey & W. Lee (Eds.), *The real life guide to accounting research: A behind-the-scenes view of using qualitative research methods* (pp. 411–432). Amsterdam: Elsevier.

Guthrie, J., Ricceri, F., & Dumay, J. (2012). Reflections and projections: A decade of intellectual capital accounting research. *The British Accounting Review*, 44(2), 68–92.

IPART. (2013). Pricing VET under Smart and Skilled, Independent Pricing and Regulatory Tribunal, Sydney.

Jamaluddin, A. (2015). *Management accounting change: A case study in Australian vocational education providers.* (PhD), University of Sydney, Sydney.

Jönsson, S., & Lukka, K. (2007). *There and back again: Doing interventionist research in management accounting.* In C. S. Chapman, A. G. Hopwood, & M. S. Shields (Eds.), *Handbook of management accounting research* (pp. 373–397). Oxford: Elsevier

Koutsogeorgopoulou, V. (2009). Enhancing educational performance in Australia. In OECD Economics Department Working Papers No. 678 (Ed.), (pp. 1–43): OECD Publishing.

Latour, B. (1986). The powers of association. In J. Law (Ed.), *Power, action and belief: A new sociology of knowledge?* (pp. 264–280). London: Routledge & Kegan Paul.

Lincoln, Y.S. & Guba, E.G. (1994). *Naturalistic inquiry* (2nd ed.). Newbury Park, CA: SAGE.

Massaro, M., Dumay, J., & Bagnoli, C. (2019). Transparency and the rhetorical use of citations to Robert Yin in case study research. *Meditari Accountancy Research*, 27(1), 44–71. doi:10.1108/MEDAR-08-2017-0202

McKinnon, J. (1988). Reliability and validity in field research: Some strategies and tactics. *Accounting, Auditing & Accountability Journal*, 1(1), 34–54.

Misko, J., & Wynes, S. H. (2009a). *Tracking our success: How TAFE institutes measure their effectiveness and efficiency*. National Centre for Vocational Education Research (NCVER).

Misko, J., & Wynes, S. H. (2009b). *Tracking our success: How TAFE Institutes measure their effectiveness and efficiency—Case studies. Support Document*. National Centre for Vocational Education Research (NCVER).

Mouritsen, J. (2006). Problematising intellectual capital research: Ostensive versus performative IC. *Accounting, Auditing & Accountability Journal*, 19(6), 820–841.

Parker, L.D. & Northcott, D. (2016). Qualitative generalising in accounting research: Concepts and strategies. *Accounting, Auditing & Accountability Journal*, 29(6), 1100–1131.

Shanks, G. (2002). Guidelines for conducting positivist case study research in information systems. *Australasian Journal of Information Systems*, 10(1), 76–85.

Tsang, E.W.K. (2014). Generalizing from research findings: The merits of case studies. *International Journal of Management Reviews*, 16(4), 369–383.

Yin, R.K. (2017). *Case study research and applications: Design and methods* (6th ed.). Thousand Oaks, CA: Sage Publications Inc.

Part 3

People, Social Systems, and Interventions— Putting It Together

9 Recruiting, Approaching, and Retaining Participants

Recruiting, approaching, and retaining participants is an ongoing challenge in qualitative research, but more so for IVR. Participating in an interview or focus group or completing an online survey does not require the same time commitment as joining an intervention team; time which many participants are unwilling or unable to give. The criteria for joining a sample cannot be compared to the skills required to help diagnose and analyse problems, and design, implement, and evaluate interventions. Moreover, the risk and trepidation associated with change can dissuade participants from entertaining an IVR project at all.

Identifying and understanding the type of social system most likely to serve the purpose of the interventionist project is the starting point for the recruitment process. In Chapter 1, we offer a basic introduction to what and who social systems and social system actors are, and we state that social systems are a proxy for research participants. Moreover, social system characteristics emphasise researcher qualities required for participant recruitment, intervention, and engagement throughout the IVR process. Therefore, in this chapter, we discuss the nature of social systems and we integrate insights on specific researcher qualities required for intervening in a variety of social systems.

The rationale for selecting specific participants normally reflects the aim of the research project and the available resources (Reybold *et al.*, 2012; Saunders, 2012; Arcury & Quandt, 1999). Keeping this in mind allows researchers to find people and social systems with attributes essential to the research project (Saunders, 2012). However, despite its importance, the IVR literature holds few meaningful insights into ways of finding, recruiting, approaching, and then retaining participants (Jimenez & Czaja, 2016; Visovsky & Morrison-Beedy, 2012; Reybold *et al.*, 2012; Arcury & Quandt, 1999).

Hence, there are four main rationales for this chapter: to understand the nature of social systems; to emphasise the importance of participant recruitment; to share strategies for recruiting participants; and to encourage other scholars to do the same.

The Nature of Social Systems

In IVR, social systems are unique in that they are both the context and the subject of the study. A common definition of a system is a set of elements or parts where relationships exist between the parts, and the parts are interdependent and organised in a way that comes together to present an integrated whole (Hall & Fagen, 1956; Robbins *et al.*, 2017). Sweetman *et al.* (2013, p. 298) define a social system as "a plurality of individuals and groups interacting in some social sphere that has a set of institutions and procedures regulating it". Organisations are bureaucratically organised social groups where the members have differentiated functions related to accomplishing organisational goal(s) (Andersen, 1990). Organisations also consist of elements, for example, individuals, groups (formal and informal), intergroups, teams, structures and authority, goals, attitudes, and motives that are interrelated. These are the elements that help achieve a specific organisational purpose (Bruhn & Rebach, 2007; Robbins *et al.*, 2017). Thus, we view organisations as social systems consisting of interdependent and interrelated individuals and secondary groups, intentionally organised to achieve the objectives of the organisation using an organisational structure that involves control and coordination mechanisms. In the context of IVR, individuals, formal and informal groups, intergroups, and organisational mechanisms are subsystems of the larger system (Argyris, 1970; Bruhn & Rebach, 2007).

Much of the knowledge about subsystems is found in the literature on social work, anthropology, organisational and social psychology, organisational behaviour, and sociology. In the social sciences, social systems are generally referred to as clients, client systems, or patients (Baard, 2010). Bruhn and Rebach (2007, p. 3) define a client system as people "who have defined the condition as a problem and may be involved in planning or participation in the intervention, and who may change or be influenced by the change from the intervention". As discussed in Chapter 3, in accounting, 'clients' are closely linked to consulting, which is reason for the suggestion of a replacement term like 'participant system' (Baard, 2010). In this book, we use the term social system consistent with accounting's sociological roots and to represent the context and the subject of the IVR project.

To enhance our understanding of what a social system is, we turn to sociology, defined as "a methodological approach to studying the social behaviour of individuals, social groups, and human institutions constituting organisations, communities, and societies" (Kammeyer *et al.*, 1994, p. 2). In sociology, practitioners use concepts, knowledge, processes, and ideologies to address social problems preserved by extant social arrangements in social systems. Similarly, interventionist researchers use discipline-specific knowledge, methods, and principles to address problems in social systems. Sociological practice is a useful place to begin understanding the nature of a social system because, like IVR, it relies on direct and active researcher involvement.

There are some other aspects of sociological practice that are consistent with intervention philosophy and Intervention Theory (IVT). For example, philosophically, sociological practice is an interventionist model of mediating between the "scientific ethos of prediction and control" and "the pragmatic orientation of everyday life" (McLain, 2002, p. 266)— roughly equivalent to Jönsson and Lukka's (2007, p. 386) "going there and back again". In terms of IVT, collaborating to solve a problem is critical to both sociology and IVR, along with all the trust and relationship dynamics that go along with that. Further, IVR relies on the role of theory primarily to underpin the intervention needed for problem-solving and to reveal theoretical relevance in the project's output. Similarly, sociological interventions remediate real social problems and construct new and advantageous arrangements in many ways by relying on sociological theory (see McLain, 2002).

Bruhn and Rebach (2007) adopt an applied sociological view to enlighten readers on social systems. Specifically, they state that social systems exist along the sociological continuum, starting with the micro-level and moving along to the meso- and macro-levels. At the micro-level, we find individuals or small social units who are members of a certain social system. We also find primary groups consisting of families and couples. At the meso or mid-level systems, we find secondary groups, such as groups, teams, departments, and divisions (work units), and small corporate structures, such as businesses, communities, government agencies, universities, clubs, and civic organisations. Macro-level systems start with large corporate structures, including national and multinational corporations; states and cities; and national systems featuring, for example, wide-ranging social infrastructures, such as education, social-welfare, and political-legal systems. They end with the world economy, where issues such as trade relations manifest. The social systems along the sociological continuum do not exist in isolation, rather they are linked. For instance, mass media, economic structures, legislation, and climate change influence individuals, their beliefs, attitudes, preferences, and jobs. Groups, for example, are influenced by the individuals within the group, their roles, organisational policies and practices, and national socio-cultural issues. Thus, we view individuals, groups, intergroups, teams, and organisations as social systems that are not distinct but interact and influence each other across levels. The vital insight here is that researchers need to be aware that intervening at one level of a social system may influence many others. Also, it is evident that the scope and complexity of social systems change as we move along the continuum. Consequently, all the characteristics of an IVR project tend to depend on where the social system, and therefore its constituents, sit along the continuum (Bruhn & Rebach, 2007).

Although not impossible, based on our experience in accounting IVR and our literature review, it is unlikely that accounting researchers will engage in interventions at the far end of the macro-level spectrum. Solving a city's problems is probably beyond the scope of one intervention, no matter how big, let alone the world's problems. However, IVR is entirely feasible at the near end, say with national and multinational companies. Social systems at the meso-level are perfect for IVR. The accounting literature mostly shows us examples in hospitals, small businesses, manufacturing firms, universities, banks, and subsidiaries of large multinational companies, but there are many others.

The two sections that follow discuss micro- and meso-level social systems in more detail: their competences and common problems, examples of interventions appropriate to each, and the researcher qualities typically needed for intervening at those levels.

Micro-Level Social Systems

At the micro-level, we have individuals enjoying membership of, for instance, a team, group, or organisation (Bruhn & Rebach, 2007). Individuals are complex social systems because they differ with respect to personalities, attitudes and values, their self-concept, expectations, tolerance for ambiguity, and their desire for growth and autonomy (Robbins *et al.*, 2017). Most individuals share three main criteria to consider themselves competent: self-acceptance, confirmation, and psychological success (Argyris, 1970). Self-acceptance refers to the extent to which they are aware of their strengths and weaknesses, have confidence in themselves, and value themselves (Shepard, 1979). Individuals who are confident and value themselves are more likely to generate and receive valid information. Confirmation justifies the confidence and value one has in themselves. Receiving frequent confirmation leads to greater confidence, which in turn often leads to greater competence.

Psychological success increases self-acceptance and confirmation (Argyris, 1970). It includes: a) the ability to define your own goals; b) the association between own goals and individual needs, capabilities, and values; c) the definition of the means to achieving those goals; and d) the extent to which achieving goals meets the aspirations of the individual (Argyris, 1970). To feel competent, people should strive to be successful in all four aspects of psychological success. Competent individuals have a greater likelihood of learning and growing, solving problems, and proficiently making and implementing decisions. Further, these qualities can have a knock-on effect, enhancing competencies in the groups and organisation that surround them. Signs of competence include taking responsibility for ideas and feelings, experimenting with new ideas and feelings, being open to the ideas and feelings of others, and helping others to experiment with theirs (Argyris, 1970). Thus, competent individuals also have a greater likelihood of accepting others and helping others with their confirmation. In many ways, this is the basis for effective work relationships in a group, team, intergroup, or organisation.

At the micro-level, social problems stem from the behaviours, emotions, and cognitions that develop from social interactions. These problems have social consequences for the individual and the organisation hosting the individual (Bruhn & Rebach, 2007). This is because social problems limit an individual's ability to meet their needs, accomplish their objectives, take action, and preserve social functioning through exchanges with or among other individuals and groups. Intervention types to address social problems are thus emotion- and behaviour-oriented. Examples of interventions at the micro-level may include but are not limited to one-on-one counselling, developing interpersonal skills, self-concept development, and intense learning experiences focused on acquiring or developing skills within their work environment (Reddy, 1994).

To intervene at the micro-level, interventionist researchers require advanced interpersonal skills centred on intellectual, emotional, and behavioural components (Argyris, 1970; Reddy, 1994). Cognitive interventions that are intellectual or idea-oriented that may, for instance, involve skill or knowledge training, may well be within the competency of the accounting researcher. Emotional/reflective interventions carry a greater risk of being rejected, given the uncertainty of participant reactions, and require a higher level of skill. Realistically, organisational behaviourists, psychologists (organisational or social), and experienced counsellors are most likely to possess these qualities (Reddy, 1994), not accounting researchers. Despite this, we see no reason why accounting researchers could not work in teams with other researchers from human sciences if there is a worthwhile IVR study with strong potential for theoretical and societal relevance.

Meso-Level Social Systems

Meso-level social systems centre on secondary groups, for instance, work units such as groups, teams, intergroups, divisions, and departments, and small corporate structures. We address groups and work units first before discussing corporate structures.

Secondary Groups

Robbins *et al.* (2017, p. 426) define a group as "two or more interacting and interdependent individuals who come together to achieve specific goals". They also differentiate between formal and informal groups. Managers create formal groups to accomplish assigned work and specific tasks to achieve organisational goals. Conversely, informal groups are established for individuals to achieve social contact and to satisfy a need for belonging—for example, a group that shares morning tea or lunch. Groups can also be assembled into departments, such as sales, manufacturing, or customer service, where most people have common functions and need to coordinate to achieve a strategic goal. Divisions are larger secondary group structures that consist of departments. For instance, a publications company can have a marketing division and an R&D division, where each division contains relevant departments.

Apart from accomplishing goals, group members interact; they outline the roles needed to support the work they do, make decisions on ideas and actions, and they fashion and influence the group member working interrelationships. These interactions are not entirely focused on the job. They also involve social arrangements and personal characteristics. Groups initiate rules on how group members think, behave, and respond to contextual factors from the larger social system they inhabit. Through roles and norms, individuals establish a group structure. Thus, groups are complex social systems that are not merely a collection of individual behaviours and personalities, but powerful subsystems that drive individual work output, individual social or anti-social actions, and organisational productivity and performance.

The idea of groups extends into the notion of teams, where a formal process brings together two or more individuals. Katzenbach and Smith (1993) find teams are significantly different from groups because: team members are accountable to themselves and the team; work is accomplished collaboratively rather than individually; the purpose of the team is to accomplish a specific complex task requiring diverse skills rather than a broader organisational purpose; leadership is shared; and team meetings feature open discussion. With teams, managers typically measure performance by evaluating collective output (Robbins *et al.*, 2017; Katzenbach & Smith, 1993). In accounting IVR, researchers are more likely to focus on formal groups, such as small groups, teams, departments, and divisions.

Argyris (1970) states that there are several criteria for competent groups. Individuals are an important constituent of groups. Thus, the extent to which individuals in the group possess a high degree of self-acceptance, confirmation, and psychological success, in part, accounts for a competent group. Another criterion is that the group needs to take responsibility for clearly defining their tasks and accomplishing challenging group tasks. Group responsibility is fostered through group members, which enhances their feelings of confidence in the group, fosters trust, and engenders high levels of psychological success. Accordingly, the group's attractiveness strengthens, as does its ability to solve problems and make and implement decisions. These are potential catalysts for change. Ongoing critical evaluation and modification of the group's processes are essential to creating a safe space where individual members feel accepted, respected, free to express their views and take responsibility for their ideas, and experiment with new ideas and feelings without negative consequence. Last, rotating group leadership based on skills and abilities, or functionally shared leadership, distributes power more equitably. In turn, groups tend to accomplish tasks more effectively, giving rise to feelings of psychological success and competence.

Argyris (1970) does not explicitly explain what the term inter-groups means. Our interpretation of his discourse on inter-groups is that they are interdependent groups drawing on important resources and interactions to achieve superordinate goals, and they exist as cooperatives within a larger social system to solve problems. Our interpretation is consistent with the competence criteria for inter-groups. First, Argyris (1970) states that between-group competency relies on individual and group competency. Second, inter-group relationships rely on interdependencies which allow groups to benefit from resources that each group has. Hence, group members need to be aware of these interdependencies because interdependencies help inter-groups contribute to and achieve a larger goal related to solving the problem. Groups cannot achieve superordinate or larger inter-group goals without cooperation and interdependency between the groups involved. Also, awareness of these interdependencies makes people feel involved, even essential to the group. They create a sense of a low power differential because each group is contributing something of importance, that is, a win-win rather than a win-lose for the groups involved. Third, groups must demonstrate a constant willingness to interact with the other connected groups because it increases the flow of valid and useful information, which is essential for problem-solving. This also creates feelings of confidence and trust between the groups.

Bruhn and Rebach (2007) and Reddy (1994) outline several social problems that may prevail in secondary groups. For instance, a groups' ability to solve problems and manage change may be compromised because group members lack skills required to effectively do their work. Ambiguity inherent in group objectives or goals inhibits the group to appropriately plan for how they are going to achieve coherent group output. Sometimes, there are issues with group diversity, where group members have their own agenda without considering others, and culture clashes disrupting group harmony and reducing group productivity. Inter-groups may experience conflict because their interdependent relationships may be dysfunctional, where groups do not trust or have confidence in each other, and thus are unwilling to interact and cooperate with other groups. Additionally, a win-lose mentality may manifest through a high-power differential.

Reddy (1994, p. 92) calls group dynamics an "iceberg" because they have levels and not all are seen. Table 9.1 provides more detail. He also states that group dynamics produce the energy for action to support group synergy, maintain group competency, help the group adapt and survive, and enable the group to achieve their goals. Although the table

Table 9.1 The Iceberg of Group Dynamics

Level	Description of the Issue	Implication
Level I: Content	The work, task, project, or service the group needs to perform	Above the surface of the iceberg and easily observable
Level II: Overt Group Issues	Group member interactions, task conflicts, interpersonal conflicts, problem-solving, and decision-making	At the surface of the iceberg and observable to a perceptive person. Group members will not explicitly refer to these issues
Level III: Covert & Core Group Issues	These issues are critical to group success: • Inclusion—group membership, affiliation, and sense of belonging • Control—power, authority, autonomy, leadership, influence, compliance, and competence • Affection—intimacy, friendship, and sexuality	These behaviours: • Are below the surface of the iceberg; they are not easily observable • Foster behaviour and dynamics in Level II • Require inference from behaviour patterns observed in Level I and Level II Disruption of these dynamics results in member dissatisfaction, absenteeism, work not accomplished, decrease in-group cohesion, and hostility
Level IV: Values, Beliefs, & Assumptions	These issues include: • Group defences, history, and personality • Basic needs for inclusion, control, and intimacy These are the basic and least changeable characteristics of individuals	These dynamics drive Level III issues Exploring Level IV dynamics is not suitable in an organisation setting May be focused on using personal growth groups and sensitivity training Group members find intervening at this level confronting and disruptive
Level V: Unconscious Dynamics	These issues relate to basic instincts, motivations, and impulses	These issues are not readily accessible and will not manifest with normal awareness Issues are potentially destructive to groups and group members

Source: Adapted from Reddy (1994)

shows the complexity of group dynamics, our view is that it also presents an account of the problems or issues that groups may experience. There is where the possibility for interventions might exist. Certainly, intervening at Levels I and II is possible, provided the researcher has suitable qualities to do so. Given the complex group dynamics and the potential issues demonstrated by Levels III, IV, and V, it is unlikely that accounting researchers will intervene at these levels unless a member of a research team is a competent psychologist or a scholar specialising in group dynamics.

Intervening in secondary groups helps groups maintain their ability to generate productive output (Argyris, 1970; Reddy, 1994). Group intervention types are mainly process-oriented—for example, approaches to conflict management, group decision-making and problem-solving techniques, and workflow coordination. Cognitive, skill, and activity interventions for entire groups are also prevalent. As with individuals, group emotional/reflective interventions are subjective and require a higher degree of skill (Reddy, 1994). As the focus of the intervention moves from Levels I to V, that is from groups to interpersonal to individual group member issues, the depth of the intervention moves from the content of the group task to covert group issues not easily observable to group member behaviours and emotions which are considered inaccessible. Thus, the risk of intervening escalates. The risk increases because intervening at the lower levels carries greater disruption for participants and increases intensity of participant reactions to interventions, which enhances the probability of intervention resistance or rejection (Reddy, 1994). Researchers seeking to intervene within groups require highly developed skills in dealing with social processes to manage confrontation, conflicts, and other group dynamics (Argyris, 1970). Groups and individual interventions are deep and risky, yet they yield the potential for emancipation and societal relevance, which is a very worthwhile undertaking.

Meso-Level Corporate Structures

The most common subjects of an accounting intervention at the meso-level are likely to be small corporate structures. Given the diverse nature of corporate structures, we use 'organisation' as an umbrella term to cover all manner of concerns: companies, corporations, universities, consortiums, government agencies, associations, clubs, networks, syndicates, and so on.

Within organisations, organisational mechanisms unify and influence individuals and groups and have short-and long-term effects on organisational behaviour and performance (Argyris, 1970). Either way, organisational mechanisms are a means of getting something done. For instance, Argyris (1970) states that formal and informal norms accentuating and rewarding an individual's competence, trust, and their internal commitment and contributions to the organisation will enhance the likelihood that an organisation will achieve their competence criteria (see Chapter 4). Similarly, norms that encourage a group to take responsibility for defining their tasks and developing skills to accomplish their tasks support the group's functionality and success. Norms influence the win-win dynamics of intergroup relationships such that successful problem-solving and superordinate goal achievement are emphasised.

Patterns of communication and socialisation are coordination mechanisms that enable people to work together to achieve goals. Control mechanisms, such as organisational policies, rules, and procedures, direct individual and group behaviour, outline boundaries of discretion, and monitor the processes and outputs of subsystems. Structural mechanisms include roles and tasks, lines of authority, and in conjunction with control mechanisms, reinforce organisational norms. Values and preferences are mechanisms influencing courses of actions and the decision-making required to get things done. Knowledge and resources are mechanisms driving capability requirements and information systems to accomplish organisational work. Therefore, following this rationale, we identify organisational mechanisms as: organisational cultures or norms; values, trust, and internal commitment; organisational policies and procedures to reinforce norms; job design; authority structures; organisational strategy; and systems, e.g., compensation, information, control, and performance measurement systems (Argyris, 1970; Beer, 1980; Robbins *et al.*, 2017). Examples of interventions focusing on organisational mechanisms include Dumay's (2010) structural intervention where a social system needed to develop a new strategic outlook, or Cullen *et al.*'s (2013) cognitive idea-oriented intervention of using quality costing to resolve reverse logistics problems. Reflecting on the nature of accounting, we infer that accounting interventions are more likely to occur in response to the problems that manifest in organisational mechanisms.

Social problems found in small corporate structures may relate to organisational competency and health (see Chapter 4); organisational mechanisms that get things done and facilitate interactions between individuals and groups; and inter-group relations including cooperation, communication, and conflict management and group harmony (Bruhn and Rebach, 2007). The researcher qualities identified in Chapters 3 and 10 should support intervention in this social system.

In summary, understanding the nature of social systems, the types of problems they may experience, the types of interventions most likely directed at these systems, and the researcher qualities required to intervene provides insights on the characteristics of a range of IVR participants. It is also important to note that each of the social systems discussed thus far are interrelated, and any intervention applied to an organisational mechanism may influence or stimulate significant change at the individual and group subsystems. Thus, interventionist researchers should not discount that intervening in one social system may result in a change in another, intended or unintended. Further, not appreciating the interrelatedness of the subsystems may render interventions ineffective or result in rejection. Accordingly, knowledge of social systems forms the starting point for participant recruitment. It provides insights into the range of participants that one IVR project may need to recruit, which in turn informs the participant recruitment process.

Recruiting IVR Participants

Recruitment is a process used to select research participants, and the literature appears to use the terms recruitment and selection synonymously. We find that recruiting participants is a very practical matter that does not receive appropriate attention in published IVR studies. The recruitment process is not without problems, but there are general strategies available to overcome the potential barriers.

Common Problems With Recruiting Participants

Recruitment problems are complex, especially when the recruiter does not have a plan, knowledge or experience with recruiting, nor an (as yet) well-developed understanding of the social system (Visovsky & Morrison-Beedy, 2012; Jimenez & Czaja, 2016; Saunders, 2012). Of course, we are not suggesting that all accounting interventionist researchers are not knowledgeable about recruitment, but since there is very little research on this topic, some might value this discussion. Jimenez and Czaja (2016) argue that researchers must be realistic in their view of participant suitability and availability, and the time and effort required for the recruitment and selection process. After gaining access to an organisation, researchers need to recruit individuals willing to provide data, collaborate, or do both.

With a clear outline of the proposed research design, the potential problem requiring solution, and the theoretical research questions to be answered, the researcher can: identify feasibly accessible organisations with likely willing participants that meet the selection criteria; and then identify the individuals, groups, or departments in organisations that are likely to provide data or join the intervention team. Our previous discussion on the nature of social systems should help researchers to construct participant selection criteria. Not being able to identify potential participants generally occurs when researchers are unaware of the problems particular candidates are likely to be experiencing, or they are ignorant to characteristics of those candidates (Jimenez & Czaja, 2016).

Turning to the accounting literature, we find extremely limited insights on participant selection criteria. Our aim is to start constructing a foundation to assist researchers in identifying participant selection criteria. On this problem, we find a helpful example from Wouters and Sportel (2005). Wouters and Sportel (2005) undertook a longitudinal IVR project to develop and implement a performance measurement system for the purposes of investigating the role of existing performance measures in an organisation. Their research site was a single case organisation, which had to satisfy some identified selection criteria. For instance, the organisation had to be medium-sized because they wanted to compare the results to a similar initiative with a very large organisation. Similarly, the site had to have a logistics function with clear links to the firm's strategy, and the senior logistics managers had to have experience with performance measurement. Hence, the researcher found and recruited an organisation that had these characteristics to align with the research project.

Another problem relates to the nature of IVR and its design. IVR is a process that requires a time and work commitment that many participants may be unwilling or unable to accommodate. Everyone who works has time demands, and the additional work that comes from committing to an IVR project requires some serious forward-thinking. Visovsky and Morrison-Beedy (2012) highlight the need for researchers to question the intervention's feasibility if it is perceived as too much of a burden. In Chapter 12, we explain the value of assessing an intervention's feasibility. Jimenez and Czaja (2016) note another recruitment obstacle, which is the lack of an effective communication strategy to inform potential research participants of the purpose and intentions of the project. Here, issues such as confidentiality, privacy, and the risks associated with change need to be addressed. Using terminology that only academics understand and telling participants how the research is going to help you will not win you any favours. Instead, ask "What can I do for you?" plainly and simply.

Participant Recruitment Strategies

We need to recognise that each intervention research project, the target participants, and the research context are distinct and, therefore, advocating a specific recruitment procedure is problematic. However, there are some general tips that can be helpful.

From a scientific perspective, recruitment strategies originate from non-probability sampling techniques. Accounting interventionists typically do not use probability sampling because it is not practical for IVR. However, IVR projects involving quasi-experiments may need to incorporate some principles of non-probability sampling. Reybold *et al.* (2012, p. 700) state: "In qualitative research, purposeful selection is legendary . . . nothing better captures the difference between quantitative and qualitative methods than the different logics that undergird sampling approaches". Reybold *et al.*'s (2012, p 700) advice equally applies to IVR because "the logic of selection is grounded in the value of information-rich cases and emergent in-depth understanding". Participant selection in IVR is embedded in researcher subjectivity and dependent on the needs of the project and the participants. Reybold *et al.* (2012, p. 701) argue that published qualitative research shows the final choice of participants but does not share how selection occurred, especially the "tried and failed" or the "discarded" that leads to the final choice. Accounts of participant selection seem so simple, easy, and effortless, whereas reality paints a very different picture. For this reason, we encourage researchers to recount stories of how they recruited and selected participants so that we might all learn from those experiences.

Purposive sampling requires researcher judgement in choosing the individuals, groups, and organisations that are most likely to answer the research question(s) (Saunders, 2012). Jimenez and Czaja (2016) state purposive strategies help researchers to advance their understanding of the opinions, experiences, needs, or problems of social systems that may be suitable for an IVR project. Convenience sampling involves selecting participants who meet the selection criteria, and who are easy to recruit or who are interested in and available to participate in an IVR study (Jimenez & Czaja, 2016; Saunders, 2012). With this strategy, participants might be selected, for example, from students in a class, accountants at professional development events, and research forums. These latter venues can be fertile ground for engaging gatekeepers and, who knows, they may be on the prowl for researchers. Researchers can contact gatekeepers through direct methods, such as personal emails, phone calls, and face-to-face meetings. Finally, referrals from family, friends, and colleagues are also useful. It is an opportunistic approach, but one that can prove to be highly effective.

Snowball sampling is another recruitment strategy where researchers use, for example, an organisation's intranet, bulletin boards, blogs, and social media. Alternatively, a gatekeeper identifies other likely participants in the organisation to support the project, which is a very common strategy in case study research when recruiting interviewees (Qu & Dumay, 2011). Similarly, community outreach through professional accounting associations and academic and professional conferences can be highly appropriate for the right kind of project. One of the benefits of both these strategies is that participants volunteer to become a part of the study on their own. Perhaps they particularly relate to the idea of the project or have strong opinions and attitudes about the issue under research (Saunders, 2012).

Saunders (2012) states that snowball sampling is useful when it is difficult to identify participants or when they are easy to identify but difficult to gain access to, such as a director or chief executive officer. From my, Vicki's, experience, when supervising a research student who was investigating highly sensitive funding and structure issues in a government agency, we found participants were extremely difficult to locate. My student received a personal referral to a senior official who, after careful negotiations, agreed to participate in the project. From this one contact, snowballing resulted in 15 additional participants. However, while snowballing can be a helpful strategy, extreme care must be applied, especially when the research topic or context is sensitive. Also, some ethics committees discourage snowballing because it can induce undue pressure on people to participate in the research.

Once the recruitment strategy has been selected, the next stage is recruitment planning. Jimenez and Czaja (2016) stress the importance of developing a recruitment plan early in the IVR project. An important component of planning is to collect information on the 'recruitment environment' that potentially suits the nature of the proposed IVR study and defines participant selection criteria. We find that having a realistic recruitment timeline that incorporates recruitment contingencies as part of the plan is important because recruitment can take longer than expected, and it is not always a 'smooth sailing' process. Visovsky and Morrison-Beedy (2012) concur that it takes time to find your potential participant(s). Researchers need to develop rapport and trust with their initial point of contact, confirm whether the participant can help you and you can help them, and then engage in negotiations with a view to successful recruitment.

As part of the recruitment planning process, Arcury and Quandt (1999) recommend that researchers make a list of the potential research sites that are relevant to the research project, for example, social clubs, organisations, and government agencies. Then researchers should think about who and what at the research site is likely to be a good source of data. For this reason, we accentuate the importance of knowledge about the participants and whether their characteristics aligned with the nature of your project. For each research site, the researcher must identify a gatekeeper to assist with the recruitment process. The gatekeeper can be the human resources director, the logistics manager of a manufacturing firm, the chair of a club, or anyone in a similar position of power and centrality.

Regardless of the recruitment strategy applied to an IVR project, the common theme is the importance of communicating key pieces of information to potential participants: be clear about the scope of the study, what the study aims to achieve, what is required of the participants, and the risks and benefits of participating. If people understand the benefits of a study, they are more likely to agree to participate. Jimenez and Czaja (2016) argue that accentuating 'the good' aspects for the participants is a powerful recruitment technique. People in organisations understanding the benefits of participating in your study and having perceptions that their participation will help them achieve their personal goals and solve the organisation's problems are more likely to agree to their recruitment. We find that face-to-face contact is an extremely effective recruitment tool. It allows researchers to interact with participants and "shed the ivory tower reputation of academia" (Jimenez & Czaja, 2016, p. 190). Moreover, we find that it serves as an important means to start building trust with potential participants.

Recruitment using online ads, particularly on social media platforms, is now becoming a very popular way to recruit participants. However, it is extremely important to create the ad with care to make sure it is understandable, ethically appropriate, culturally sensitive, and offers an unambiguous account of the nature of the IVR project and the potential value for its participants (see Chapter 6). In our experience, university ethics committees and marketing services are extremely helpful in guiding the content of personal emails and online ads for IVR. Further, researchers are normally required to provide examples of the communications with potential participants as part of an ethics application. Depending on the nature of your IVR study, this can take time, especially if there is a large degree of ambiguity in your recruitment strategy and plan.

Complementary to participant recruitment, and our last thoughts on the subject, is the matter of the research design and research resources. Visovsky and Morrison-Beedy (2012) recommend having discussions on one's research design and approach to recruitment with colleagues or practitioners not associated with the study. This is helpful because it is another way of assessing the project's feasibility and your recruitment approach before taking action. Jimenez and Czaja (2016) remind us that recruitment requires resources, including researcher time, effort, and money. Beyond any remuneration for the participants, there are also travel and training costs and perhaps a research assistant to help support the process, which are essential to account for in the budget (see Chapter 6).

In this section, we discussed some useful strategies to think about for recruiting participants. Some strategies target social systems first; others target the participants and the social system follows—finding both simultaneously is also possible. Given the diverse nature of IVR projects, it is very difficult to prescribe which order recruitment should happen in. The best approach for your study is at your discretion, but the common thread is that it should be motivated by the nature of the study, your experiences from previous IVR projects, feedback from an ethics application, and, dare we say, acting on instinct. Next, we discuss how to approach IVR participants.

Approaching IVR Participants

Access is another hurdle in the recruitment process. Access involves approaching people and organisations with information about the scope, aims, and anticipated outcomes of the study, but there are several considerations to keep in mind. Visovsky and Morrison-Beedy (2012) point out that people and organisations can receive many requests to accommodate research, which means you could be in competition with other studies— IVR, case studies, or other methodologies. If participants prefer another study, they may be reluctant to engage in yours. This is also true for the gatekeepers and, given their control over access to the organisation, losing the interest of this key player will probably result in a polite 'thank you, but no'. Another concern is that the research may be viewed as intrusive or focussed on issues that are too sensitive. Alternatively, the organisation may have concerns about confidentiality. Trust comes into play here, too. People in the organisations, including the gatekeeper, may view you with scepticism because you are an outsider: How could you possibly understand the nature of the organisation, its operations, and problems? Your competencies are unknown to them, and the idea of IVR may be foreign. Lastly, the people who need to be involved in the research may not have time to help with the research, plus accomplish their everyday work. So how do we go about accessing participants with all these potential barriers?

The Gatekeepers

There is demonstrated value in using gatekeepers to approach participants (Campanale *et al.*, 2014, Cullen *et al.*, 2013; Chiucchi, 2013; Saunders, 2012; Dumay, 2010; Davis & Albright, 2004). Argyris (1970) refers to the gatekeeper as a salient point of entry, which should ideally be at a high level in an organisation because this person provides an anchor for IVR effectiveness. Executives or senior managers have the power to stimulate "changes in attitudes, values and behaviour which can lead to changes in administrative controls, structure and organisational policies" (Argyris, 1970, p. 25). This power helps to spread word of the intention behind the research project throughout the organisation and signal the organisation's commitment and to making change, which results in fruitful IVR. Although the conversation on gatekeepers does not stop here, we have, in a previously published book chapter, discussed the value, importance, and role of the gatekeeper in approaching participants that is still relevant to IVR as this book is being written (see Dumay & Baard, 2017).

Approaching IVR Participants: Evidence and Action

The first source of guidance on approaching IVR participants comes from the accounting literature, although coverage insights are somewhat limited. Campanale *et al.* (2014) report that they gained access through existing relationships between their university and the participants. Chiucchi (2013) reports a similar gateway, although she explains that several meetings with the general manager (the gatekeeper) were required before access was granted. Cullen *et al.* (2013) appear to have gained access through workshops and industry forums, forming part of a larger multidisciplinary research project, but they offer no explicit explanations on the access process. Dumay (2010) explains that his entry was through a pre-existing academic relationship with a board member. He paved the way because he was interested in Dumay's doctoral work and saw some potential for collaboration.

Davis and Albright (2004) state that they gained access to their case organisation, a bank, because they were acquainted with someone employed at the bank, who turned out to be a gatekeeper and opened doors to other people in the bank to further their research efforts. Lohman *et al.'s* (2004) project stemmed from a university program on international logistics. However, they offer no details on their recruitment process or exactly how they accessed the participants. Wouters and Roijmans (2011) report that their longitudinal action research study was part of a larger research effort with a beverage manufacturing firm spanning four years, but, again, there is no explicit discourse on the path from the firm to the specific participants.

In our literature review, we find no evidence of general strategies to help researchers access participants. However, outside of the accounting literature, Saunders (2012) has some useful views. For instance, taking an opportunistic approach to participant access, facilitated by colleagues, friends, and family may lead to success, noting that there is also an element of luck with this approach. Saunders (2012) also states that when meeting the gatekeeper, it is helpful to offer to collect data that might not be relevant to your research but is of interest to the organisation. Although the work of Argyris (1970) occurred some time ago, he finds that organisations are known to approach a university requesting assistance with a specific problem. We infer that this might well have been the case with Campanale *et al.* (2014) and Lohman *et al.* (2004).

Argyris (1970) states that there are two main reasons for organisations approaching universities. First, the organisation may have identified a problem and its origins correctly, but they lack clarity on the exact nature of the problem and, therefore, a feasible solution. Second, a solution to the organisational problem exists, but managers seeking to implement it may not have the expertise to do so. Third, managers might not be willing to implement their solution because doing so may involve making unpopular decisions or generating political instability in the organisation. Researchers collaborating with these organisations can help with problem diagnosis and solutions. However, Argyris warns scholars that people in organisations may be seeking to transfer the responsibility of effective diagnosis and action to them, rather than engaging in productive collaboration. Without collaboration, the researchers might be regarded as consultants. Consequently, in this case, because the participants 'outsourced' implementation rather than committing to the solution, there is greater potential for the intervention to fail or be rejected. Likewise, their problems might re-emerge, benefits might not manifest and, if they do, they might not last.

Given the gaps in the literature on this important topic, there is an urgent need for accounting IVR scholars to outline how they accessed their participants in greater detail. In the interim, some of the strategies we offered may help. For instance, direct contact methods, starting with email or social media, are helpful because the participant is under no pressure to respond; they can decide for themselves if they are interested in your project. Do not forget that the content of your communication when recruiting and accessing participants, including evidence that your request is legitimate, is critical. In our experience, the opportunistic 'foot-in-the-door' approach with referrals from people you know has been especially helpful in gaining access to participants. Assuming recruitment and access is successful, the next hurdle is participant retention.

Retaining IVR Participants

Participant retention in IVR is challenging. Jönsson and Lukka (2007) state that IVR necessarily needs to be longitudinal, since the deep immersion and collaborative style of empirical work simply takes time. Visovsky and Morrison-Beedy (2012) argue that participant retention needs to be prioritised when designing the research project, and that it is the researcher's responsibility to devise strategies to retain their participants. They point out that retention strategies should incorporate: gathering the participants' contact information; plans for how to maintain contact with the participants during the study; communication plans to foster ongoing collaborations between researcher(s) and the participants including maintaining trust; and monitoring the intervention work to ensure that the demands on people's time and/or effort are not excessive. We also argue that participant retention must receive attention before and during intervention design and before implementation (see Chapters 11 and 12). Jimenez and Czaja (2016) state that participant attrition may occur if participants lose interest in the project or experience dissatisfaction because the study is not meeting their expectations. Participation attrition is influenced by the extent to which a sound retention strategy and operational plan is in place early in the project's pipeline. Additionally, recruiting participants whose characteristics, needs, and values are closely aligned with the nature of the research, and who will ultimately benefit from collaborating with researchers, is critical for successful participant retention.

Concluding Remarks

Participant recruitment, access, and retention is challenging when undertaking IVR. We have outlined the characteristics of a variety of social systems that contain research participants. Additionally, we identified the problems associated with recruitment, access, and retention and offered general strategies to achieve success with this vital IVR activity. "Recruitment and retention of participants remains one of the character builders of IVR", say Visovsky and Morrison-Beedy (2012, p. 209). Organisations depend on their customers, clients, or patients in the same way that interventionist researchers cannot solve real-life problems without participants. Breakthroughs in IVR projects in the medical and behavioural sciences have resulted in great improvements to people's health and quality of life. While accounting IVR may not have the same visible impact on people's lives, the people working in organisations are influenced by real-life problems that impinge on their ability to make decisions, feel emancipated and empowered, and achieve their personal and career aspirations. Interventionist researchers in accounting can be a part of this process by selecting and accessing participants aligned with the nature of their project and retaining participants until the intervention is implemented and evaluated.

References

Andersen, R.C. (1990). A technique for predicting intraorganizational action. *Clinical Sociology*, 8, 128–142.

Arcury, T.A. & Quandt, S.A. (1999). Participant recruitment for qualitative research: A site-based approach to community research in complex societies. *Human Organisation*, 58(2), 128–133.

Argyris, C. (1970). *Intervention theory and method: A behavioural science view*. Reading, MA: Addison-Wesley Publishing Company.

Baard, V.C. (2010). A critical view of interventionist research. *Qualitative Research in Accounting and Management*, 7(1), 13–45.

Beer, M. (1980). *Organization change and development: A system view*. Glenview, IL: Scott Foresman.

Bruhn, J.G. & Rebach, H.M. (2007). *Sociological practice: Intervention and social change*. New York, NY: Springer Science.

Campanale, C., Cinquini, L., & Tenucci, A. (2014). Time driven activity-based costing to improve transparency and decision making in healthcare. *Qualitative Research in Accounting & Management*, 11, 165–186.

Chiucchi, M.S. (2013). Intellectual capital accounting in action: Enhancing learning through interventionist research. *Journal of Intellectual Capital*, 14, 48–68.

Cullen, J., Tsamenyi, M., Bernon, M., & Gorst, J. (2013). Reverse logistics in the UK retail sector: A case study of the role of management accounting in driving organisational change. *Management Accounting Research*, 24, 212–227.

Davis, S. & Albright, T. (2004). An investigation of the effect of balanced scorecard implementation on financial performance. *Management Accounting Research*, 15, 135–153.

Dumay, J. (2010). A critical reflective discourse of an interventionist research project. *Qualitative Research in Accounting and Management*, 7(1), 46–70.

Dumay, J. & Baard, V. (2017). An introduction to interventionist research in accounting. In Z. Hoque, L.D. Parker, M.A. Covaleski, & K. Haynes (Eds.), *The Routledge companion to qualitative accounting research methods* (pp. 265–283). New York, NY: Routledge.

Hall, A.D. & Fagen, R.E. (1956). Definition of system. *General Systems*, 1, 18–28.

Jimenez, D.E. & Czaja, S.J. (2016). Recruitment and retention: Two of the most important, yet challenging tasks in behavioural intervention research. In L.N. Gitlin & S.J. Czaja (Eds.), *Behavioral intervention research* (pp. 177–194). New York, NY: Springer Publishing Company LLC.

Jönsson, S. & Lukka, K. (2007). There and back again: Doing interventionist research in management accounting. In C.S. Chapman, A.G. Hopwood, & M.S. Shields (Eds.), *Handbook of management accounting research* (Vol. 1, pp. 373–397). Oxford, UK: Elsevier.

Kammeyer, K.C.W., Ritzer, G., & Yetman, N.R. (1994). *Sociology: Experiencing changing societies* (6th ed.). Boston: Allyn & Bacon.

Katzenbach, J.R., & Smith, D.K. (1993). *The wisdom of teams*. New York, NY: McKinsey & Co.

Lohman, C., Fortuin, L., & Wouters, M. (2004). Designing a performance measurement system: A case study. *European Journal of Operational Research*, 156(2), 267–286.

McLain, R. (2002). Reflexivity and the sociology of practice. *Sociological Practice: A Journal of Clinical and Applied Sociology*, 494, 249–277.

Qu, S.Q. & Dumay, J. (2011). The qualitative research interview. *Qualitative Research in Accounting and Management*, 8(3), 238–264.

Reddy, W.B. (1994). *Intervention skills: Process consultation for small groups and teams*. Johannesburg, South Africa: Pfeiffer and Company.

Reybold, L.E., Lammert, J.D., & Stribling, S.M. (2012). Participant selection as a conscious research method: Thinking forward and the deliberation of "emergent" findings. *Qualitative Research*, 13(6), 699–716.

Robbins, S., Bergman, R., & Coulter, M. (2017). *Management* (8th ed.). Frenchs Forest, Australia: Person Australia Group.

Saunders, M. (2012). Choosing research participants. In G. Symon & C. Cassell (Eds.), *Qualitative organizational research* (pp. 35–52). London, UK: Sage Publications.

Shepard, L.A. (1979). Self-acceptance: The evaluative component of the self-concept construct. *American Educational Research Journal*, 16(2), 139–160.

Sweetman, J., Leach, C.W., Spears, R., Pratto, F., & Saab, R. (2013). I have a dream: A typology of social change goals. *Journal of Social and Political Psychology*, 1, 293–320.

Visovsky, C. & Morrison-Beedy, D. (2012). Participant recruitment and retention. In B.M. Melnyk & D. Morrison-Beedy (Eds.), *Intervention research: Designing, conducting, analysing, and funding* (pp. 193–212). New York, NY: Springer Publishing Company LLC.

Wouters, M. & Roijmans, D. (2011). Using prototypes to induce experimentation and knowledge integration in the development of enabling accounting information. *Contemporary Accounting Research*, 28(2), 708–736.

Wouters, M. & Sportel, M. (2005). The role of existing measures in developing and implementing performance measurement systems. *International Journal of Operations & Production Management*, 25(11), 1062–1082.

10 Selecting and Managing the Intervention Team

Although a researcher can undertake an IVR project individually depending on its scope and nature, it is generally unrealistic to suppose that a researcher will have all the requisite qualities for a successful intervention. To do IVR successfully, we find that IVR researchers usually need to collaborate with other scholars, professionals, and experts in specific areas. Hence, we refer to an intervention team rather than a research team. For some introductory insights on selecting and managing an intervention team and, specifically, the sorts of experience to look for in a researcher, identifying the gatekeeper, a 'go-to' person, key informants, and leveraging organisational skills, we refer readers to Dumay and Baard (2017).

In Chapter 3, we discuss how interventionist researchers tend to need different qualities and skill sets compared with other qualitative and quantitative researchers. Beyond the standard 'scientific' qualities most scholars hold, interventionist researchers also need practical knowledge of the social systems, operations, and processes they are studying, to the extent that they can make as sound judgements as practitioners would in the course of their duties. Hence, because IVR occurs in the field in real-life with real consequences, carefully selecting and managing the intervention team is paramount. Further, the researcher(s) must move back and forth between the emic and etic perspectives. This makes for a distinctly multi-faceted role of participant, expert, team member, comrade, theorist, and/or protagonist. Being aware of the many roles you play and empathising with what your participants are experiencing is critical to effective intervention activities.

Therefore, in this chapter, we focus on three main situations that may arise in IVR and the researcher qualities needed to cope with these situations. Thereafter, we discuss how to recruit and select team members accompanied by a real-life example of key roles and responsibilities.

'There and Back again': Managing Field Situations

One would think that moving there, to the emic world, and back again, to the etic world, would be easier if you have spent time working in professional accounting practice. However, in our experience, entering the emic world as an interventionist researcher is a very different venture from starting a new job as a practitioner. You enter intending to help people solve problems, and in helping people, you hope you can affect constructive change that increases efficiency or effectiveness, or emancipates and empowers the people within the organisation, provides them with new competencies, or whatever your noble goal may be. To accomplish these goals, interventionist researchers need to be aware of the field dynamics that surround them and be able to manage challenges arising from the field.

In his discourse on intervention theory (IVT), Argyris (1970) uses his and others' experiences from the field to offer insights on these challenges, referring to them as the conditions the interventionist researcher is likely to face in the field. Adding to the conversation, Suomala *et al.* (2014, p. 305) refer to conditions in the field as a "battlefield" containing potential conflicting agendas and interests between and within the organisation and the research team. While they note that the battlefield analogy should not "be construed in an overly combative manner", our thinking is that a battlefield signifies an insurmountable obstacle for researchers new to IVR. Obstacles, yes. Insurmountable, no. We do, however, agree with Suomala *et al.* (2014) that challenges found in the field can potentially provide a rich source of data and opportunities for knowledge exchange between practice and academia and, in turn, theoretical and practical IVR outputs. For simplicity, we use the term 'situation' hereafter to mean the conditions, challenges, controversies, or circumstances that may be present in the field. Additionally, we follow Argyris' (1970) notion of conditions being what those involved in the intervention experience.

We acknowledge that knowing about potential challenges and tensions in the field is no substitute for real IVR experience in the field. However, being accountants, we like to be prudent and take comfort in the adage 'forewarned is forearmed'. This awareness means researchers will be better able to recognise situations when they present. Over time and through experience, researchers can develop skills to balance the demands of existing situations, identify and note new or unexpected situations, manage any negative consequences resulting from them, and use what they learn to generate theoretical, practical, and societally-relevant IVR.

It is also important to remember that organisations need challenges and controversies. Without them, nothing would progress, and nothing would change. For example, in Dumay and Rooney (2016), the researchers were helping to develop an intellectual capital report for a government department. At the time, controversy was raging about the emphasis of numbers versus narratives in the report. However, they viewed the controversy as positive, not negative:

> The controversy becomes productive in its own right because it is a catalyst for the development of IC practices and the inscriptions

contained in the ICS and the debate allows managers to adopt and adapt their accounts of IC. As the Director General outlined in a 2009 interview, the existence of the controversy created tension, contributing to progress as the supporters and detractors of numbers or narrative work through the controversy "while we still have significant tensions in the organisation, sometimes they're more healthy than not, because you don't make progress unless you have some tension".

Thus, conflicts and controversies, especially those related to the IVR project, can have significant benefits and, perhaps, need to be managed rather than resolved.

Awareness and experience are not the only ways to manage situations in the field. There are many different skills that can be used, but which to use often depends on the situation. Obviously, there are too many different situations to discuss in detail, but Argyris (1970) identifies three common situations researchers may encounter and their consequences. These are: discrepancies of view between the interventionist and the participants on the nature of the problem, the most effective intervention to apply, and what is realistically achievable; researcher marginality; and mistrust leading to confrontation. Each is discussed in more detail next, along with some indispensable qualities that can help ameliorate each situation. Additionally, more insights should come to light if interventionist researchers publish their research 'warts and all' (see Suomala *et al.*, 2014; Lyly-Yrjänäinen *et al.*, 2017).

Discrepancies in View

Finding convergence between an organisation's interests and the endeavours of the researcher can be an ongoing challenge and a source of stress (Suomala *et al.*, 2014). Typically, these differences manifest in three different ways, as discussed next.

Houston, We Have a Problem . . . Do We?

There are differences in views over what the problem is, why it is a problem, the cause(s) of the problem, and where or with whom ownership of the problem lies. These differences may even be antagonistic. The participants may think they have identified the problem and its causes, but you may suggest otherwise. People do not always like to be wrong, so conflict may ensue. Additionally, when people do not clearly understand the problem or how to solve it, it is common to be defensive to counteract their perceived threat, or to avoid admitting failure, inexperience, or ineptitude (Argyris, 1970). It is discomforting to be aware of a problem and then to accept and take ownership of it. Additionally, people do not always like to admit that a problem even exists. It may be that ignorance is bliss or that an oversimplified view has taken hold in the hopes of a relatively swift and/or incremental solution rather than radical, long-term change. Alternatively, preliminary investigations may reveal a much more complex problem than initially assumed, which strikes at the heart of the organisation's competence. Lastly, on this point, the academic world prizes individuality, expressing new ideas, taking interest in the ideas of others, taking risks, and experimenting (Argyris, 1970). Encouraging these notions in participants can be extremely potent and may stimulate change, especially when the problem is likely to require an innovative or non-routine response. Conversely, that potency may lessen if it turns out there is a fairly routine solution or little change is likely to result. As researchers, these qualities can be powerful motivators drawn from the etic world.

Related to the difference in views on the nature of the problem is that a researcher adopting a divergent view thereon is perceived by participants as an outsider. It takes time to move from being a tourist to becoming 'one of us' with a position of trust within the system. The organisational culture may not be predisposed to experimenting with new ideas because new ideas are risky, which is understandable. As an outsider, it is more likely that any idea on the problem you come up with will be considered 'new'. One way around this situation is to experiment with new ideas to clarify the nature of the problem. This approach may generate new information or reveal a different view of the problem not previously considered. Regardless, the organisation may still view the researcher's ideas with scepticism because they have a low tolerance for risk and experimentation. Likewise, the organisation's degree of openness, that is, the extent to which they incorporate new information into their operations or enlarge the scope of their boundaries for new ideas, may differ significantly from that of the researcher. This can also be a function of a conservative approach to risk given the potentially serious consequences of being wrong in a competitive business environment.

Indirectly influencing discrepant views on the social system problem is a difference of opinion as to what constitutes an effective or ineffective social system. In Chapter 4, we discussed that, for social systems to be effective, they must: a) define and achieve their objectives; b) maintain their internal environment; c) adapt to their external environment, and d) accomplish a steady state. Further, a social system must have the capacity and capability to solve its problems in such a way that the chances of a problem recurring are very low. If the participants have an inaccurate perception of the problem, then it is likely that the organisation may not be as effective or as competent as it should be. Further, this means that the organisation may not be able to manage external forces and threats to its survival and stability because its processes, resources, control systems, and other structural mechanisms promoting internal coherence are unable to protect the organisation from the external environment. If the participants perceive their organisation to be effective, they may not be open to any intervention or the potential for change resulting from intervening. Participant views of social system effectiveness may be at odds with researcher views, which may yield resistance to the researcher. Resistance to interventionist researchers is a constant threat that researchers should be aware of when conducting IVR because it will influence the nature of the intervention and its potential to stimulate change.

Implementing Change: Whose Job Is It?

The second divergence between a researcher and an organisation relates to the view on the effective implementation of change (Argyris, 1970). Your task as an interventionist researcher is to generate valid information, help organisations make free, informed, and responsible choices, and cultivate an internal commitment to those choices. Argyris (1970, p. 129) argues that initiating, encouraging, and facilitating change is not the remit of the researcher—the "interventionist's job is to create all sorts of water holes", but researchers cannot force participants to drink. Opening the door for change is the participants' responsibility. Researchers conceiving the problem as encompassing and requiring change may mean the organisation perceives their problem(s) as those of change (Argyris, 1970). Additionally, participants may perceive your actions as simultaneously promoting change while attempting to manipulate the organisation to do so. This may inadvertently place the organisation in a submissive or dependent position, which compromises their free choice and internal commitment to the change process.

Also, imposing change on an organisation may provoke defensiveness, hostility, and resistance. The participants may perceive this as a threat to the stability and security of the organisation and, in the worst case, withdraw from the study (Bruhn & Rebach, 2007). If not for this reason alone, the organisation must choose to own the problem and then decide whether to make changes to solve it at their discretion. For them, there is more at stake than just an outcome; they need to contemplate their available resources, the associated costs, and the effort and processes required. As part of the intervention team, you can help them with the work required, but the organisation must have developed an internal commitment to their choices for the intervention to achieve its intended objectives.

Idealism versus Realism

The third discrepancy is an internal fight within the researcher—a conflict between what you would idealistically like to achieve versus what is realistically achievable (Argyris, 1970). The degree of conflict depends on several things. The divergence between the organisation's and the researcher's views on the nature of the problem, previously discussed. Moreover, is the problem well known to you. Does a solution already exist, or will you need to create a new one? Do you possess or have access to the capabilities needed to achieve your ideal objectives? To what extent are you likely to accept that your current capabilities may be at odds with those needed for effective intervention activities? Is your previous research or IVR experience compatible with accomplishing your ideal intervention activities?

The greater the degree of internal conflict, the greater the feelings of ineptitude, insecurity, and anxiety. This will inevitably influence your ability to conduct the IVR project effectively. However, knowing that there is potential for this problem to arise likely means you can more easily reconcile your aspirations with the reality of what is possible. Further, this challenge can be thought of as a prompt to be: a) honest with yourself about the capabilities required for different types and depths of interventions; b) open to continuous learning and skill development; c) open to adjusting your ideal objectives to align with what is realistically achievable; and d) able to terminate a relationship with the organisation if the problems are unreconcilable. The discrepancy of views, discussed here, may lead to researchers experiencing marginality and participants demonstrating mistrust and confrontation.

Interventionist Researcher Marginality

Transitioning between the etic and the emic realms requires researchers to conduct themselves and respond to situations in each realm with different approaches. Additionally, as an academic, your behaviour will be different from the participants, and you must accept that. That said, there is a delicate balance between fitting in and being your normal scholarly self, so keeping a constant vigil is wise. Transitioning between these realms also frequently requires 'taking sides'. Behaving according to your own world view may elicit reactions, ranging from perplexity to antagonism to alienation. Alienation occurs when a researcher maintains a theoretical perspective in the field, without modifying their behaviour, and does not modify their behaviour to translate their views into practical terms that are unambiguous to the organisation. Conversely, behaving as though you hold the same views as the organisation to be perceived as "one of their own" (Argyris, 1970, p. 132) can also have negative effects, especially if organisations are in denial about the problems they have. Participants may no longer generate valid information for diagnosing or solving the problem, or they may see less of a reason for change.

There is no safe ground in the middle either. Researchers straddling both realms can be misinterpreted as being conflicted, indecisive, and lacking confidence. Subtle cues from the participants may make you yourself begin to experience feelings of doubt and incompetence while in the field. Clearly, the stronger these feelings, the less effective your work will be. This is a downward spiral, where their feelings impact your feelings, which further reinforces their feelings, and on it goes. However, the real danger is in 'going native', burying yourself deeper into the social system in the hopes of making greater sense of the research context and that things will work out. Whichever the cause, experiencing marginality should be a foreboding warning to very quickly examine whether the IVR project should continue.

Mistrust and Confrontation

The third situation that may present in the field is when the participants do not have trust or confidence in the researcher. Participants must view you as a 'competent and trustworthy' insider because it fosters collaboration and helps you to understand the problems from their perspective (Suomala *et al.*, 2014). The people within an organisation may adopt the researcher's worldview when they:

- do not know exactly what the problem is;
- are under pressure to solve the problem quickly;
- are not clear which solutions are feasible; and/or
- lack the willingness to implement a solution because it involves an unpopular action, or they want to transfer the responsibility for problem-solving entirely to the researcher.

In adopting the researcher's world view, the participants can begin to also straddle the etic and emic realm. This is not behaviour consistent with their status quo (Argyris, 1970). The result is usually feelings of confusion, ambiguity, conflict, and doubt on the part of the participants. That is, they become marginalised, not you. In this situation, it is highly probable that people will preserve their self-acceptance, and that might mean they turn against you. After all, people like to feel strong and confident in their own abilities and decisions, and they tend to not enjoy facing their own shortcomings. Moreover, confirmation bias is always a factor. It is very common for people to interpret information in a way that is consistent with their values and the norms of their organisation, rather than the interpretation you intended. When combined with the need to preserve self-acceptance, participants following their own interpretations can result in mistrust and confrontation for the researcher. Again, a downward cycle of reinforced anxiety on both sides ensues, and participants are more likely to withdraw from the project.

To assess and manage these three situations—discrepancies in the scope and nature of the problem, becoming marginalised, and losing the trust of the participants—researchers must be self-aware, self-accepting, and conscious of their ability to influence others (Argyris, 1970). Having the right qualities to deal with these situations is an important part of this process, which we discuss in more detail next.

Qualities Needed by an Interventionist Researcher

Beyond self-acceptance and self-awareness, there are four other qualities that can help prevent challenges from becoming bad situations. These are confidence in your intervention strategy, an accurate perception of a stressful reality, acceptance that mistrust and confrontation are relatively commonplace, and trust in your experience of reality.

The Intervention Strategy: Confidence and Cognitive Maps

Argyris (1970) argues that, to manage IVR situations, having confidence in one's intervention strategy requires a cognitive map and being clear about one's motives for intervening in a social system.

A very broad definition is that cognitive mapping is a process consisting of mental, emotional, and intellectual changes whereby a person acquires knowledge, stores it in memory, and decodes that knowledge into the characteristics associated with experiences, events, and observations in their everyday lives (Downs & Stea, 1973). In other words, a cognitive map is a concept or idea that we have in our minds to help think about how we know, understand, and navigate the world around us. Further, Golledge and Timmermanns (1990) maintain that cognitive maps are knowledge structures that develop and expand with age and education. Downing (1992, p. 442) extends this idea through stating that cognitive maps

> suspend impressions, thoughts, feelings and ideas until, for some reason, consciously or unconsciously, the mind solicits, changes, and often distorts or manipulates its contents for some immediate purpose. In this way, cognitive maps (images) allow us to bridge time, by using past experiences to understand present and future situations.

Thus, our experiences influence how our cognitive map is constructed. Kitchin (1994) also views cognitive maps as dynamic because when we combine diverse knowledge structures and information using perception, memory, recall, and reorganisation, we form cognitive maps for specific tasks or specific events, including IVR and its associated activities.

So how does a cognitive map enable researchers to generate an intervention strategy? First, it helps us assess and navigate the emic landscape to help an organisation with its problems (Argyris, 1970), because cognitive maps contain knowledge, images, and attitudes about our environment that assists us to make sense of, simplify, and create order where complexity prevails (Kitchin, 1994). Second, we are better able to see how the individual components of the problem connect by using the knowledge structures and information stored in our cognitive map. Third, it helps when managing change as it enables researchers to ponder the benefits and challenges of a change program resulting from intervention, and thus sustains researcher autonomy and avoids researcher marginality. A cognitive map encapsulates experiences and stores information about the etic and emic environments used in making everyday decisions which guide behaviour. Four, we can use past knowledge and experience to identify a range of interventions, likely to be most effective in solving organisational problems.

A well-articulated and internalised intervention strategy shows consistency when intervening, which is important for developing trust and esteem. Consistency implies that interventions have specific objectives and are based on a specific set of purposeful values. Consistency also helps participants to understand exactly what is going on and what the researcher's intentions are, which means they are better able to make informed decisions about whether or how to collaborate with the researcher to solve problems. These dynamics help build credibility, which, in turn, translates to a reputation for competence, that is, someone who knows what they are doing. Without credibility, there is a much higher risk of the participants rejecting the intervention, withdrawing from the research project early, or marginalisation on either side of the fence. Further, an informed and prudent intervention strategy provides insights into one's limitations concerning the repertoire of skills and behaviours needed to see the project through. It can also act as a kind of forecast as to what difficulties might be on the horizon, both generally and due to lack of skills, and to put contingencies in place or take another route accordingly.

Knowing your own motives for undertaking IVR also boosts confidence, internally and externally. Based on our interpretation of Argyris (1970), we find that researchers should ask themselves the following questions. Why do I want to do IVR? Am I trying to fulfill my desires to be a hero and help others who are experiencing significant problems? Fulfilling personal needs can lead to manipulative behaviour, conscious or otherwise. That undermines the ability of the participants to make a free and informed choice and all the consequences that come with that. Other questions are: Do I want to engage in IVR because it is different and presents an opportunity to make a strong theoretical contribution to the literature? This motive might mean you need to be careful about excluding the practical contributions IVR should be making. Do I want to help others solve their own problems now and in the future by building skills and competencies? How do my motives relate to the theoretical, practical, and societal output of the IVR project? How might my motives influence how I intervene in a social system? Ideally, fulfilling your own needs and improving the competencies of others should be the overriding motivation for conducting IVR. Hence, consider your motives and make sure they are, first, aligned with the objectives of the project and, second, those objectives are embedded in the intervention strategy.

Accurate Perception of Stressful Reality

Possessing and developing a cognitive map helps researchers to generate a considered, internalised, and flexible intervention strategy. Accordingly, this provides researchers with the capacity to perceive the reality of the emic environment and intervention accurately, especially when the environment is stressful (Argyris, 1970). The emic environment may present difficulties and challenges that create stress; this is equally applicable to the etic world. Further, an accurate perception of the worlds inhabited under stress build researcher awareness of potential defence mechanisms that may inhibit the intervention. Additionally, the manifestation of researcher defence mechanisms may cause participants to question the researcher or become confrontational. Or it may give the impression of incompetence, insecurity, and an inability to control one's behaviours.

The interventionist researcher must be able to explain the reality they are immersed in while conducting IVR, regardless of whether the situation is stressful or not. Explaining reality is useful because IVR must generate valid and useful information, even when under strain. An accurate perception of the stressful reality also enables the researcher to select suitable skills and behaviours to address the difficulties in the emic environment to better cope with stress. Again, this creates a perception that the researcher is competent, confident, and flexible in the participants. From all these things, two fundamental benefits are likely to emerge: less of a divergence between the participants and the researcher and reconciliation of your ideal objectives and what is realistically achievable.

Acceptance of a Social System's Mistrust

Mistrust and confrontation are generally undesirable. While confrontation can be healthy, confrontation from mistrust and resentment is probably going to jeopardise an effective intervention. Argyris (1970) states that researchers must value this undesirable situation. For instance, Suomala *et al.* (2014) argue that IVR challenges provide the potential for meaningful knowledge exchanges between the researcher and the participants, as well as the constructive generation of innovative knowledge. Thus, researchers should encourage participants to articulate their frustrations, reservations, and antagonisms about the problem, how to solve it, and indeed your own shortcomings as they perceive them. Articulating mistrust is often an effective way of reducing participants' anxiety about a problem.

Similarly, a confrontation sustains participants in dialogue with the researcher, which provides an opportunity for both the researcher and the participants to explore and discuss feelings, problems, and other differences. It may also help when implementing the intervention (see Dumay & Rooney, 2016). When participants confront the researcher, it "is a sign that the interventionist is being taken seriously" (Argyris, 1970, p. 147). For researchers, confrontation presents the possibility not only for self-assessment, reflection, and an experience of self-growth and development, but also for integration into one's cognitive map.

Argyris (1970) argues that everyone engaged in the intervention must use every dilemma, every difference in view, and every conflict as a potential opportunity for learning. Thus, those 'stressful situations' can be converted into a state of psychological success, strengthen collaborations, and increase participants' self-confidence to mobilise effective problem-solving activities. Demonstrating an acceptance of mistrust and confrontation and using this to sustain dialogue with the participants may help the researcher address situations stemming from mistrust and confrontation.

Trust in One's Own Experience of Reality

A researcher needs to trust their own experience of their world and their qualities to manage situations in the field and mobilise themselves to conduct effective IVR (Argyris, 1970). For a researcher to have a reasonably high degree of self-trust, they must: a) have a well-thought-out, internalised, and flexible intervention strategy supported by an internally consistent cognitive map; b) be able to accurately perceive reality even under stress; c) have clear motives for intervening that serve their own and the social system's best interests; and d) be capable of learning and help others learn through respect and acceptance of a social system's confrontations and mistrust. Trusting in your experience of reality during an IVR project helps to develop a cognitive map as does developing the intervention strategy and constantly endeavouring to improve one's skills in IVR. Moreover, it enables researchers to reduce concern about their marginality and the potential for ongoing social system mistrust and confrontation.

An Intervention Team

In previous chapters, we discussed that IVR is challenging because the research process can take time. Further, IVR requires complex decision-making at various stages. Designing and developing an intervention in collaboration with participants requires careful negotiation. The researcher needs to adopt multiple roles during the IVR process, and a successful project requires diverse skills. In short, IVR may not be for everyone (Gitlin & Czaja, 2016).

Outside of the range of individual attributes, experience, and knowledge we identified in Chapter 3, Gitlin and Czaja (2016) state that interventionist researchers require a sound belief that the intervention has value and can make a real difference in a person's life. Additionally, interventionist researchers require "action skills", which include: selecting and recruiting members for the intervention design team; developing an intervention strategy; building and sustaining the intervention team to meet the demands of the IVR process; communicating, collaborating, and negotiating with multiple stakeholders throughout the project; managing research budgets and monitoring expenditure; managing any problems arising during the project, including participant selection, recruitment, and retention issues; and leading others through all phases of the intervention process. While a single researcher can undertake IVR, the nature of the project and intervention, the participants, and the researcher qualities needed may dictate otherwise. I, Vicki, came to understand this when embarking on Project A as discussed in Chapter 11.

Selecting and Recruiting the Intervention Team

The discussion in this section is based on my experience when working on Project A. It spans selecting and recruiting the intervention team, identifying team member roles and responsibilities, and managing the intervention team during the IVR process. Regardless of whether a researcher is a novice or expert, in our view, this discussion may be helpful as it presents a real-life example of selecting and managing an intervention team in the absence of other explicit examples in the IVR literature.

There are numerous matters to ponder before selecting and recruiting the intervention team. In my experience in both my doctoral work and Project A, the nature of the intervention is the dominant driver in determining who is going to be part of the team. If researchers intend to design and develop a novel intervention, you may need team members with specialised skills. Note, however, that bringing in specialists can be expensive, so consider your budget here. If funds are constrained, you will need to adjust your intervention or reconsider it entirely to ensure you can afford the required skills. Using an existing intervention in a different context with some minor modifications may not require specialised skills. You may already have sufficient qualities to undertake minor design and construction work.

The project or intervention objective(s) and the project deliverables the researcher needs to achieve will also direct team composition and the associated critical objectives, activities, and tasks that must be done in each phase of the project. This informs who, and just as importantly when, specific team members will be required. I found that I needed both permanent and temporary team members. Roles such as the co-investigator, project coordinator, teaching assistant, quality assurance specialist, and mentors were permanent because I needed to confer with them throughout the project. Temporary team members were brought in to handle very specific aspects of the project, such as developing the graphics and building the website. In reflecting on the nature of the team, I realised that I had assembled an intervention team rather than a pure research team made up of academics, professionals, and technical experts, each with a unique role, different responsibilities, and corresponding work-loads as discussed next.

The principal investigator and any co-investigator(s) will probably have the heaviest workloads. As such, balancing commitments to the existing academic responsibilities of these investigators with the demands of the IVR project can be problematic. Much depends on the amount of funding the project attracts, and the restrictions imposed by your institution about what scholars can or cannot do when working on a large research project. My employer, for instance, did not want an experienced teacher out of the classroom to work on an IVR project. So, I had to carefully think about what aspects of my teaching work I could outsource that would respect their position. I had to make sure that no student was disadvantaged by my outsourcing any teaching work, and I had to free up time to complete my IVR activities within the confines of a time-sensitive project.

Using the Interventionist Research Framework (IRF) to guide planning your IVR project can help to identify the roles, responsibilities, and the requisite skill set amongst the team. Project management techniques, such as setting milestones and preparing Gantt charts (see Chapter 12), show what work is required, how much time is available to do the work, and the deadlines: they provide a relatively complete picture of which team members need to do what and by when. Hence, potential team members can realistically assess the commitment that will be required of them and accept or not. Researchers must ensure they meet a project's milestones notwithstanding team member turnover or personal crises; therefore, a considered approach to team recruitment and selection is critical.

Part of project planning entails having an idea of your budget. Research-ers intending to apply for competitive grants will have an idea of the available funds. Because you must present your budget and its rationale as part of the application, applying for funds will help in configuring the intervention team and determining the associated cost of using specialised and routine skill sets to accomplish the required work. For Project A, I probably under-budgeted a little because I did not want to present what could be construed as an overly ambitious project. Nor did I want to be in a position where I would have unspent funds that someone else could use. Forfeiting unused grant funding has reputational implications. My tactic was to leverage the psychology that $4.99 is far cheaper than $5.00 or $5.50. Anecdotally, to my surprise, progress on Project A was receiving attention from the wider academic community, in part because of frequent postings on a blog about the project and because the value of the work performed was perceived as significant. Also, notably, the 'discounted' 51¢ found its way into the research grant account for some project extras. It also provided some relief after a very busy year juggling the project and other academic responsibilities, including writing this book. An important lesson that I learned from an associate was that you might not get the funding you want, so it's wise to have a plan B for your IVR project because the outcomes from grant funding may vary.

The last point I want to make about selecting and recruiting your IVR team is about myself as an interventionist researcher. Be honest with yourself about what you can and cannot accomplish, including the researcher qualities you do or do not have. My self-awareness and self-reflective abilities are important skills that I learnt when studying for my MBA. This has stood me in good stead in my professional life and the challenging and dynamic environment of academia. I am persistent, tenacious, and confident, yet cautious in my approach to my work. I am flexible, creative, adaptable, and a good trouble-shooter, but I'm not always as patient as I should be. I can also be risk-averse, and I am highly respectful of diversity and culture. I have well-developed listening and oral communication skills, although these are always a work-in-progress. I am a fair negotiator and reasonably adept at preventing and managing conflict. Plus, I am a meticulous management accountant, always seeking ongoing professional development. If my research project work needs a capability that I do not have, I am not shy or embarrassed to admit it, and I engage team members whose skill set embraces what mine does not.

So how do we recruit team members? Each institution has its procedures and policies related to staffing. Often there are specific templates for posting job opportunities. Roles have set descriptions. There are requirements for who may or may not recruit and interview staff. For my part, I am subject to a well-developed enterprise bargaining agreement that applies to a range of job titles, classifications, general responsibilities, and associated remuneration. On the downside, it can be restrictive; on the upside, it means you don't have to reinvent the recruitment wheel, and it's useful for project budgeting. On another note, always be prepared that hiring processes can take time. If you have a time-sensitive project, this could cause serious delays, which in turn can affect your funding, and other staff you may have secured who cannot or will not renegotiate their time window. For Project A, some of the team members had an Australian Business Number and, hence, issued invoices for the work done, which obviated the need for a lengthy, formal hiring process. Some team members were full-time academics or professionals who did not require payment. The project coordinator was someone I knew with extensive project management experience in a high-pressure information technology environment. Although a formal hiring process was required, it was streamlined because they had previously worked at the university. It took about four weeks to complete the process, which was one week less than the five weeks I had allowed. I also recruited a teaching assistant I knew and trusted, and who had worked with me before. Again, pre-approval was in place, so no formal recruitment process was needed.

To find the two higher degree research (HDR) students in organisational psychology, I used an internal advertisement supported by their department. There were nine applicants that I and the co-investigator interviewed in a group. Given the role, the responsibilities, and the essential skill set required, we identified one strong candidate. Having worked as a research assistant on another project, the hiring process was again substantially simpler. Although we ideally needed two students, we only engaged one at first. Halfway through the project, the HDR student was offered full-time employment and could not continue working on Project A. The student was replaced with a candidate from an official higher education placement program who had professional experience, the requisite qualities, who was upscaling their academic qualifications, and was immediately available.

For me, three important recommendations arose from the recruitment and selection experience. One, be aware of and prepared for a range of factors that will influence the recruitment process. Two, know the approximate recruitment time required to build your intervention team then, if possible, use a variety of recruitment methods to avoid any delays. Three, know the exact role, responsibilities, and skill set that your team members will need to accomplish their IVR work. More on this is discussed next.

Team Roles and Responsibilities

My professional experience and my scholarly knowledge of teams and teamwork have taught me several important things—specifically, that team members work interdependently because they depend on each other to do their work, and they share knowledge and efforts to achieve the project objectives and deliverables. Team interdependence extends into a team's workflow, which encapsulates how the project work is executed and how the team works together. To a large extent, harmonious workflows depend on clearly delineating people's roles and responsibilities (assuming they have the requisite qualities). Levi (2017) argues that team roles are crucial building blocks of performance because people know what is expected of them and how their roles relate to what other team members are doing. I found that stating the responsibilities attached to each role and outlining the essential qualities required to do well in that role were instrumental in retaining most team members. Additionally, I shared the project plan with everyone on the team. As a result, there were minimal delays in the project and team member turnover was very low.

Early in the project, when I was assembling Project A's team, I had a meeting where team members introduced themselves to each other and explained what they did and when. These introductions helped establish a rapport and harmonious workflows between the team members. I strongly believe this influenced the success of the project. Table 10.1 identifies the team roles, their main responsibilities, and their requisite qualities.

Table 10.1 Project A's Intervention Team

Role	Main Responsibilities	Qualities
Project Lead	• Write the grant application • Prepare the project budget • Construct the project plan • Identify potential team members • Collect valid and useful information • Create the framework for the intervention, including design activities • Lead the intervention team	• IVR knowledge and experience • Project A content expertise • Experience in competitive grant writing • Teamwork and team management skills • Ability to exercise financial control • Excellent interpersonal skills—collaboration, communication, negotiating, and conflict management • Critical and analytical thinking • Flexibility and adaptability • Troubleshooting skills
Co-investigator	• Evaluate all aspects of Project A • Assess the feasibility of the intervention • Assess the ethical aspects of Project A • Engage in quality assurance work	• Excellent communication skills • Relevant intervention content expertise
Project Coordinator	• Coordinate the production of the teaching and learning materials, incl. video, graphics, and web designer • Monitor project progress using Microsoft Project • Generate project progress and budgetary reports • Coordinate team member recruitment • Complete timesheets, collect invoices, and coordinate payments • Coordinate team meetings	• Project management experience and skills • Excellent communication skills • Sound knowledge of higher education processes and systems, incl. generating timesheets and processing invoices • Ability to use Microsoft Word, Excel, and Project • Ability to work in teams • Flexibility and adaptability • Excellent problem-solving skills • Excellent organisation skills • Ability to work under pressure
Learning Designer	• Work closely with the project lead, organisational psychology students, and the graphic and web designer • Evaluate the design of teaching and learning materials • Create teaching and learning materials • Quality assure resources and the assessment portfolio • Map learning outcomes, teaching activities, and assessment tasks	• Knowledge and experience in designing learning experiences • Broad and deep knowledge of current trends in learning technologies, online education, and adult education • Excellent communication skills • Problem-solving skills • Ability to work with others • Critical and analytical thinking skills

Teaching Assistant	• Mark assessments for the two postgraduate units • Monitor support students with the online learning components • Provide ad hoc student consultation	• Knowledge and experience in teaching postgraduate management accounting students • A command of the unit content • Excellent oral and written communication skills • Knowledge and experience to manage online learning components using a learning management system • Good problem-solving skills • Excellent organisation skills
Media Students (four)	• Design, shoot, and produce three, three-minute live-action videos • Source students for the videos • Draft production schedules to meet Project A milestones • Prepare a detailed budget • Coordinate with the Learning Designer to incorporate approved production principles	• Previous or current enrolment in a Bachelor of Media degree • Experience in producing short creative and corporate videos • Ability to manage and edit educational media • Knowledge and experience in post-production work • Time management skills • Attention to detail • Flexibility • Good communications and teamwork skills

Organisational Psychology Students (two)	• Create the following teaching and learning materials:
	  – Module notes and readings
	  – Brief vignettes (sourced/developed)
	  – Three small case studies (500–800 words).
	  – Five quizzes of 10 to 15 questions
	  – Three scripts for educational videos on a range of teamwork skills (350–400 words)
	• Work with Project Lead and Project Coordinator to ensure materials meet intervention requirements
		• A Bachelor's degree in Organisational Psychology
		• Currently enrolled in a Master's or Doctoral Organisational Psychology degree
		• Work experience in the education sector
		• Well-developed knowledge of teams, teamwork, team theory, and teamwork skills
		• Excellent written and verbal communication skills
		• Excellent organisation skills
		• Ability to use Microsoft Word
		• Ability to work independently and as part of a team
		• Flexibility and adaptability

(Continued)

Table 10.1 (Continued)

Role	Main Responsibilities	Qualities
Graphic/ Web Designer	• Undertake the following design work for Project A: – A concept logo. – Three cover concepts for the teaching and learning materials and assessment portfolio – Templates, forms, and other interactive graphic materials – "Quick guides" with graphics for use by multiple stakeholders • Programming with Moodle	• Academic qualifications in graphic and web design • Experience in graphic and web design for diverse stakeholders • Working knowledge of programming • Some knowledge of working with target users • Excellent problem-solving skills • Creative thinking skills • Flexibility and adaptability • Ability to work with others and independently • Excellent communication skills • Excellent time management skills
Research Assistant	• Assist with identifying readings and resources centred on teams and teamwork • Create and maintain Endnote with teams and teamwork literature • Write and maintain field notes from intervention activities	• Previous research experience at a Master's or Doctoral level. • Excellent written and oral communication skills • Demonstrated ability to work independently
Quality Assurance Specialist	• Assess all Project A teaching and learning materials and assessments, applying overarching quality assurance principles and using quality standards • Provide advice on quality assurance improvements when required	• Expertise in adult education • Expertise in quality assurance
Project A Mentors	• Provide advice to the Project Lead on Project A intervention activities as required • Offer contemporary insights on intervention design to incorporate feasibility issues for multiple stakeholders	• Expertise on Project A content including teams and teamwork

This list is specific to Project A; your roster will inevitably be different. For instance, team members may include people responsible for: a) conducting interviews and observations within organisations; b) recruiting and selecting participants; c) entering and checking data, doing data analyses, and interpreting the results; and d) practitioners, managers, and other professionals from the organisation under research. In Chapters 1, 4, 5, and 12, we identify the role of the gatekeeper and the role of the go-to person. The gatekeeper's responsibilities may vary, but normally he or she helps the researcher access the participants, identify resources, and monitor the implementation. Typically, the gatekeeper has management experience and good people and technical skills. The go-to person is an ally (Dumay & Baard, 2017) who may or may not be part of the intervention team. Selecting and establishing your team is one critical aspect of the intervention team. However, maintaining and motivating them to persist through the IVR process is another.

Managing the Intervention Team

Each project lead has a different approach to managing the intervention team. This is the way I approached this critical task.

As the leader of Project A, I saw my responsibility to the team as entrenching and sustaining a shared sense of purpose, a shared mission, and articulating team goals aligned with the overall intervention objectives and what each team member wanted to accomplish from their experience working on the project. It was my job to set an enthusiastic and collaborative tone, energise people, and help them appreciate the importance of the project and the significance of their contributions to it. During the entire project from recruitment to close-out, I fostered a strong sense of the value of teams and teamwork. Notably, it would have been hypocritical not to since Project A was about cultivating teamwork skills in students.

I also created an atmosphere of open and honest communication and psychological safety. Team members were encouraged to offer ideas and make suggestions on the direction and content of the project and to freely and openly agree, disagree, or agree to disagree with each other on project work. Doing so assisted in building a climate of trust, where team members could communicate their feelings and reactions, respectfully, and with trust and confidence in each other. I achieved this by being approachable and available to team members when they needed to talk or needed help and through frequent team meetings. Levi (2017) states that regular team meetings are essential for sharing information, reviewing project progress, saving time, and improving team effectiveness.

The frequency of team meetings may vary from one IVR project to another and be subject to the needs of and problems faced by team members when doing their project work. I found that clearly articulating an expectation for team meetings and offering reasons for this expectation during the recruitment process was useful. During Project A, team meetings were sporadic, but Skype helped when team members could not attend in person. Despite this, the members welcomed team meetings because they: a) provided an avenue to discuss project work and share experiences; b) validated the hard work that team members were doing; c) recognised and celebrated team member wins, commiserated their losses and frustrations, and reinforced the value of their contributions and their role in the project; d) provided an opportunity for discussions and decisions on key issues; and e) provided an excuse to eat double chocolate Tim Tams and drink too much coffee. Team meetings were very important for the media and psychology students because working in a real-life intervention project was an investment in their professional development. So, it was important to nurture their learning experiences, ensure their well-being throughout the project, and reinforce their equality as important and valued team members.

Overall, managing a team relies on maintaining open communication, listening and paying attention to all team members, acknowledging good work, figuring out collectively how to move forward when problems and frustrations manifest, and being real about the need for discipline when it comes to managing time, money, and delivering on one's responsibilities. As the project leader, I also shared leadership with team members when I had no expertise with the task required. For instance, the media students assumed responsibility for and made strategic decisions on behalf of the team about producing the videos. Similarly, the organisational psychology HDR student developed the module about team respect, trust, and professionalism because she had practical experience and knowledge in that area.

Concluding Remarks

This chapter presented three common situations researchers may face when undertaking IVR. Over time, and as your repository of knowledge grows, dealing with these challenges becomes normalised. We hope that accounting scholars will endeavour to share these situations in their publications to help build that body of knowledge. The same goes for insights into qualities that can counter problematic situations in the field. Suomala *et al.* (2014, p. 306) state that the situations that present in the field when doing IVR, although challenging, offer a "rich and inspiring field of opportunities for knowledge exchange between researchers and practitioners and the potential conflicts between the collaborating parties can offer significant seeds for generating innovative knowledge". In our opinion, mobilising knowledge exchange and generating new knowledge occurs through selecting and managing an effective intervention team.

References

Argyris, C. (1970). *Intervention theory and method: A behavioural science view.* Reading, MA: Addison-Wesley Publishing Company.

Bruhn, J.G. & Rebach, H.M. (2007). *Sociological practice: Intervention and social change.* New York, NY: Springer Science.

Dumay, J. & Baard, V. (2017). An introduction to interventionist research in accounting. In Z. Hoque, L.D. Parker, M.A. Covaleski, & K. Haynes (Eds.), *The Routledge companion to qualitative accounting research methods* (pp. 265–283). New York, NY: Routledge.

Dumay, J. & Rooney, J. (2016). Numbers versus narrative: An examination of a controversy. *Financial Accountability & Management*, 32(2), 202–231.

Downing, F. (1992). Image banks: Dialogues between the past and the future. *Environment and Behaviour*, 24(4), 441–470.

Downs, R.M. & Stea, D. (1973). Theory. In R.M. Downs & D. Stea (Eds.), *Image and environment* (pp. 1–7). Chicago, IL: Aldine.

Gitlin, L.N. & Czaja, S.J. (2016). *Behavioural intervention research: Designing, evaluating and implementing.* New York, NY: Springer Publishing Company.

Golledge, R.G. & Timmermanns, H. (1990). Applications of behavioural research on spatial problems I: Cognition. *Progress in Human Geography*, 14(1), 57–99.

Kitchin, R.M. (1994). Cognitive maps: What are they and why study them? *Journal of Environmental Psychology*, 14(1), 1–19.

Levi, D. (2017). *Group dynamics for teams* (5th ed.). Thousand Oaks, CA: Sage Publications.

Lyly-Yrjänäinen, J., Suomala, P., Laine, T., & Mitchell, F. (2017). *Interventionist management accounting research: Theory contributions with societal impact.* London and New York: Routledge.

Suomala, P., Lyly-Yrjänäinen, J., & Lukka, K. (2014). Battlefield around interventions: A reflective analysis of conducting interventionist research in management accounting. *Management Accounting Research*, 25, 304–314.

11 Intervention Design and Construction

Using interventions to solve real-life practical problems is the fundamental difference between IVR and other research paradigms. Despite its centrality to the methodology, the accounting literature offers little insight into what should be considered when designing an intervention (Baard, 2010; Dumay & Baard, 2017). Mullen (1994) states that intervention design is a planned approach to achieving organisational and social change through solving problems. There are multiple considerations in intervention design, including but not limited to: its theoretical underpinnings; the intervention type, focus, and intensity; researcher views and actions; the expertise and capabilities of people who will use the intervention; financial constraints; the nature of the problem; and the nature of the social system, its culture, values, structure and control mechanisms, and its everyday operations. These are important considerations because they assist with designing effective interventions and because they influence how an intervention is implemented. Additionally, they contribute to IVRs' reliability, validity, and ultimately its legitimacy. Unfortunately, intervention design and construction are the least developed aspects of this methodology to this day (Mullen, 1994; Baard & Dumay, 2018). Therefore, in this chapter, we follow on from Chapter 5 and explain the critical objectives and activities associated with designing interventions in greater detail. The chapter concludes with the case of an intervention in a university that followed the IRF.

Problem-Centred Intervention Design

So, how do we systematically and deliberately design relevant accounting interventions for real-world contexts? Using the IRF, Phase 3's activities span scientific, technical, and practical knowledge and are influenced by the politics of the organisation, that is, how and where power, status, and authority sit; key stakeholders—academic and non-academic; economic constraints; researcher qualities and social system capabilities; and resources. Moreover, intervention design also depends on researchers collaborating with the research participants before, during, and after the design process (Mullen, 1994; Fawcett *et al.*, 1994). Accordingly, intervention design and construction require a multi-faceted and considered approach. Next, we briefly revisit social problem specification and information synthesis because they are antecedents to intervention creation.

Social Problem Specification and Information Synthesis

Social problem diagnosis, analysis, and information gathering provide the foundation for all design activities as they identify a problem requiring intervention. That is, during Phase 1 and Phase 2 of the Interventionist Research Framework (IRF) discussed in Chapter 5, a social problem or need is specified, requiring an intervention. Mullen (1994) states that during these phases and before engaging in design activities, researchers should investigate whether there is an existing intervention with potential utility for their IVR project. If an existing intervention has the potential to solve the problem, researchers should use these phases to assess the intervention for its strengths, weaknesses, and potential efficacy. Following an intervention assessment, researchers must decide whether any modifications or further development is needed to make the intervention fit-for-purpose. Any further intervention development is addressed in Phase 3. When a suitable intervention does not already exist, researchers will need to think about designing and constructing a new one.

Regardless of whether an existing intervention undergoes further development or a novel intervention is designed, researchers must further ascertain if the proposed intervention, is feasible (Mullen, 1994; Thomas, 1984). That is, its ability to effectively solve the problem in the real world (Baard, 2004). Taking this approach is both practical and sensible as it increases the chances of success and may reveal constraints, participant opposition, or other unforeseen problems (Baard, 2004). Thomas (1984) identifies several factors that are important to assessment, which we have adapted to the accounting IVR context, as shown in Table 11.1.

In the next sections, we follow the remainder of the intervention design activities in Phase 3 of the IRF.

The Design Objective

Closely associated with the social problem specification is outlining the design objective. Researchers must distinguish between intervention objectives and design objectives (Mullen, 1994). An intervention objective is a statement about the development of an intervention or social technology aimed at solving a particular social system problem. The design objective refers to the tasks to be accomplished, comprising the intervention. The term social technology is interesting because it can be an artefact used by practitioners or researchers to achieve an intervention objective; a process, strategic plan, idea, method, or policy to be tested; or, for example,

Table 11.1 Feasibility Assessment Factors

Feasibility Factors	*Description*
Technical	The extent to which an intervention has a technical foundation using: • Theory and/or a conceptual framework • Research findings from the problem diagnosis • Research participant personal and professional experiences and professional knowledge in relation to the problem and their social system • Technical knowledge relevant to accounting, e.g., international financial accounting standards or auditing • Interdisciplinary knowledge outside of accounting • Current practice in the researcher's area of accounting • The researcher's personal experiences with the problem or context • The researcher's professional experiences from working in the field
Organisational	The extent to which people or organisations have competences to design and develop interventions: • Researcher(s) qualities and social system actors' competences. • Leaders, managers, and supervisory support • Research and administrative support • Researcher and social system time, material, and technology resources
Economic	The extent to which the benefits of intervention design and construction are likely to exceed the associated costs: • Monetary cost, e.g., software, research assistant time, and costs incurred by the social system • Qualitative human factors, e.g., people's effort, knowledge, experience, power, status, commitment, values, emancipation/de-emancipation, and empowerment/disenfranchisement • Benefits, e.g., likelihood of solving the problem, sustained effectiveness, improved performance (financial and non-financial), and theoretical and practical contributions
Political	The extent to which the proposed intervention: • Includes design contributions from the people in the social system • Is acceptable to people with the power to authorise design, development, adoption, and implementation • Is compatible with the system culture and values
Utility	The extent to which the intervention: • Will be adopted and used by the people experiencing the problem • Is easy to use • Requires training people before use

Source: Adapted from Baard (2004) and Thomas (1984)

a product, machine, software, or information system (Graham & Neu, 2003). Thus, an intervention can be either tangible or intangible, which is an important design consideration.

While the accounting literature does not reveal specific design objectives, we derived examples from recently published accounting IVR. For instance, Dumay's (2010) intervention design objective was to create a strategic plan that would communicate a new marketing strategy to all a university's stakeholders. This is an abstract social technology designed to address the need for an organisation to explain how it creates value. Cullen *et al.* (2013, p. 215) state that the objective of their overarching reverse logistics research was to "develop a set of diagnostic tools to assist organisations implement effective reverse logistics operations". This intervention relied on the abstract nature of expert knowledge, and the diagnostic tools developed were tangible technologies to address reverse logistics issues. Campanale *et al.* (2014, p. 170) explicitly identify their objective as "a system which could provide information able to trace the consumption of resources to patient needs and support a fair assignment of fixed available resources to activities". Although implied, Chiucchi's (2013) objective was to design a system that could measure the amount and performance of different components of IC to improve the firm's performance in these areas. Thus, all forms of intervention have either explicit or implied design objectives.

Design Domain

The design domain defines the bounds of the intervention and, as shown in Table 9.2, it consists of a set of interacting components. There are three notable aspects of the design domain. First, interventions do not necessarily constitute solutions to problems; they can also address a need, for instance, back burning to prevent catastrophic fires or one of many other objectives as outlined in the table. Second, outlining the design domain may happen before, or concurrently with, developing the design objective(s); this is not necessarily a linear sequence of activities. Third, the components provided in Table 11.2 are the essential ones, but this is not an exhaustive list. Each IVR project is different, and there may be many more relevant components.

Design Specifications

Design specifications are the characteristics an intervention must have to solve the diagnosed problem (Fawcett *et al.*, 1994), such as the training needed to use intervention (Rothman & Thomas, 1994) or how compatible the intervention is with the current organisational processes (Baard, 2010). Some examples of real-world interventions include Campanale *et al.* (2014), who prescribed that their costing system had to: produce information consistent with a hospital's current workflows; support the individual responsibilities of the clinicians; and produce the information

Table 11.2 Design Domain Components

Components	Description	Examples
Research Setting	Considering the intervention objective, where will your intervention occur?	A small-medium privately-owned firm, a hospital, a community mental health centre, a public school, a large accounting firm, a non-profit organisation, residential aged care facility, a services or manufacturing organisation, government agency, a specific department in a large retail store
Objectives for Change	Solve a problem (remediation)	Install a surveillance system to stop excessive stock theft in a warehouse
	Improve functioning or performance to a level (enhancement)	Modify current reward systems to enhance customer service satisfaction from the industry average of 90% to 95%
	Improve a social systems' ability to manage difficulties or solve own problems (competence)	Provide graduate employees with training on changes in auditing standards to avoid unnecessary delays during time-sensitive audits
	Deliver knowledge and information for better understanding (education)	Create an interactive information system to help small business owners understand how changes in government taxation regulations influence their firm
	Eliminate potential difficulties before they become problems (prevention)	Modify a reverse logistics system for a major department store to avoid excessive returned goods costs from its new online purchasing system
	Provide material and financial resources	Provide pro-bono accounting services to a non-profit organisation having difficulties raising donations
Targets	Who or what is the target of the intervention?	Individuals, behaviour, groups, processes, competencies, systems, control mechanisms
Participants	Who is going to participate in intervention design?	Individuals, teams, groups, organisations, communities. Participants may grow during intervention design or as problems arise
Roles	What are the roles of the researchers and participants in the intervention?	Objective setters, intervention designers, implementers. Again, roles may change during design or as problems arise

Source: Adapted from Thomas (1984) and Baard (2004).

those clinicians needed. Moreover, budgets were tight, so time and money taken to establish and, more importantly, maintain the intervention had to be minimal. Chiucchi's (2013, p. 52) intellectual capital (IC) intervention had to "measure overall IC elements and their performance, promote discussion on IC, and improve overall financial performance". Chiucchi does not discuss compatibility requirements, and not considering this factor— in this case, some non-negotiable management controls—meant the IC management system could not be implemented. Data needed to be re-categorised and IC performance indicators needed to be recalculated—all of which was very time-consuming. Although implied, Dumay (2010) provides some evidence of design requirements—for example, professional and academic staff needed to be involved in developing the intervention to ensure that it incorporated both the themes common to all stakeholders as well as their diverse needs. Further, the strategic document had to be developed and written such that people without accounting and business expertise could understand the document.

Other Design Considerations

In contemplating, other design consideration, Thomas (1984, p. 97) asks: "What makes for a good intervention?". Thomas identifies several criteria, which he argues researchers can use to design and implement a successful intervention. In examining all these criteria, we find that some of them are only applicable to human services (i.e., social work), but they do offer food for thought when designing accounting interventions. We identify and discuss the criteria most applicable to accounting IVR.

First, the intervention must possess *objective capability*, that is, it must be effective and efficient. This means it must have a high probability of producing the desired outcomes without wasting resources or requiring excessive time or effort to use. Thomas (1984) notes that an intervention's effectiveness is a proxy for its validity. Second, the intervention must be *ethically suitable*. In all instances, regardless of discipline or research paradigm, the rights of the participants must be protected. Generally, in protecting participants, the researcher should minimise any risks to them that arise from harmful intervention outcomes. In Chapter 4, we identified one intervention type, 'modified existing interventions' that is especially risky because of its potential to cause participants harm. Researchers should make sure that the benefits of any intervention outweigh the risks. Consideration of these issues and undergoing formal ethics approval can be very helpful here (see Chapter 6). Third, the intervention should have good usability, which means it is compatible with the research context, it serves the needs of the people using it, and there is a high probability that the participants will adapt to the intervention (Thomas, 1984; Baard, 2004). A more comprehensive list of usability criteria is given in Table 11.3.

Table 11.3 Intervention Usability

Usability Criteria	Description
Relevant	The intervention and the problem's solution must be aligned. The ability of an intervention to solve a problem must be contingent on collaborative design.
Codified	The way in which the intervention is presented, for example, in writing, audio, and visual. Appropriate codification makes it easier for people to adopt and use the intervention.
Simple	The intervention must be relatively easy to use, so people can understand how and why it works. An overly complex intervention is less likely to be used and more likely to be rejected before, during, or after implementation.
Flexible	The intervention should be able to be modified or reconfigured without changing the essence of its design and the objective to be met. A delicate balance between flexibility and standardisation should be observed. Flexible interventions encourage creative involvement and foster a sense of ownership and commitment.
Cost-effective	The intervention should not be costly to use. Reflect on the time and money involved in acquiring the skills to use the intervention and the potential cost of implementing it. Expensive interventions can be justified if their effects are positive or there is more than enough funding.
Sustainable	The intervention should be capable of being integrated into the everyday life of the social system to achieve positive long-term outcomes (see Chapter 12).
Socially Compatible	The intervention must be consistent with the existing values, past experiences, customs and practices, and needs of potential users. This is also relevant when considering the potential for the participants' emancipation or de-emancipation.

Source: Adapted from Thomas (1984).

Intervention Concept

The next step is to create an intervention concept or concepts, that is, the two- to three-word phrase that best encapsulates what the intervention is. For example, Campanale *et al.*'s (2014) intervention was a time-driven, activity-based costing system. Chiucchi's (2013) was an IC performance measurement and management system. Baard (2004)'s was an interactive learning system to facilitate strategic management control. From this basis, one can begin to transform the concept into a prototype.

Conversion: From Intervention Concept to Prototype

At this point in Phase 3, researchers and participants are deeply immersed in intervention design. The design tasks, previously discussed, constitute the intervention concept or conceptual plan that outlines the form of the intervention to satisfy the intervention and design objectives. Converting an intervention concept into a prototype is an essential design activity (Rothman & Thomas, 1994). Mullen (1994, p. 173) argues that conversions "require creativity and imagination" because tangible or intangible interventions cannot be inferred from information and design concepts for pilot testing or implementation.

Moving an intervention from a concept through construction into a prototype exemplifies the intervention's feasibility (Baard, 2004). Further, it reduces the likelihood that an intervention will be rejected and helps to ensure the intervention will be implemented in the optimal fashion (Fawcett *et al.*, 1994). For instance, wildlife volunteers seeking to reduce possum fatalities after dark design a circular net-like tube for attachment to streetlight poles on either side of the road. Hence, possums can use the tube to cross the road, where their risk of fatality is reduced. Instead of encouraging local councils to use their intervention concept to reduce possum fatalities, the volunteers develop prototypes of the tube and enlist council assistance to erect them close to areas abundant with possums. This intervention is then pilot tested to ascertain its feasibility to reduce possum fatalities, with a view to implementation in areas with high possum fatalities.

Accordingly, conversion puts accounting researchers in touch with reality because conversions move the intervention from a theoretical idea to social technology to solve problems or address a situation with a need. Moreover, converting an intervention from a concept into a prototype for pilot testing and implementation also fosters intervention quality, reliability, and validity. Explicit accounts on how accounting interventions are converted from a concept to social technology are largely absent from the accounting literature, excepting Campanale *et al.* (2014) who offer a fairly detailed account of an intervention conversion.

Notably, an intervention does not need to proceed to construction. It can remain a theoretical idea that never leaves the etic domain because such an intervention constitutes a logical inference in the world of pure reason, delivering a theoretical contribution to the literature without demonstrating any practical utility. Without conversion, the research-practice gap persists because such research does not offer a practical contribution and thus will not deliver research with practical relevance. Hence, we recommend that accounting researchers provide explicit accounts of intervention conversion from concept to prototype. So how do we put all these conceptual design activities into practice? That is discussed in the next section.

An Intervention to Enhance Student Employability

This section describes the design of an intervention for a large, public university undertaken by me, Vicki Baard. The goal of the project was to design, develop, and deliver a teamwork experience, in line with the teaching and learning strategies of higher education, to increase employability by developing transportable teamwork skills. Transportable, also referred to as transferrable skills, are competencies students can use in diverse situations and contexts (e.g., Oliver *et al.*, 2011). The project, dubbed Project A for this book, was funded by a competitive university grant.

The project was motivated by the enormously rapid changes in business and society, as a result of globalisation, technological advancements, and intense competition. To survive today, organisations must be able to: a) change the way they operate; b) reduce costs while improving quality; and c) enhance customer and other key stakeholders' satisfaction. Hence, it is now equally as important for a graduate to have the skills to cope with complexity, uncertainty, and interdependence as it is for them to know facts, figures, and their tradecraft (Levi, 2017). Today's workforce must be innovative and flexible (Bunney *et al.*, 2015), which demands research skills, problem-solving capabilities, and interpersonal skills including conflict management, teamwork, communication skills, and a willingness to embrace life-long learning. These skills are sometimes referred to as generic or soft skills (Lim *et al.*, 2016; Bunney *et al.*, 2015; Oliver *et al.*, 2011; Kennedy & Bull, 2008). These are the skills employers expect graduates to have (Lim *et al.*, 2016). However, employers were finding students did not have these skills they needed on graduation (Levi, 2017; Lim *et al.*, 2016; see also Paguio & Jackling, 2016; Bunney *et al.*, 2015).

Employability is currently a topic on everyone's lips in the education sector (Kalfa & Taksa, 2015). Employability relies on people possessing transferrable skills and reflects a person's capacity to find and retain a job, remain employable, and respond to diverse employment possibilities (Bunney *et al.*, 2015; Kalfa & Taksa, 2015; Castillo, 2014). Additionally, employability involves a person's ability to live and work in a complex global environment (Lim *et al.*, 2016). In Australia, the United Kingdom (UK), the United States of America (USA), Canada, and the world over, governments and educational institutions alike are emphasising student employability as *the* benchmark for a successful education (Kalfa & Taksa, 2015).

The new nature of work demands expertise on many fronts to solve challenging problems, which may not be realistic for one person to have. Hence, teams and teamwork are becoming increasingly important (Levi, 2017). Teams are a critical means for organisations to respond quickly to the dynamic global environment and meet the demands of the new nature of work (Levi, 2017; Kozlowski & Bell, 2013; Kennedy & Bull, 2008). Therefore, teams are an important component of a contemporary workforce working in an adaptive organisational environment, and teamwork is a transferrable skill that organisations require (e.g., Levi, 2017; Kalfa & Taksa, 2015). However, employers see significant deficiencies in the teamwork capabilities of graduates (Paguio & Jackling, 2016). Hence, the purpose of Project A was to develop soft skills in students, particularly teamwork skills.

A thorough literature review confirmed that there was no existing intervention that would provide a suitable solution, which meant a novel solution had to be designed from scratch. The project commenced in December 2017, and intervention design had to be completed by January 2019. Thus, the project was time-sensitive. Following the IRF, specifically, Phase 3 helped in this regard because it laid out a systematic roadmap that avoided time-wasting pitfalls. In the next section, we outline the sequence of critical objectives, activities, and tasks that were undertaken in practice to arrive at a fully designed Project A.

Preliminary Work: Social Problem Specification & Information Synthesis

Beyond the motivation for designing and developing Project A, the idea was informed by four aspects of my academic and professional background. First was my interdisciplinary research on teamwork, team management, and management controls since 2010, and how I could transform that theoretical and empirical knowledge into a practical form, that is, knowledge utilisation (see Chapter 5). The second was my service in curriculum development, where teamwork had to be an integral aspect of the course work. Third, I worked in industry for ten years before becoming an academic as a management accountant in the banking, commodity trading, and entertainment sectors, where working in teams was common practice. Fourth, I am a certified chartered accountant with Chartered Accountants Australia and New Zealand (CAANZ), which keeps me in touch with industry at forums and events.

Information Sources

Here, the primary tasks were to obtain an accurate diagnosis and analysis of the problem, that is, developing teamwork skills in undergraduate students. Some of the questions that needed to be answered to more clearly specify the problem included: Were there skill benchmarks that needed to be reached? What was the current level of skill? Did teachers and students feel there were any barriers to developing teamwork skills? What were teachers currently doing to instil teamwork skills in their students? The preliminary information-gathering work included:

- Assembling and reviewing an up-to-date repository of literature from organisational and social psychology, organisational behaviour, group dynamics, healthcare, and human resources (managed by a research assistant using EndNote);

- Reviewing the higher education literature on generic skills and employability;
- Examining strategy and policy documents on higher education in Australia;
- Examining under and post-graduate program structure and content in multiple fields;
- Quantitative and qualitative data obtained from university teaching and learning student evaluations and anecdotal evidence from students kept as field notes; and
- Conferring with academics in organisational psychology who were doing some research on teaching and learning with teams.

Applying for the teaching and learning grant was an interesting aspect of this project because it significantly changed the focus of Project A. It influenced the nature of my initial ideas behind Project A and, therefore, the information gathering that was to follow. There was an initial call for expressions of interest in applying for a teaching and learning grant around August of 2017. Given my background, I was motivated to apply. I thought: "Why not develop teamwork skills across a range of undergraduate and postgraduate accounting units and programs? You have a demonstrated track record . . . maybe give it a go".

Applying for research grants is very different compared to applying for teaching and learning grants; I learnt that the hard way and my application was unsuccessful. As part of the application process, all applicants had to present a five-minute pitch in front of a highly knowledgeable and experienced panel . . . and all the other applicants. The experience was quite intimidating! Despite being unsuccessful, I received an overwhelming number of emails from academics from different fields across the education sector, expressing an urgent need for a cohesive and comprehensive approach to developing student teamwork skills. As many units and programs (i.e., Bachelor's and Master's degrees) had learning outcomes directly related to teamwork or teamwork skill development, this need was significant. Nineteen academics from multiple fields (psychology, engineering, education, physics, astronomy, software engineering, marketing, and management), as well as university career services staff, generously volunteered a significant and valuable amount of information during brainstorming sessions. In those sessions, we discussed existing teaching and learning approaches that other academics were using. This included sharing the activities, materials, and assessments they currently use, how they use them, and what outcomes they have achieved. They also offered information on the problems they experienced in developing student teamwork skills and what they needed to help overcome these problems.

Unexpectedly, another round of funding presented in November 2017. This time, I was informed, prepared, and successful in my pitch. Fully funded, I embarked on designing an intervention to cultivate team-capable, employable students across multiple fields. Bunney *et al.* (2015) find that supporting the need for generic skills development in graduates encompasses diverse disciplines (management, economics, finance, accounting, science, and engineering) in an international context.

Findings from Information Sources

Several findings emerged from synthesising all the information gathered during the data collection phase.

Beginning with the facts, I found approximately 30 under- and postgraduate programs have learning outcomes centred on 'working effectively in teams' or 'applying/developing teamwork skills'. The units within these programs are offered face-to-face, online, or in blended formats. According to Stevens and Campion (1999), teamwork skills consist of two main components: interpersonal skills and self-management. Interpersonal skills include conflict resolution, communication skills, listening, distinguishing between verbal and non-verbal cues, open and supportive dialogue, and collaborative problem-solving. Self-management involves planning, establishing team member roles and responsibilities, setting team goals and objectives, monitoring and evaluating team performance, and providing feedback to individual team members. Strategy and policy documents show that teamwork skills are highly prized by employers across a wide range of industries from health care to software development to telecommunications. Moreover, employers believe that graduates should be able to identify what generic skills they have and provide examples of how or when they have used them.

From feedback and anecdotal evidence, I observed an interchangeable use of the terms 'group work' and 'group project' with 'teamwork' and 'working in teams' without a clear distinction between the two. Working in groups is not the same as working in a team (e.g., Katzenbach & Smith, 1993), and conflating the two confuses students as to exactly what teams are, how they function, what skills team members must have to work effectively with others, and how exactly groups are different from teams. Additionally, it raises the question of whether group work or teamwork is being cultivated within curricula. Kennedy and Bull (2008) argue that too much group work and not enough teamwork may account for why academics wrestle with structuring and managing effective student teams.

I also discovered that many students are required to complete team assessments with little or no instruction on how or what it means to work in teams. Further, the assessments are focussed on the team product, not the teamwork process. Teamwork processes are complex and include forming teams, adopting roles, collaborative problem-solving, making collective decisions, interpersonal communication, and managing conflict. At university, interactions are commonly done through tweeting, texting, exchanging comments on Facebook, or not communicating at all until the deadline looms, as opposed to the face-to-face meetings and emails common of real-world teamwork. Therefore, students may not be experiencing authentic teamwork dynamics nor developing the process skills employers want to see.

Generally, students do not seem to like working in groups or teams and prefer individual work and assessments. Kalfa and Taksa (2015) argue that this may illustrate the ongoing emphasis on students developing technical expertise rather than generic skills. Based on the valid and useful information generated, I find that students are unable to distinguish between group work and teamwork; their perceptions of what it means to work in a team are ambiguous. Students do not like group work or teamwork, and unproductive experiences make them reluctant to engage in it. It is not surprising that their experiences are unproductive when they have been given no instruction on: a) the challenges of coordinating and communicating in teams; b) what teamwork skills encompass; c) working collaboratively as opposed to 'everyone doing his or her part' and then 'pasting everything to a single output'; d) how to resolve the inevitable conflict that arises when working collectively; and e) why the outcomes of a team effort are better than the outcomes produced individually or by a group. In fact, some students don't even know that employers expect them to have teamwork skills.

Given the widespread requirement for teamwork learning outcomes, unit coordinators must incorporate these skills into the course curricula. This is usually a solo effort, but generating resources, designing assessments, and creating teaching activities is time-consuming, so unit coordinators spend a lot of time reinventing the wheel only to achieve the same outcomes. Some coordinators may choose to incorporate teamwork into their units for various reasons, while others are tasked with this because the program learning outcomes require it. Moreover, teamwork is not likely the coordinator's research interest or area of expertise; many are at sea with the fundamentals of teamwork as the students and resources and support are scarce. Hence, their frustration is intense. The most common suggestion for alleviating this frustration was shared resources focused on developing teamwork skills. Lastly, I confirmed that no sufficiently generic intervention could solve this problem across a range of learning fields.

Designing Project A

With the salient aspects of the problem analysed and diagnosed, the next step was to design an intervention. Following Phase 3 of the IRF, the first step was to establish my design objectives for Project A—to create a flexible, generic teamwork experience comprising teaching and learning activities, authentic resources, and an assessment portfolio that could be incorporated into existing under- and postgraduate courses.

Design Domain

From Table 11.2, the project setting was a higher education social system, and the change objectives were:

1. To address employers' needs for team-capable students by developing transportable teamwork skills in students (competence).
2. To give students the abilities to distinguish between teams and groups, understand and manage teamwork processes and challenges, and create and promote productive student team experiences (remediation).
3. To deliver knowledge about teams, present opportunities for team-work, and mobilise their ability to work effectively in teams inside and outside the classroom (education).
4. To help unit coordinators deliver a teamwork experience with shared teaching resources that deliver the required learning outcomes attached to teamwork skills (competence).

The targets of the intervention were individual students (their teamwork skills). Additionally, I targeted the unit coordinators' competence in embedding teamwork learning activities into curricula, and their ability to develop teaching and learning strategies that support teamwork skills development.

Most of the grant funding was used to create a diverse intervention design team—a highly competent collection of people without whom the intervention would not have been as successful as it was (see also Chapter 10). Apart from myself, the team consisted of a unit coordinator (UC1) who had no knowledge of teams but had been tasked with embedding teamwork skills into a postgraduate unit. UC1's role was to evaluate the feasibility of Project A and its capacity to help unit coordinators develop student teamwork skills even when they had little or no expertise in this area. The rest of the team comprised two research students in organisational psychology, one doctoral student and one master's student. They worked with me to develop the teaching and learning materials and assessments and to create or source authentic resources. The idea was to involve students as proactive collaborators in the design of a learning journey aimed at influencing teaching and learning strategy. But it was also to produce an intervention designed by students for students. In the same vein, I engaged a team of media students to produce teaching and learning resources centred on teamwork skills in the form of live-action videos. The teamwork skills included team communication, collaborative problem-solving, and conflict management.

I also engaged several support staff. A project coordinator helped me: monitor progress on milestones; identify and manage any issues arising during design; and control the finances and other ad hoc project work.

A teaching assistant provided administrative support to keep on top of my normal duties. A highly innovative web designer (WEB1) and trusted colleague for over ten years created interactive web formats on the learning management system used to host Project A. Additionally, WEB1 developed interactive templates and sourced or created graphic materials to enhance the functionality and aesthetics of the materials. Volunteers with whom I formed informal collaborations included two organisational psychology academics, one engineering academic, one career services professional, and a senior learning designer. Their input was invaluable (and I will always be grateful for it).

Quality assurance was extremely important to the reliability and validity of Project A. I also conferred with a highly experienced senior quality assurance specialist, who specialised in the education sector, through all stages of the design process. This person was instrumental in organising the pilot test for Project A. I found overall that stipulating the design domain offered me a structured framing of Project A and its design activities.

Design Criteria (Requirements/Specifications)

Identifying the preliminary design specifications is extremely helpful for guiding the scope and boundaries of construction efforts (Thomas, 1984). The specifications for Project A were that it must:

1. Be a stand-alone and a flexible teamwork experience with the capacity to interact with existing programs and existing units of study, regardless of field and format.
2. Be generic in nature so that it does not favour any specific field but still retains its capacity to support students and unit coordinators in learning about teams and developing teamwork skills.
3. Have the capability and capacity to provide high-quality teamwork skills to students, which includes an informed understanding of what it means to work in teams and clarity on the difference between groups and teams.
4. Be able to be hosted on a learning management system for easy access by all unit coordinators.
5. Incorporate relevant technical, organisational, and economic feasibility criteria (see Table 11.1) and a range of academic and student insights for connectivity purposes.
6. Be ethical, sensitive to cultural diversity, and politically feasible (see Table 11.1).
7. Follow a modular approach that covers: an introduction to teams and teamwork; a theoretical framework underpinning team functioning and effectiveness; and three practical modules centred on developing teamwork skills. Each module would include a guide, an

assessment portfolio, grading rubrics, a range of learning activities and materials, and relevant and authentic resources. The modular approach has the following advantages:

a) It gives unit coordinators complete discretion on how they want to use Project A.
b) It means any part of Project A can be incorporated into a course.
c) Students develop skills using a scaffolded approach.
d) It makes trials and piecemeal implementation easier (see Chapter 12).
e) It supports future micro-credentialing of modules for complete inclusion into a program, where each module can be delivered as a 'bite-sized' chunk to support developing proficiency in teamwork and teamwork skills.

Thus, the intervention concept was 'a novel, flexible and modular approach to developing student teamwork skills'.

Project A Design: In Conclusion

Reflecting on the design experience in creating, developing, and delivering Project A, I adopted a highly disciplined approach guided by Phase 3 of the IRF. Despite the seemingly structured approach, there was enough flexibility in the method to support worthwhile deviations from the plan and to address any unexpected challenges that arose during design. In any project, there are inevitably a range of challenges that arise—time pressures, administrative issues, team members unable to fulfil their obligations when you need them most, underestimating the time needed for a design task or how much effort it will consume, and some conflicts here and there. Harnessing the creativity and competences of all design team members, Project A was successfully converted from a concept into a live program. Currently, Project A is being used by 41 different unit coordinators from a range of fields across higher education. Some are piloting parts of it, but most are implementing what they need in their 2020 curricula. A feedback system has been established to collect evidence that will indicate the extent to which Project A's change objectives are being achieved, although I expect this will take some time to become evident. Designing novel interventions with a large team is not easy.

Most interestingly, the parallels between the soft skills of teamwork and employability and the competencies required for successful IVR have not escaped our attention. You need persistence, resilience, and confidence, as well as excellent skills in problem-solving, organising, negotiation, and communication to mount a fruitful intervention. Most importantly, you need to be able to listen, interpret non-verbal messages and, above all, have patience. These are the skills we refer to Chapter 3, and I learned many of them though Project A.

Designing and developing a novel intervention is an awfully big adventure. It is both scary and exhilarating, but well worth embarking on the adventure. Every IVR project is different, and it certainly helps to have and to follow a method outlined by Phase 3 carefully. However, do know that you are most likely going to need to improvise along the way to manage any risks that inevitably arise and capitalise on unexpected prospects that present. Alongside a flexible method, your researcher qualities are critical. It is important to be honest with yourself about what you can and cannot accomplish; it is an unrealistic expectation for one person to possess all the capabilities required for a complex IVR project. Thus, accomplishing innovative intervention design and construction is best served by working with a strong, competent team.

References

Baard, V.C. (2004). *The design and implementation of an IT consulting system in South African small businesses.* (Doctor of Technologiae), Central University of Technology, Bloemfontein, South Africa.

Baard, V.C. (2010). A critical view of interventionist research. *Qualitative Research in Accounting and Management*, 7(1), 13–45.

Baard, V.C. & Dumay, J. (2018). Interventionist research in accounting: Reflections on the good, the bad and the ugly. *Accounting and Finance*, Advance online publication. https://doi.org/10.1111/acfi.12409

Bunney, D., Sharplin, E., & Howitt, C. (2015). Generic skills for graduate accountants: The bigger picture, a social and economic imperative in the new knowledge economy. *Higher Education Research & Development*, 34(2), 256–269.

Campanale, C., Cinquini, L., & Tenucci, A. (2014). Time driven activity-based costing to improve transparency and decision making in healthcare. *Qualitative Research in Accounting & Management*, 11, 165–186.

Castillo, R.C. (2014). Employability skills of graduating business and accounting students of Batangas State University. *International Journal of Sciences: Basic and Applied Research*, 13(1), 303–315.

Chiucchi, M.S. (2013). Intellectual capital accounting in action: Enhancing learning through interventionist research. *Journal of Intellectual Capital*, 14, 48–68.

Cullen, J., Tsamenyi, M., Bernon, M., & Gorst, J. (2013). Reverse logistics in the UK retail sector: A case study of the role of management accounting in driving organisational change. *Management Accounting Research*, 24, 212–227.

Dumay, J. (2010). A critical reflective discourse of an interventionist research project. *Qualitative Research in Accounting and Management*, 7(1), 46–70.

Dumay, J. & Baard, V.C. (2017). An introduction to interventionist research in accounting. In Z. Hoque, L.D. Parker, M.A. Covaleski, & K. Haynes (Eds.), *The Routledge companion to qualitative accounting research methods* (pp. 265–283). New York, NY: Routledge.

Fawcett, S.B., Suarez-Balcazar, Y., Balcazar, F.E., White, G.W., Paine, A.L., Blanchard, K.A., & Embree, M.G. (1994). Conducting intervention research—The design and development process. In J. Rothman & E.J. Thomas (Eds.), *Intervention research: Design and development for human service* (pp. 25–54). Binghamton, NY: Haworth Press.

Graham, C. & Neu, D. (2003). Accounting for globalisation. *Accounting Forum*, 27, 449–471.

Kalfa, S. & Taksa, L. (2015). Cultural capital in business higher education: Reconsidering the graduate attributes movement and the focus on employability. *Studies in Higher Education*, 40(4), 580–595.

Katzenbach, J.R. & Smith, D.K. (1993). *The wisdom of teams*. New York, NY: McKinsey & Co.

Kennedy, F.A. & Bull, R.B. (2008). Transferable team skills for accounting students. *Accounting Education: An International Journal*, 17(2), 213–224.

Kozlowski, S. W. J., & Bell, B. S. (2013). *Work groups and teams in organizations: Review update* [Electronic version]. Retrieved September 28, 2017 from Cornell University, School of Industrial and Labor Relations site: http://digitalcommons.ilr.cornell.edu/articles/927

Levi, D. (2017). *Group dynamics for teams* (5th ed.). Thousand Oaks, CA: Sage Publications.

Lim, Y., Lee, T.H., Yap, C.S., & Ling, C.C. (2016). Employability skills, personal qualities, and early employment problems of entry-level auditors: Perspectives from employers, lecturers, auditors and students. *Journal of Education for Business*, 91(4), 185–192.

Mullen, E.J. (1994). Design of social intervention. In J. Rothman & E.J. Thomas (Eds.), *Intervention research: Design and development for human service* (pp. 163–193). Binghamton, NY: Haworth Press.

Oliver, B., Whelan, B., Hunt, L., & Hammer, S. (2011). Accounting graduates and the capabilities that count: Perceptions of graduates, employers and accounting academics in four Australian universities. *Journal of Teaching and Learning for Graduate Employability*, 2(1), 2–27.

Paguio, R. & Jackling, B. (2016). Teamwork from accounting graduates: What do employers really expect? *Accounting Research Journal*, 29(3), 348–366.

Rothman, J. & Thomas, E.J. (Eds.). (1994). *Intervention research: Design and development for human service*. Binghamton, NY: Haworth Press.

Stevens, M.J. & Campion, M.A. (1999). Staffing work teams: Development and validation of a selection test for teamwork skills. *Journal of Management*, 25(2), 207–228.

Thomas, E.J. (1984). *Designing interventions for the helping professions*. Beverley Hills, CA: Sage Publications.

Part 4

Intervention Implementation and Dissemination—In Touch With Reality

12 Intervention Implementation

Ultimately, the success of an intervention depends on effective implementation. However, that is often easier said than done as we have discovered. The work is labour- and resource-intensive, it demands people's commitment, and requires creative problem-solving skills. It also requires careful planning and coordination and, most importantly, in the end, the intervention must be normalised into the social system's everyday operations.

Unfortunately, there is no one optimal method for ensuring a successful implementation because there are so many variables at play. The Interventionist Research Framework (IRF) offers some practical ideas on implementation, see Phase 4 in Chapter 5. The problem we face as IVR researchers is that we know very little about implementing interventions. Therefore, in this chapter, we contemplate the meaning and definition of implementation. We introduce normalisation process theory (NPT), which is an implementation science framework used in healthcare IVR that can be applied to accounting. We also show how project management can be used as a structured approach to implement an intervention. To further illustrate how IVR can work, or not as the case may be, we offer a critical reflection on a successful intervention project, followed by some lessons learned from two failed implementations.

The Meaning and Purpose of Intervention Implementation

Several definitions of implementation in the IVR context have been put forward. Damschroder *et al.* (2009, p. 3) define implementation as:

> The constellation of processes intended to get an intervention into use within an organisation; it is the means by which an intervention is assimilated into an organisation. Implementation is the critical gateway between an organisational decision to adopt an intervention and the routine use of that intervention; the transition period during which targeted stakeholders become increasingly skilful, consistent, and committed in their use of an intervention.

Gitlin and Czaja (2016) state that implementation involves using strategies to integrate interventions into practice settings to change current practices, and that implementation bridges intervention adoption and its routine use in organisations. Hence, some factors influencing intervention implementation are, for example, available resources (people, material, and financial); resistance to change; people's workload, roles, and capabilities; culture and values, leadership; and control mechanisms.

Linton (2002, p. 65) states that:

> Implementation involves all activities that occur between making an adoption commitment and the time that an innovation either becomes part of the organisational routine, ceases to be new, or is abandoned [and the] behaviour of organisational members over time evolves from avoidance or non-use, through unenthusiastic or compliant use, to skilled or consistent use.

May *et al.* (2007) define implementation as a series of organised, dynamic, and contingent interactions where individuals and groups work with an intervention to put it into practice in a specific context over time. Further, an effective implementation means that interventions have workability (ease and efficiency) and can be integrated into everyday operations. Baard (2004) views implementation as a change process that occurs when an intervention, designed to solve a problem or alter an organisational practice, is introduced into an organisation's everyday activities or work (see also Scheirer, 1981).

Beyond definitions, scholars have raised other important contingents for a successful implementation. For instance, Cook and Odom (2013, p. 138) argue that implementation represents a critical link between effective research and practice in yielding desired outcomes, also shown as: "Effective interventions x Effective implementation = Improved outcomes". Gitlin and Czaja (2016) state that the impact of an intervention depends on its adoption and sustained use. Jönsson and Lukka (2007) argue that it is only through implementation that IVR attains practical relevance; without implementation, the ideas and solutions to the problem are destined to remain in the etic realm. Practical, effective, valid and reliable interventions also depend on a well-planned and structured approach to implementation (Baard, 2010). However, from the perspective of the organisation, implementation success is more likely to relate to the take-up of the intervention, how deeply it becomes embedded in practice, whether it maintains or improves competencies, and whether it solves the diagnosed problem.

Definitions are helpful, but what is more important is how they inform our understanding of implementation. Implementation is a process of dynamic and dependent interactions between individuals that become part of the everyday work of an organisation. It moves a workable intervention from adoption to integration to achieve long-term change. In this way, implementation transitions the intervention from research into practice, which produces relevant practical research outcomes that can be reported. Moreover, the reliability and validity of an intervention is also contingent on a design that facilitates effective implementation. Hence, identifying the factors that might influence implementation early in the process is prudent because they may present barriers to implementation.

Additionally, the term implementation should not be used interchangeably with the terms 'adoption' and 'diffusion' (Gitlin & Czaja, 2016; May *et al.*, 2007). Adoption involves an explicit decision to make use of an intervention (Rogers, 2003), but it does not mean the intervention becomes entrenched in the organisation's everyday operations (May *et al.*, 2007), nor that it creates the intended change (Scheirer, 1981). Diffusion is the passive spread of knowledge, practices, and technologies between participants and to the academic and professional zeitgeist (Tucker & Parker, 2013; May *et al.*, 2007; Rogers, 2003). Dissemination is the purposive distribution of knowledge and information on evidence-based interventions specific channels, for example, academic journals, and practitioner conferences and journals (Gitlin & Czaja, 2016) (see Chapter 13). Hence, while these terms are related, their meanings are subtly different, and thus we use the term 'implementation'.

Implementation Science—A Healthcare Perspective

Given the limited coverage of intervention implementation in accounting and social science literature, we turned to the healthcare literature for guidance. Broadly speaking, the view on implementation in healthcare is that it is a complex and understudied problem, and that poor implementation can easily undermine well-conceived interventions. Additionally, there are clear calls for more detailed and specific implementation theories, models, frameworks, and strategies.

Gitlin and Czaja (2016) present the idea of implementation science, which is emerging in healthcare as a significant way to transition evidence-based, research-inspired interventions from conception to development and evaluation, to incorporation into a real-life setting. Eccles and Mittman (2006, p. 1) define implementation science as "the scientific study of methods to promote the systematic uptake of research findings and other evidence-based practices into routine practice". Straus *et al.* (2009) find that implementation science is synonymous with the terms of knowledge utilisation, knowledge translation, implementation research, and diffusion. Cook and Odom (2013) state that implementation science is not the science of implementation; rather, it is a scientific field of inquiry that examines implementation issues. Further, these authors argue that implementation science aims to investigate and understand how interventions are adopted and maintained, thus implementation transitions from "letting it happen" to "making it happen" (Cook & Odom, 2013, p. 140).

Gitlin and Czaja (2016) state that implementation science investigates how interventions can be implemented and sustained in social systems through exploring the best implementation strategies and identifying the social, behavioural, economic, or organisational obstacles that are barriers to implementation. Proctor *et al.* (2013, p. 2) define implementation strategies as "methods or techniques used to enhance the adoption, implementation, and sustainability of a clinical program or practice". Here, sustainability means that an intervention should have the material and cognitive resources to continue delivering beneficial outcomes to people and organisations after the IVR project is complete (Gitlin & Czaja, 2016). Implementing interventions using strategies that provide for obstacles is more likely to achieve sustained positive change and other beneficial outcomes within real-life settings (Cook & Odom, 2013). Gitlin and Czaja (2016) argue that for an intervention to achieve sustained beneficial outcomes for people and organisations, we need to understand the complexities or downstream challenges of implementing an intervention in a real-life setting. These challenges include, for example, the characteristics of people, groups, and organisations; their workflow patterns and systems; financial and other resource considerations; the organisational climate; any workforce training requirements; and the readiness of people to change. Understanding the downstream challenges will influence upstream challenges, specifically intervention design and evaluation. Thus, implementation is highly contingent on intervention design.

In the context of behavioural intervention research, Gitlin and Czaja (2016) identify 13 commonly used implementation science models and theoretical frameworks that are helpful for advancing intervention implementation in a real-world setting. A detailed account of how each one fits with accounting IVR falls outside the scope of this book. However, some had merit, so interested readers should refer to Gitlin and Czaja (2016). Based on our experience with IVR, we identified Normalisation Process Theory (NPT) as the most appropriate implementation science framework for advancing our understanding of implementing interventions in accounting IVR.

Normalisation Process Theory

NPT is a proven applied theory from sociology that centres on collective social action. In our context, collective social action means the things that people do when they implement an intervention (May *et al.*, 2007). NPT is also a middle-range theory of action (see Chapter 1). May and Finch (2009) state that 'normalisation' refers to work that the project's participants perform as they engage in intervention activities, for example, new or modified ways of thinking, acting, making decisions, organising, etc. Normalisation also considers how these activities become embedded in "the matrices of already existing, socially patterned, knowledge and practices in organisations" (May & Finch, 2009, p. 540). Thus, new knowledge, technologies, programs, and practices become routinely embedded in organisations because of the individual and collective work people do to enact them. Murray *et al.* (2010) state that normalisation is not irrevocable as participants may reject the intervention or the intervention may no longer be needed if the problem is effectively solved.

NPT consists of three main things (May *et al.*, 2007; May & Finch, 2009). First is implementation, which involves the relationships, processes, or the work people need to do to put an intervention into practice. Second is the process of embedding an intervention in the everyday practices of the people in an organisation. It is the work that people accomplish and how they operationalise the work through four generative mechanisms: coherence, cognitive participation, collective action, and reflexive monitoring. Understanding these four mechanisms is useful for explaining factors that promote or inhibit intervention implementation into an organisation's everyday operations (Murray *et al.*, 2010; May & Finch, 2009). Murray *et al.* (2010) state that these mechanisms are not linear. Rather, they are dynamic relationships among the organisational structure, social norms, and group processes. Third is integrating the intervention into the organisation so it becomes sustainable. The intervention or material practice resulting from intervening achieves sustainability in a social context, specifically through people's continued investment in work, activities, and processes. May and Finch (2009, p. 539) define material practices as "the things that people do to perform certain acts and meet specific goals". Scheirer (2005) states that an intervention achieves sustainability when it: a) continues to produce good outcomes for the participants; b) maintains a current identifiable or modified form; and c) maintains the capacity for an organisation to effectively operate and function. These three components—implementation, embedding, and integration—combine to form the primary principle of NPT, which is to capture the work, understanding, and commitment of people to achieve a goal (May & Finch, 2009).

Murray *et al.* (2010) argue that NPT serves as a "sensitising tool" that prompts researchers to consider implementation during its design. Thus, NPT offers a sound framework to plan for, explain, and enable intervention implementation.

NPT—Constructs and Components

The work that people do to bring an intervention into their everyday practices is operationalised through four main generative mechanisms, as shown in Figure 12.1. The generative mechanisms are also referred

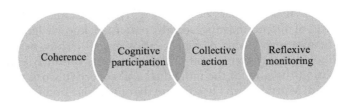

Figure 12.1 The Constructs of NPT

to as interactive constructs because combining all the tasks forming the work people do generates outcomes from intervention implementation. Each construct has several components that are useful to reflect on when designing and developing an intervention and when planning its implementation.

Coherence refers to the sense-making participants do when operationalising an intervention. May & Finch (2009, p. 542) describe this as people developing a "cognitive and behavioural ensemble of the intervention". Practically, 'ensemble' refers to the intervention as a recognisable and novel package that can attach to the everyday work of an organisation. Participants also need to invest time to grasp the meaning and the nature of the intervention because their understanding of the intervention increases and evolves over time. Table 12.1 outlines the coherence components.

Cognitive participation is the work people do to enrol and engage themselves in putting the intervention to use. It usually starts with 'intervention champions', that is, the initiators, who promote and create awareness of the coming change. Enrolment involves recruiting people into a community of practice who collectively participate in the work associated with the intervention but, obviously, this work is tempered by the skill sets of those involved. Participants need to apply Argyris' (1970) principle of internal commitment to the intervention. They need to 'buy into' the intervention because they need to see it as central to their everyday work. The projected benefits must be obvious to them, and they must believe they can make a valid contribution to bringing about those benefits. Moreover, all participants need to share this commitment. Once organised and committed to the intervention, participants need to communally delineate actions and procedures to sustain the work required and remain actively involved in the project (activation and legitimisation).

Collective action is the actual work that people do to put the intervention into practice using their skills, resources, and knowledge of how the intervention supplements their everyday work. This construct points to

Table 12.1 Coherence Components

Component	Description
Differentiation	The work people do to understand how the intervention is distinguishable from their existing ways of doing things. People attempt to understand how doing things differently is likely to help them in their everyday work.
Communal Specification	The work needed to obtain a shared understanding of the intervention's purpose and the associated value of the expected change resulting from the intervention. Collectively, participant understanding of the intervention's aims and benefits may differ from the intervention's aims and benefits. A high degree of communal specification means that intervention normalisation is advantageous.
Individual Specification	Individuals try to understand how their specific work and responsibilities fit in with the work needed for the intervention. Hence, this component relates to the work of thinking about and quantifying the expected time, effort, and resources needed to operationalise the intervention, from an individual's standpoint. Understanding the task requirements to make the intervention happen does not mean that suitably proficient participants are willing or available to participate.
Internalisation	The work participants do to comprehend and interpret the nature of the intervention and how it relates to their own beliefs, values, experience, and the culture within a group, or organisation. This component is consistent with Argyris' (1970) third IVR principle of internal commitment.

Source: Adapted from May *et al.* (2009), May and Finch (2009) and Murray *et al.* (2010)

the factors that may help or hinder implementation and relies on four components, outlined in Table 12.2.

The general implication of this construct is that an intervention can be implemented into an organisation if it is practicable and easily integrated into everyday practice by the people in the organisation.

Reflexive monitoring is the evaluating work people do to appraise the value of the intervention—this value appraisal can be accomplished by participants individually, collectively, or both. It involves using a systematic and informal approach to collecting and organising valid and useful data to ascertain the effects of the intervention. Additionally, participants may decide to modify or reconfigure the intervention based on the outcomes of their evaluation. This construct is consistent with Phase 5 of the IRF.

Table 12.3 provides a range of issues to consider when researchers are seeking to put NPT and its four generative mechanisms into practice.

Table 12.2 Collective Action Components

Component	Description
Interactional Workability	Refers to the work that people do with each other when they are putting the intervention into practice.
	This component directs people on how to do the required work and the extent to which putting the intervention into use helps or hinders their everyday work. It is helpful to think about whether any formal or informal rules within the organisation may influence how to accomplish the work.
Skill Set Workability	The skill sets people possess to do the work to put the intervention into practice. Thinking about the knowledge, skills, attitudes, and capacity of people working on the intervention is important because training, knowledge, information sources, and new equipment may be required to accomplish the work.
	This component refers to the work of allocating tasks and distributing resources and rewards, that is, who gets to do what work. Thus, it also identifies who has the power to make decisions on allocating tasks and resources.
Relational Integration	The work that relates to fostering and sustaining accountability, trust, and confidence in an intervention, and in each other's skill and proficiency to successfully operationalise the intervention. The work may lead to a change in existing relationships and networks.
	Accountability relies on knowing who has the knowledge needed to do the work and the required contributions from each person involved. Confidence relates to self-assurance in one's own knowledge and practical utility and that of others to operationalise the intervention.
Contextual Integration	This work involves integrating the intervention into the existing social, cultural, or political environment of an organisation.
	This component relates to the practicalities of integration. For example, making decisions about allocating money, equipment, people, and other resources and the associated costs and risks; providing leadership support; and assessing current infrastructure including policies, procedures, and other protocols.

Source: Adapted from May *et al.* (2007), May *et al.* (2009), May and Finch (2009) and Murray *et al.* (2010)

Table 12.3 NPT—Putting NPT into Practice

Constructs	Operationalising Implementation: Generative NPT Mechanisms			
	Coherence	*Cognitive Participation*	*Collective Action*	*Reflexive Monitoring*
Focus	What work is to be done?	Who does the work?	How does the work get done?	How is the intervention understood and assessed by the participants doing the work?
Factors Inhibiting/ Promoting	Intervention mobilisation	Participant commitment to and engagement with the intervention	Putting an intervention into use or practice	Intervention assessment
Issues to Consider	• Is the intervention easily described? • How is the intervention conceptualised or understood by people? • To what extent is the intervention distinguishable from current practices? • To what extent does the intervention have a clear purpose, and do people know this purpose? • To what extent do people understand the intervention's potential value and benefits? • For whom or what are the benefits of the intervention? • What is the likelihood that people will value the intervention's benefits?	• How are people likely to respond to the intervention—will they think it is a good idea? • Who is willing to drive or initiate the work to make the intervention happen? • Are people likely to view the intervention as research and central to the everyday work they do? • What is the likelihood of people easily knowing the purpose of the intervention? • Are people likely to be motivated to invest time, effort, and work in the intervention? • To what extent are people willing and have the capacity to define actions required to sustain the intervention?	• To what extent are people capable of putting the intervention into use? • To what extent is intervention work suitably allocated to people? • Will people maintain accountability and confidence in each other when working on the intervention? • To what extent will the intervention help or hinder people's everyday work? • Will existing policies, procedures, and protocols help or hinder intervention work? • Will people need training to do the work needed to operationalise the intervention? • What is the likely impact on resources, power and values, responsibilities, and authority levels of people? • To what extent is the intervention work supported by managers and new/existing resources?	• Are individual and/or collective appraisals going to be used? • What is the likelihood of the intervention being perceived as beneficial for users? • How are users likely to perceive the intervention after it is in use for some time? • Can people provide feedback while intervention is in use? • What are the intervention's effects? • To what extent can the intervention be modified/reconfigured based on people's experience of using it?

Source: Adapted from Murray *et al.* (2010), May and Finch (2009), May *et al.* (2007) and May *et al.* (2009).

We also view this table as an instrument to support planning for and contemplating issues related to intervention implementation.

NPT—Next Steps

NPT is a good guide for implementing an intervention for several reasons. Foremost, it has methodological rigour and has been empirically validated in real-world health care settings. It is also an applied theory—a theory of action, rooted in sociology, but conceptually suitable for use in accounting IVR. NPT is also open to theoretical debate, which provides an excellent opportunity to fulfil that side of IVR's duality of output. Its generalisability to different settings gives it broad utility when designing, developing, and planning projects, whether that is for a hospital, a business, a government agency, bank, school, or cricket team. Moreover, using NPT can help researchers decide whether or not to proceed with the IVR project.

The IRF and Pilot-Testing

Phase 4 of the Interventionist's Framework, implementation, begins with pilot-testing. According to Rothman and Tumblin (1994), pilot-testing in IVR serves two purposes: to establish viability and to test for intended and unintended consequences. Establishing an intervention's viability includes assessing its quality, feasibility, and observing how it will perform prior to 'live' implementation. To be viable, an intervention must: a) be able to solve the problem in question; b) be ethical; c) fit within the organisation's capabilities, resources, climate, and leadership attitude); d) be compatible with normal operations; and e) be simple and easy to use.

Testing for consequences prior to full-scale implementation is just common sense. If problems arise, it is easier to contain the impact, and fixing them will not waste as much time or resources. It also minimises the risk of failure for the researchers who are accountable for the intervention's outcomes. Ultimately, pilot-testing provides the opportunity to refine or modify the intervention for its best chance of success. There are different ways to test an intervention and the implementation method, but each depends to a large extent on the intervention design. For instance, a case study at the department level could be pilot tested with a few people or at the organisational level with just one department. Similarly, quasi-experiments could be run on a small sample of the full population. However, people in the pilot test should not participate in the live experiment to preserve its integrity. Some of the basics of pilot-testing follow (Baard, 2004):

- The pilot test should be small enough to be manageable but sufficiently large to show significance and to instil confidence in the intervention throughout the organisation.

- The participants involved in pilot-testing should be willing to commit for the duration of the test and must be made aware that problems could arise during testing. Hence, researchers should establish a feedback system to manage, document, and resolve any issues that may arise.

- Planning and scheduling the pilot-test with the people involved is just as important as planning for the live implementation. The intervention materials, instructions, and so on must be provided and explained to the participants, along with anything specific to the pilot-test—for example, notification of a post-pilot test interview or a feedback form for logging issues, recommended changes, and rating features and benefits.

- The feedback, and any other data emerging from the pilot-test, should be preserved for later reference if required.

A Project Management Approach to Intervention Implementation

As mentioned, the literature does not advocate a one-size-fits-all implementation method, although Phase 4 of the IRF offers some practical insights. However, a project management approach is generally workable in some situations. I, Vicki Baard, used this approach to implement an intervention for small businesses during my doctoral study. This is my experience.

While studying for my master's degree, I met an architectural engineer, a highly creative problem-solver who designs buildings to improve people's standard of living while ensuring sustainable work and recreation environments. In conversation with him at a challenging and stressful time during my doctoral work, I expressed grave concerns about how to implement my intervention. Almost instantaneously, he responded, "Why not use project management? We use it successfully all the time. It's a structured way to manage a project regardless of complexity. Microsoft Project is a great tool to help you manage your implementation".

The practical nature of a project is fairly consistent with an intervention. I am a practical person and so, using a project management approach, I configured an implementation methodology consisting of four main steps, see Figure 12.2. Given the critical importance of implementation planning and preparation, the discussion that follows centres mostly on this.

Step 1 Planning and Preparation

Underestimating the importance of preparing for implementation can have undesirable consequences as implementing an intervention into an organisation can be easily undermined without a sound work plan. As a doctoral student doing research using IVR, an approach that my fellow

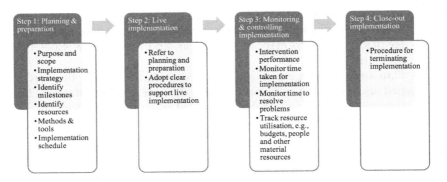

Figure 12.2 An Implementation Methodology

students had never heard of before and doing a quasi-experiment no less, I found myself subjected to many unappreciated comments that generally exemplified a perception that my thesis was 'a disaster in the making'. After all the work afforded to finding, negotiating, and collaborating with participants to design and develop a new intervention, I was not about to jeopardise everything with an implementation approached with haste and nervousness. Careful planning helps to map out the project scope, its objectives, and establish strategies to achieve those objectives. Additionally, it is likely that you will use time and resources more efficiently and properly allocate responsibilities to the people best suited to those roles. Planning should include stipulating ways to identify problems, monitoring implementation activities and their outputs/outcomes, and following the overall progress and status of each task. Some specific activities in this phase include: a) outlining the implementation concept; b) formulating an implementation strategy; c) identifying milestones and developing an implementation schedule; d) identifying the resources needed; and e) identifying the methods and tools to be employed.

The Implementation Concept

As opposed to the intervention concept, which is the briefest summary of what the intervention is, the implementation concept incorporates the purpose, scope, and objectives of the intervention, plus the basic issues that may or will arise during implementation. Table 12.4 provides more detail.

The Implementation Strategy

Even though every implementation strategy is different, there are some common elements. These are: how to move participants beyond adoption

Table 12.4 The Implementation Concept

Purpose of Implementation	**Why?** Establishes the foundation for defining implementation scope, formulating objectives, and identifying basic issues influencing implementation. To establish if the intervention: • can be embedded into a real-life setting and achieve integration with everyday work and activities • is simple to use, a practical method or tool, and adaptable to and compatible with participant norms and values • demonstrates efficacy within an organisation to solve a problem • has the capability to provide tangible and/or intangible benefits for social system long-term survival and prosperity
Implementation Scope	**Why?** Specifies implementation boundaries and identifies elements of work. The scope should consider: • Where will the implementation occur? • How long will the initial implementation take and, after that, how long will the intervention be embedded into the organisation? • What advice, technical assistance, or other support will participants require for optimal implementation?
Implementation Objectives	**Why?** Formulating objectives supports achieving the overall goal of the implementation. The objectives are contingent on the nature of and type of change anticipated by the intervention, and they are unique to each project. Examples include: • Enhancing management accounting and strategic and operational management practices to increase organisational competency • Establishing intervention effectiveness as a practical methodology to support strategic planning and implementation
Basic Implementation Issues	**How?** Anticipating and identifying likely problems and developing proactive approaches to managing them. Examples of potential issues, their impact, and the means to overcoming the issue follow:

Issues	*Impact*	*Solution*
Underestimating the level of effort required for implementation	Insufficient resource allocation will result in project delays	Set realistic resources targets for each task and include some contingency
Misunderstandings about the implementation activities	May result in delays, demotivate the participants, generate resistance to doing the work required, and rejecting the intervention	Establish regular communications before and during implementation. Create a psychologically safe forum for discussing issues

and implement the intervention; how to overcome resistance by participants; and how to do the live implementation.

Moving a small business owner beyond adoption to implementation depends on having them recognise that the goal of the intervention is something they need. This is a function of marketing but, as a management accountant, marketing was not my speciality. However, my husband is very good at it, and he shared some practical insights with me. The first step was to gather information on what the participants wanted, needed, and preferred. I was doing a quasi-experiment, so that meant doing a pre-test survey to glean valid and useful information about the problem, the dynamics of the environment, and the participants' ideas for solving the problem. Here, the problem was that small firm owner-managers were using information systems that were unable to support them in generating managerial information for planning and decision-making (decision-facilitating) and motivating their employees (decision-influencing). Information from the pre-test survey was valuable because it helped to diagnose the problem and align the solution with the needs of the people who were ultimately going to use the intervention and, in turn, the owners of the business. Using a marketing perspective appealed to the self-interest of owners while my research offered a solution to their problem. After the pilot-test, I was 95% confident that using this approach as part of my implementation strategy was likely to be successful, partly because, beyond promoting the benefits of the intervention, it prepared participants for the coming change and mobilised them to take ownership of the project.

Resistance to change is always a likelihood. Here, the pre-test surveys were also 'a-foot-in-the-door strategy' for building collaborations with participants. Communication is vital in addressing any form of resistance to change, so I shared information with them: the nature of the piecemeal implementation aimed at minimising inconvenience and disruption to daily operations and what would be required of them. I was also honest with the participants and discussed with them that, while participants would most likely experience very few or no disruptions to their daily routines during implementation, some unforeseen disruptions may occur. I offered an open invitation for anyone to contact me as needed to discuss any issues, and I 'did the rounds' daily to informally chat with the participants to see how they were doing. These conversations were extremely useful because they established an atmosphere of trust and support. It was also an effective strategy because resistance to the intervention and its implementation were low, the owners were excited about the potential changes to come, and there was an overall positive feeling about the intervention.

The 'live' implementation followed the traditional 'by-time' approach, which divides the full implementation into a sequence of smaller interventions—six in my case. This approach simplifies the implementation process and minimises confusion and misunderstandings by the participants. When broken down, it is also easier to allocate an appropriate amount of time to implement each task in each segment, which dictates the overall length of the implementation process. I was able to estimate the time for each phase fairly accurately given my prior experience in industry. However, it is best to err on the side of allocating too much time rather than too little.

Identify the Project's Milestones

Milestones are an important component of project management. They represent a logical sequence of the main goals, important decisions, and stages in an implementation (Lientz & Rea, 1999). However, milestones also help to identify areas of risk because they are typically linked to deliverables or outcomes—risks such as whether the project is progressing on schedule and, if not, why not. Has the scope changed? Is there resistance? Are problems brewing that have not yet surfaced? Therefore, milestones represent good points to conduct a review of the implementation so far.

Identify the Resources Needed

Identifying the research team, participants, equipment, material supplies, facilities, and budgetary requirements of the implementation ensures those resources are on hand when needed (Lientz & Rea, 1999). There is a saying known as the 5 Ps of planning, "Proper Planning Prevents Poor Performance", that is never more true than resource planning for an intervention. It prevents unnecessary delays, ensures resources are used in an optimal fashion, and helps to ensure that each member of the team knows their responsibilities and the limits of those responsibilities. Additionally, resource planning harks back to one of the fundamental tenets of IVR, which is to be honest about the capabilities of both the researcher and the social system. As the researcher, you are one of those resources. Hence, this is the time when you should really consider whether you have the qualities necessary to implement your intervention. With a project management strategy, one of the most important questions to answer is: Are you a project leader? Table 12.5 lists three general approaches to leadership. Scholars must make free and informed decisions about which one best suits the needs of your IVR project; I adopted the 'Facilitating' leadership approach.

Identify Methods and Tools Employed

Selecting the methods and tools to support the implementation should reflect its size, the backgrounds, cultures, and values of the participants, and the research context. Project management encompasses a range of

Table 12.5 Implementation Leadership Approaches

Approach	Advantages	Disadvantages
'Stay-out'	Ownership of the implementation process remains with the participant	It is possible that the implementation activities required to complete implementation may not occur, thus influencing intervention rejection
	Maximised opportunities for the participant to learn and develop by taking responsibility for the implementation	Participants may feel that there is no support from the researcher. This may reduce the extent of their commitment to intervention implementation and create conflict between the researcher and participant(s)
	Reduced dependency of the participants on the researcher	The implementation may not be carried out effectively, or the participant(s) may not have a suitable level of expertise to optimally complete intervention implementation
'Hands-on'	Implementation is completed properly	The participant may be denied a significant learning opportunity
	Less time required for implementation	The participant dependency on the researcher is increased, which may impinge on free and informed choices and inhibit an internal commitment to the intervention and its implementation
	Reduced risks for the participants	There are low levels of participant ownership of the implementation, resulting in a reduced level of commitment and an increase in resistance to the intervention
	Greater satisfaction over the implementation for the researcher	Control over and responsibility for the implementation is taken away from the participant, resulting in intervention rejection
Facilitating	Maximise a significant learning opportunity for the participant	The implementation may take longer to accomplish
	Decreases participant dependence on the researcher, and the participants feel supported by the researcher	It is a more difficult approach for the researcher to adopt; you are balancing 'stay-out' with 'hands-on'
	The researcher can oversee the implementation and anticipate any major issues the participants may experience	The reduced levels of 'interference' by the research will improve the validity of the results achieved from intervention implementation
	Participants are empowered, and resistance to the implementation and associated change diminishes	

Source: Adapted from Baard (2004)

methods and tools that are well suited for implementing interventions—many of which are functions of Microsoft Project. Some examples are provided in Table 12.6.

By integrating and using all the knowledge acquired during the above five activities, researchers can develop a detailed plan for converting a project into an operating schedule for the implementation.

Table 12.6 Implementation Methods/Tools

Implementation Task	Methods/Tools	Details
Creating a Schedule	Gantt charts, calendars, and task sheets	<u>Advantages:</u> Easy to use, use as a control mechanism to monitor progress, easy to maintain
Addressing & Managing Issues	Design appropriate forms, for example, Management Issue Form	<u>Criteria for forms:</u> • Describe the issue • Assign a low, medium, or high priority • Identify the impact of an issue • Show potential solutions, i.e., do nothing, use extra resources, restructure tasks, obtain additional researcher support • Identify actions required or taken • Show follow-up work to solve the issue if required
Communications	Identify the communication strategy used during implementation Design a communication log (useful for field notes, record-keeping, and transparent communication)	<u>Advantages:</u> Discuss and review implementation progress, problems, and unexpected benefits; avoid and/or resolve crises efficiently <u>Approaches:</u> telephone, email, texts, tweets, Facebook, face-to-face, discussion forum, and blogs
Monitoring & Controlling Implementation	Implementation and intervention performance Track with a Gantt chart Cost and resource performance Monitoring budgets—using accounting software or Excel spreadsheets	<u>Advantages:</u> Monitors unexpected problems, the frequency that milestones are not achieved, time for implementation, and time to solve problems <u>Advantages:</u> controls financial resources to support implementation

Source: Adapted from Baard (2004)

The last step is to 'close-out' an implementation, also referred to as terminating the implementation. Closing-out means the intervention has been integrated into the everyday work life of the organisation, and the researcher(s) can withdraw. Retreating to the etic realm, this is the time to update field notes, compile reports, preserve project records, and take satisfaction in the fact that the intervention is now happily owned and ensconced with the participants. Time and budget permitting, researchers can monitor the impacts and changes from the intervention. In my doctoral research, I continued to meet with the participants weekly for four months post-'close-out'. We discussed issues, possible modifications to the intervention, and the benefits it had brought to the owners and employees. For my doctoral project, implementation was successful with some minor issues arising during the process. It was incredibly hard work, but a very rewarding experience that changed the way small business owners adopt information systems to support critical planning and management controls.

Critical and Cautionary Tales From the Field

We are often reminded of the saying, "I want to move to theory. Everything works in theory". So, while we have covered intervention implementation theory in detail, the next hardest thing is to take what we have learned in theory and think about how we can implement that theory in practice. After all, if everything did indeed work in theory, then why would we need proof that it works in practice? In our experience, we, as researchers, need to be careful not overstep our bounds and create havoc in the very organisations we are trying to help.

Here, again, reflecting on one's skills is crucial. As we keep saying, IVR projects demand both academic skills and professional skills. However, many academics have never worked in industry, and so may never have had to solve problems inside an organisation before. If that is you, then leading an IVR project may not be for you. Or you might try starting with a small intervention that carries few risks and working your way up as you gain more experience. As Jönsson and Lukka (2006, p. 37) illustrate, there are serious risks associated with IVR:

> The researcher also needs to consider the various risks [their] interventions may cause for those co-operating with [them], and to the entire host organisation. Making interventions carelessly may lead to the "elephant-in-the-glass-store" effect, where the researcher causes a lot of damage to the target organisation.

Dumay (2010, p. 63) stresses that we must think about the scale of the intervention when considering the risks because every intervention is unique in its scope and potential impact. For example, on the low-risk end, a researcher can be a 'comrade' who provides moral support or acts as a sounding board for a project. At the high-risk end, interventionist researchers assume a role akin to a manager, who is ultimately responsible for the success of the intervention (Jakkula *et al.*, 2006; Suomala & Lyly-Yrjänäinen, 2009b). Understandably, the skills required to be a comrade are distinctly different from those required to be the buck stop (Dumay, 2010).

Having an academic researcher responsible for the outcome of an IVR project can also have some serious methodological and practical ramifications. As Suomala and Lyly-Yrjänäinen (2009a, p. 8) warn:

> It could be possible that a strong researcher would be able to contribute to a state of affairs, which could be seen as unnatural otherwise in that particular setting [the] researcher is not facilitating a change but rather manipulating one. As a result, the suggested implications would only contain anecdotal value.

Hence, it is important for the interventionist researcher not to forget that they have two fundamental responsibilities: they must deliver a practical outcome, and they must derive significant theoretical insights. We must not forget the connections between research and practice. By working in the field, researchers have the opportunity "to learn from those interesting new management accounting innovations and their functionality in real-life settings" (Suomala & Lyly-Yrjänäinen, 2009a, p. 8). As such, sharing those insights with accounting professionals and the academic community is also a valid outcome, as we explore more in Chapter 13.

A Critical Reflection of a Successful Implementation

The following reflections of a successful implementation are based on the experiences of this book's second author, John Dumay, who had run a successful consulting business for 15 years before joining academia. He returned to study to improve his consulting skills, which led to an MBA in 2001 immediately followed by a PhD in Accounting. His success and joy for academia saw consulting fall by the wayside, and he is now an accounting teacher and researcher. His recollections, in his own words, follow.

Background

The project occurred in 2008 while I transitioned from completing my PhD to beginning my academic career and has been the subject of two articles and two book chapters (Dumay, 2010; 2014; Dumay & Baard, 2017). These publications contain more detailed reflections on a project management approach to IVR and, in some cases, insights into how the method could be improved. The four-step framework in Figure 12.4 closely aligns with my prior experience as a project manager in industry and so is used to structure this account.

The project was to help develop and write a new strategy for the University of Sydney Conservatorium of Music. I was given the opportunity to undertake this project because one of my PhD mentors sat on both the Advisory Committee of the (now) University of Sydney Business School and the Conservatorium of Music. He was to be the gatekeeper of the project.

Step 1: Planning & Preparation

Purpose and Scope

The Sydney Conservatorium of Music is a world-class musical education institution with a long history of developing some of the finest Australian and international musicians (Collins, 2001). At the time the intervention took place, the Conservatorium and its new Dean were under considerable pressure to make major changes to the way the Conservatorium was run. The Dean was also under personal pressure from some members of academia, the music profession, and music lovers, as they did not support her appointment (Alexander, 2013). However, the Dean met that challenge head-on by commissioning a project to develop a new strategy for the Conservatorium. The primary goal of the strategy was to build on the Conservatorium's past success and enhance its reputation as a world-leading musical educational institution. To develop a rallying point and focus for the strategy, the Dean chose the upcoming centenary of the Conservatorium's founding, which was to occur seven years later in 2015. Thus, the Dean wanted to develop a long-term and comprehensive strategy. More importantly, the Conservatorium already had a well-defined mission statement Dumay *et al.* (2008, p. 4):

> The Sydney Conservatorium of Music is a cultural catalyst inspiring the study, research, creation and performance of music in all its forms, to prepare students for artistic, innovative performance and scholarship at the highest level of excellence, to foster lifelong commitment to music and culture and to provide enjoyment and enlightenment to all people.

To develop the new strategy, the mission statement also needed to fit in with the University of Sydney's strategic directions and the recommendations of the accrediting bodies. Six areas were identified as being crucial for business planning purposes, with a pervasive three-year rolling review: Academic and Artistic Excellence; Education Programs and Services; Community Outreach and Communications; Institutional Technology;

Business, Enterprise, and Institutional Effectiveness; and Development and Advancement.

Implementation Strategy

One of the main concerns with developing the intervention was how to get Conservatorium employees to help and adopt ownership of the process and then the eventual strategy. Thus, it was decided that the following people were to be directly involved in giving input to the project: a representative from the Board of Advice to the Conservatorium, the researcher (me), the academic staff of the Conservatorium, and some professional support staff. Involving these people in developing a strategic conversation is a prime example of using theory to underpin the implementation strategy and the overall success of the project. I relied on micro-sociological theory (Westley, 1990) to address "the need to reflect the desires and ambitions of the organisation as articulated by its people and stakeholders" (Dumay, 2010, p. 60).

Identify Milestones

The key tasks in the intervention, i.e., the project milestones, were to:

- Conduct interviews with key stakeholders;
- Organise interview transcripts;
- Analyse and report the findings of key stakeholder interviews;
- Prepare material for a strategic workshop;
- Liaise with university staff over access to the financial and KPI information needed to develop the strategic plan;
- Write the first draft of the strategic plan;
- Edit the draft based on comments and feedback from the workshop participants;
- Present the draft for comments to the Dean; and
- Create a final draft for printing.

The Sydney Conservatorium was required to:

- Schedule face-to-face interviews with the stakeholders;
- Arrange and coordinate resources for the strategic workshop;
- Print and distribute the workshop material;
- Provide secretarial support and distribute material generated from the workshop;
- Coordinate university staff to discuss financial and KPI data with me;
- Print and distribute the first draft of the strategic plan; and
- Print and distribute the final draft of the strategic plan.

Identify Resources

To conduct any research project successfully, including an intervention, the researcher needs to access resources and people (Jönsson & Lukka, 2006, p. 16). The main resources required for this project were human resources.

The first and most influential resource was the gatekeeper. As I outlined, "In this case, the gatekeeper was a member of the Board of Advice to the Conservatorium, a semi-retired businessman who was involved in constructing the previous strategic plan." (Dumay, 2010, p. 54). He had a longer association with Conservatorium than the Dean and so was good to talk to about historical issues. Second was the 'go-to' person—a Conservatorium insider who became my 'right hand'. In addition to being an important ally, this person became responsible for delivering the project internally. With an established tenure at the Conservatorium, the 'go-to' person knew everyone, and the internal politics, and could help me become part of the Conservatorium's everyday life. Additionally, the 'go-to' person helped me find interviewees and a person with both access and authorisation to use key organisational resources, such as the accounting systems, human resource information, and key documents relating to strategic development. Without such a person, interventions are extremely difficult to mount, if not impossible.

Other key human resources included the senior administrative and academic staff at the Conservatorium. Because the project commenced in July, several key staff members were not available for interviews. However, in any IVR project, you need to assess whether some missing people are key to undertaking the project. Here, it would have been helpful to have more participants, but it was not possible, and so intervention work continued. The senior administrative and academic staff were asked to participate initially in an interview and then to participate in a strategy development workshop.

The strategy development workshop built upon the data collected from the interviews and was a key mechanism for involving the professional and academic staff in creating the new strategy. Staff involvement was essential because the previous strategic plan was developed in isolation, and we recognised that any new strategy needed to synthesise individual staff inputs into a more cohesive 'voice' of the Conservatorium. Using both human and organisational resources enabled us as a team to develop the first draft strategic plan through several iterations of feedback, redrafting, and editing with the Dean, gatekeeper, researcher, professional staff, and academics.

Methods and Tools

The methods and tools in this IVR project consisted of interviews, a workshop and document analysis, and "walking the halls" of the Conservatorium. In IVR, I call this aspect of the research process "catalytical", defining it as a research process based on the emic and etic perspectives, "whereby the researcher intervenes within the organisation and allows the existing organisational processes, both formal and informal, to take their normal paths while observing and analysing the results in preparation for future interventions" (Dumay, 2010, p. 61). However, the catalytical is more than just the emic and the etic because it allows the researcher to probe inside the organisation and elicit responses from the participants (Brown & Eisenhardt, 1997; Kurtz & Snowden, 2003; Snowden & Boone, 2007). Once analysed, these responses can be a catalyst for organisational change. Hence, the interviews and the interview questions were designed to elicit responses about the strategy and spark strategic conversations among the staff (Westley, 1990). By asking probing questions, the interviewees were now engaged in strategy development and put strategy on their agendas. In other words, each interview question was a micro-intervention acting as a catalyst for personal thought, conversation, and action. Therefore, the interviewees' responses needed to be analysed instantly and taken into consideration before asking another question (Qu & Dumay, 2011).

After analysing the interviews, the 'future, backwards' strategic workshop was conducted. This was a multi-directional strategic conversation among the participants where they shared their knowledge and ideas about the strategy. It was part of the sense-making process and a way to stretch the strategic conversations beyond the initial interview to keep refining the strategy. This workshop was an essential part of confirming the analysis of the interviews and keeping staff involved. The workshop also linked individual inputs into that common voice for the Conservatorium, which was so important.

In a nutshell, 'The future, backwards' workshop method is (Dumay, 2014, p. 74):

> an alternative to scenario planning and is designed to increase the number of perspectives a group can take on understanding their past and a range of possible futures. Done properly, it can help participants to discover entrained patterns of past perceptions about their workplace that are then used for determining its future. This allows participants to compare and contrast their different aspirations for the present and the future, which then becomes linked to strategy.

The workshop involved 12 of the 28 staff members who participated in the interviews and intentionally did not include the Dean. The workshop had two steps.

The first unique step in this process was a game with 'hexies'— hexagonal-shaped post-it notes, custom made especially for this process. Hexies come in different colours, and I used six to represent different aspects of the past, present, and future as perceived by the participants.

The reason for the hexies, as opposed to normal post-it notes, is that the six-sides of the hexagon create richer connections when posted on a wall. The reason for using post-it notes is they can be moved around as the workshop progress (see Figure 12.3).

Playing 'the hexie game' has four phases. First, participants were asked to think about where the Conservatorium was at present, write whatever came to their minds on a yellow hexie, and stick it to the wall. They were encouraged to post each hexie next to another hexie with a related idea and move the hexies around as new ideas were posted. During this initial phase, I also explained the rules of the game, which are as follows:

- There is no right or wrong answer;
- Be as creative, imaginary, and extreme as you can;
- Consider all behaviours, processes, characteristics, events, newspaper headlines, pictures, anything that helps describe the future state;
- Do not channel all discussions/postings through one person—everyone contributes; and
- Discuss items and perspectives and experiences while posting—no silence!

Then, participants were asked to look back in time to connect the series of events that led to the present and post these on the wall on blue hexies. There was no time limit to this; they could go as far back as they wanted. Third, participants must think of what heaven (utopia) or hell (dystopia)

Figure 12.3 The Completed 'The Future, Backwards' Wall

would be when working at the Conservatorium in 2015. Green hexies were for heaven; pink hexies for hell. Last, they had to identify the series of events needed for either heaven or hell to occur: light-green hexies for the path to heaven, and light-pink hexies for the path to hell. The idea is that the events connecting the past and present to heaven can be used to devise actions to be taken while the events leading to hell can be used to devise preventative actions.

Another key tool was to allow all staff members participating in the interviews and workshop to give feedback on the first draft of the new strategy. The request for feedback had two purposes. First, it consolidated staff involvement so that they could see that their voice had been heard, further cementing their involvement (Westley, 1990). Second, it helped to validate the strategy for me and the Dean, which gave additional confidence that the outcomes were achievable and the staff had internally committed (Yin, 2017).

What this recounting should emphasise is that the research methods selected must be purposeful. They were in the Conservatorium project, designed to be the interventions in themselves. The IVR literature does not adequately address the impact of research methods as interventions. Instead, the focus is on outcomes, not process (Dumay, 2010).

Implementation Schedule

Unlike many IVR projects that have long timelines, the Conservatorium project had to be delivered in six weeks, despite its seven-year lifespan. As shown in Figure 12.4 below, I was onsite for most of those six weeks, so it was fortunate that the time coincided with the semester break. The schedule highlights how IVR projects can be very time-consuming and usually require the researcher to fully immerse themselves in the project.

Step 2: Live Implementation

This section presents a brief reflection on the live implementation, which was somewhat of a blur considering the short timeframe. Certainly,

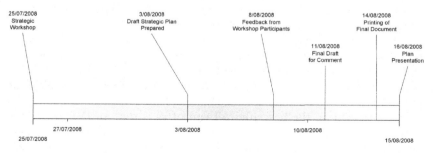

Figure 12.4 The Conservatorium Project: An Implementation Schedule

projects with longer timelines would have much more scope and necessity to trace live implementation. However, the main reflection is that the project was successful because it had the full support of the Dean and the involvement of the professional and academic staff. Such a short timeline and the quality of the eventual strategy document reflects their involvement because it provided adequate detail, brought forward realistic concerns, and proposed strategic initiatives that would otherwise not have been possible if the strategy was developed in isolation of their involvement. Moreover, it promoted a real team effort and eventual buy-in of the strategy that the staff owned as much as did the Dean.

Another reflection on live implementation is the skill sets required by the interventionist research, and key people such as the go-to person, the Dean, and the gatekeeper. All these key people have well-developed management and people skills, along with their appropriate technical skills. It greatly highlights the need to have the right people in the right place at the right time for such a project. It also reflects on the ability of the researcher to involve their academic skills and their ability to deal with the emic in the etic aspects. It also highlights that the education of the key people plays a significant role in implementing an IVR project. In this case, IVR was just a catalyst to help get the job done, while at the same time allowing for an academic outcome alongside the managerial outcome.

Step 3: Monitoring and Controlling Implementation

The Dean and the gatekeeper controlled intervention performance and kept a close eye on the project implementation. As soon as we analysed the data from the initial interviews and then the workshop, we sent the results to the Dean and the gatekeeper for their comments and input. Additionally, as soon as the initial draft of the strategy was completed, the Dean forwarded it to the university leadership to ensure the strategy we were developing was in keeping with their overall plans and policies. Thus, there was continuous monitoring of the quality of the evolving strategy so that when the final document was eventually published, it had already passed through a series of checks and balances to ensure success.

Monitoring the time taken for implementation was part of the above process as was resolving any problems along the way. For example, the go-to person developed the financial analyses for the project. Being able to access and understand the university's financial reporting and management accounting system was difficult at times, but together we were able to develop key metrics for the budget and key performance indicators for the strategy.

Upon reflection, the best advice I can offer is that an IVR project is multifaceted with many tasks occurring at the same time. In the case of the Conservatorium, writing and editing the strategy document were happening simultaneously, all while the work to analyse the data, develop budgets and forecasts, identify and confirm key performance indicators, and so forth continued. It did not seem like any one task was ever finished until the final crescendo of the published strategy document.

Step 4: Close-Out the Implementation

The procedure for terminating implementation was as quick as it had started. As soon as the strategy document was complete, it went to the university for approval and my work was complete. The approval process took almost as long, if not longer, than preparing the document. However, arguably, the real implementation was the strategy itself because, even though the aim of the project was to prepare a strategy document, it was now up to the Dean and the staff of the Conservatorium to put the strategy into action.

To the best of my knowledge, the Dean was committed to the strategy and implemented it as it was designed. For example, one key strategic initiative was *Sounds of the Century: "100 Commissions for 100 years"*. The first performance of a commissioned work was presented in September 2009 with John Corigliano's Mr Tambourine Man, based on the poetry of Bob Dylan. I was invited back to the Conservatorium for several more performances and one post-performance party where the Dean formally acknowledged my presence and my contribution to the genesis of the Conservatorium's current strategy. Like Vicki, I also feel that IVR can be very rewarding.

Reflections on Unsuccessful Implementations

What I have described above is an example of a successful implementation, but not all projects are successful. In my experience, it is very difficult to set up a project and carry it out even when all the participants have the best intentions. For example, I was part of the team about to embark on a project installing a new point-of-sale accounting system for the restaurants and bars in the student union in a major Australian university. However, even after getting the ethics approval and the cooperation of the managers at the student union, the month before the project was to commence, the gatekeeper was made redundant. With the gatekeeper gone, so too was the project. This failure highlights how projects can radically change in scope and outcome with the simple change of one key player. Bernardi (2015) reports a similar situation where the head of the division under study suddenly left, and the incoming head radically changed the project. Thus, interventionist researchers need to be cognisant that all IVR projects are subject to changes in personnel and particularly in industries where employee turnover rates are upwards of 20%.

IVR projects are also subject to disagreements over what the purposes and the eventual outcomes of the project should be. One example of internal issues that ultimately led to the demise of an IVR project was at a small technology company. This company employed about 20 people with a turnover of several millions of dollars from selling a speciality product to a worldwide customer base. The business was owned and managed by a husband and wife team, with the husband taking care of technical and marketing aspects and the wife taking care of the personnel and overseeing the accounting. They were in their mid-50s and looking at succession planning for their retirement. Perhaps their son would move into the business or perhaps they would sell it.

I was introduced to the company by an accountant from a small second-tier accounting firm in Sydney. They had been struggling with the client for many years, trying to explain that their poor performance was because, like many small businesses, they seemed to be doing a lot of work and not earning that much money. However, the real difficulty was that this poor performance made it difficult to determine what the business was worth. I was asked to help explain what value was in the business. The accountant who recommended me had seen me speak at an industry event about the value of intangibles as drivers for business value. He thought that if I could unlock what the intangible value of the business was, we would be able to put forward a value that was not just based on financial outcomes. Understanding and identifying intangibles was the subject of my PhD, so this seemed like a great IVR project.

As such, after conferring with the accountant and a meeting with the business owners, I drew up an ethics application. Once I received approval, I arranged another meeting to review the company's financial performance. While I understood the financial performance was poor, what happened next was something I didn't expect. I remember sitting in the office reviewing the balance sheet and the profit and loss statements when I noticed a line item, which was an adjustment to the cost of sales of several hundred thousand dollars. This was a significant portion of their cost of sales expense. I immediately interjected into the meeting that there must be a problem with the account-keeping system or its review. The wife openly admitted that there were problems. One of the main ones was that their employees had been loyal for years but felt they had not been fully trained. So, unlike the Conservatorium, where the people were professional and highly educated, the staff of this firm, including the husband and wife, had technical knowledge, but little managerial and accounting experience. The accounting system was a well-known software package, but the only training that had ever happened was with one staff member by the person who had installed the software a few years prior. Most staff, especially newer staff, had almost no training but were being asked to perform specific accounting tasks without knowing why these tasks were needed or, often, how to carry them out properly.

Unfortunately for the wife, my observations about cost adjustment played into the hands of the husband who was not a firm believer in accounting and accounting systems. Much to the dismay of the accountant and the wife, the husband's bookkeeping approach was simple—so long as there was money in the bank, the business was doing okay. He was a firm believer in cash accounting and didn't care much for balance sheets, profit and loss reports, debtors and creditors listing, or stock takes. Moreover, he didn't care much for accountants because he thought they charged too much. The only need for an accountant was lodging tax returns, after minimising what the company had to pay of course. Thus, there was an immediate challenge in this project because the husband, who should have been a willing participant and had initially indicated support for the project, was now withdrawing.

Yet the accountant talked him into starting the project. He explained that selling the business would be very difficult without such a project: that it was in the best financial interests of he and his wife to get me to help. I was somewhat hesitant about the project and worked on it for several weeks trying to get to the bottom of what was required to understand the true intangible value of the business. One of my main challenges was to understand if the accounting system was truly broken, or whether it could be easily repaired so the financial information was timely and relevant. However, my continued presence at the site only seemed to create a bigger divide between the fully supportive wife and the increasingly resentful husband. She was trying to learn from my investigations, while he saw it wasting more and more time.

In the end, I took a break from the project to attend a conference overseas. When I returned, I tried to make a further appointment, and the wife told me they were going overseas themselves for a few weeks holiday, but they would contact me again. They never did and, even after a follow-up, nothing eventuated.

The lessons learned here is that there is no certainty that an IVR project will be successful, and one of the leading causes of failure is the people surrounding the project rather than the project itself and, try as we might, people cannot be forced to drink. As highlighted in the case of the Conservatorium, the project had a tight-knit group of people determined to work together to achieve the outcome, which increases the likelihood of success, but does not guarantee it. When key people come and go, it puts the project in jeopardy. As in Bernardi (2015), the research project did not completely stop. However, the scope significantly changed, and therefore the implementation process was severely disrupted, and the final outcomes were not as intended. On the bright side, there are learnings in these failures. Ensuring the project begins with the right people and the right skills and a solid motivation in place is a good start. Proper planning for resources is next and, above all, be cognisant of the organisational realities. Regularly stand back to reflect on the project and critically observe the people within it.

In Summation

The two most important take-aways from this chapter are that interventions require planning and testing. In terms of planning, we recommend following NPT because it gives you insights on how to plan an implementation. However, the best-laid plans can often go astray, so make room for contingencies to help manage any unforeseen circumstances. Also, pilot-test to see how the implementation might work on a small scale and make changes as needed so that minor blunders do not become huge disasters.

Further, we must always learn from past failures as well as successes. What we have outlined in this chapter demonstrates successful projects and highlights lessons learned from the field on unsuccessful projects. We need to emphasise that human resources are a key part of success and, specifically, matching the right people to the right project. In the Conservatorium project, it was quite evident that the project was a success because all the people involved took it upon themselves to help. However, this may not have happened if the gatekeeper was not so good at rallying people to the cause; if the Dean was not committed to a long-term vision; and the go-to person was working in conjunction with the research. Together, these people marshalled what was required to get the project off the ground and keep it working, which included the help of the academics and support staff. Likewise, the unsuccessful projects failed because they could not cross the hurdle of enrolling people. If the key participants cannot maintain their enthusiasm, the researcher cannot maintain the project. Winning the hearts and minds of your participants is just as important as having a good plan.

References

Alexander, H. (2013, February 14). Uni made me unemployable, says ex-dean. *The Sydney Morning Herald*. Retrieved from: www.smh.com.au/education/uni-made-me-unemployable-says-ex-dean-20130213-2eddd.html

Argyris, C. (1970). *Intervention theory and method: A behavioural science view*. Reading, MA: Addison-Wesley Publishing Company.

Baard, V.C. (2004). *The design and implementation of an IT consulting system in South African small businesses*. (Doctor of Technologiae), Central University of Technology, Bloemfontein, South Africa.

Baard, V.C. (2010). A critical view of interventionist research. *Qualitative Research in Accounting and Management, 7*(1), 13–45.

Bernardi, C. (2015). *Integrated reporting: Insights, critical issues and future research agenda*. (PhD), Roma Tre Universita Delgi Studi, Rome.

Brown, S.L. & Eisenhardt, K.M. (1997). The art of continuous change: Linking complexity theory and time-paced evolution in relentlessly shifting organizations. *Administrative Science Quarterly, 42*(1), 1–34. Retrieved from: http://search.epnet.com.ezproxy.library.usyd.edu.au/login.aspx?direct=true&db=buh&an=9706191514

Collins, D. (2001). *Sounds from the stables: The story of Sydney's conservatorium*. Crows Nest, NSW, Australia: Allen & Unwin.

Cook, B.G. & Odom, S.L. (2013). Evidence-based practices and implementation science in special education. *Exceptional Children*, 79(2), 135–144.

Damschroder, L.J., Aron, D.C., Keith, R.E., Kirsh, S.R., Alexander, J.A., & Lowery, J.C. (2009). Fostering implementation of health services research findings into practice: A consolidated framework for advancing implementation science. *Implementation Science*, 4(50), 1–15. Retrieved from: https://link.springer.com/article/10.1186/1748-5908-4-50

Dumay, J. (2010). A critical reflective discourse of an interventionist research project. *Qualitative Research in Accounting and Management*, 7(1), 46–70.

Dumay, J. (2014). Developing a strategy to create a public value chain. In J. Guthrie, G. Marcon, S. Russo, & F. Farneti (Eds.), *Public value management, measurement and reporting* (pp. 65–83). Bingeley, UK: Emerald.

Dumay, J. & Baard, V.C. (2017). An introduction to interventionist research in accounting. In Z. Hoque, L.D. Parker, M. Covaleski, & K. Haynes (Eds.), *The Routledge companion to qualitative accounting research methods* (pp. 265–283). Oxfordshire, UK: Routledge and Taylor and Francis.

Dumay, J., Walker, K., Greenwood, L., & Wauchope, B. (2008). *Strategic outlook 2008–2015*. Retrieved from: www.music.usyd.edu.au/docs/Conservatorium_LiteFINAL19Dec_2008.pdf

Eccles, M.P. & Mittman, B.S. (2006). Welcome to implementation science. *Implementation Science*, 1(1), 1–3.

Gitlin, L.N. & Czaja, S.J. (2016). *Behavioural intervention research: Designing, evaluating and implementing*. New York, NY: Springer Publishing Company.

Jakkula, V., Lyly-Yrjänäinen, J., & Suomala, P. (2006, December 14–16). *Challenges of practically relevant management accounting research: The scope and intensity of interventionist research*. Paper presented at the 5th New Practices in Management Accounting Research Conference, Brussels.

Jönsson, S. & Lukka, K. (2006). *Doing interventionist research in management accounting*. Gothenburg Research Institute, Gothenburg.

Jönsson, S. & Lukka, K. (2007). There and back again: Doing interventionist research in management accounting. In C.S. Chapman, A.G. Hopwood, & M.S. Shields (Eds.), *Handbook of management accounting research* (Vol. 1, pp. 373–397). Oxford, UK: Elsevier.

Kurtz, C. & Snowden, D. (2003). The new dynamics of strategy: Sense-making in a complex and complicated world. *IBM Systems Journal*, 42(3), 462–483. Retrieved from: www.research.ibm.com/journal/sj/423/kurtz.html

Lientz, B.P. & Rea, K.P. (1999). *Project management: Planning and implementation*. New York, NY: Harcourt Professional Publishing.

Linton, J.D. (2002). Implementation research: State of the art and future directions. *Technovation*, 22(2), 65–79.

May, C.R. & Finch, T. (2009). Implementing, embedding, and integrating practices: An outline of normalisation process theory. *Sociology*, 43(3), 535–554.

May, C.R., Finch, T., Mair, F., Ballini, L., Dowrick, C., Eccles, M., . . . Heaven, B. (2007). Understanding the implementation of complex interventions in health care: The normalization process model. *Implementation Science*, 7(148), 1–7. Retrieved from: https://bmchealthservres.biomedcentral.com/articles/10.1186/1472-6963-7-148

May, C.R., Mair, F., Finch, T., MacFarlane, A., Dowrick, C., Treweek, S., . . . Montori, V.M. (2009). Development of a theory of implementation and integration: Normalization process theory. *Implementation Science*, 4(29), 1–9. Retrieved from: https://implementationscience.biomedcentral.com/articles/10.1186/1748-5908-4-29

Murray, E., Treweek, S., Pope, C., MacFarlane, A., Ballini, L., Dowrick, C., . . . May, C. (2010). Normalisation process theory: A framework for developing, evaluating and implementing complex interventions. *Implementation Science*, 8(63), 1–11. Retrieved from: https://bmcmedicine.biomedcentral.com/articles/10.1186/1741-7015-8-63

Proctor, E.K., Powell, B.J., & McMillen, J.C. (2013). Implementation strategies: Recommendations for specifying and reporting. *Implementation Science*, 8(39). 1–11. Retrieved from: https://implementationscience.biomedcentral.com/articles/10.1186/1748-5908-8-139

Qu, S.Q. & Dumay, J. (2011). The qualitative research interview. *Qualitative Research in Accounting & Management*, 8(3), 238–264. http://dx.doi.org/10.1108/11766091111162070

Rogers, E.M. (2003). *Diffusion of innovations* (5th ed.). New York, NY: The Free Press.

Rothman, J. & Tumblin, A. (1994). Pilot testing and early development of a model of case management intervention. In J. Rothman &and E.J. Thomas (Eds.), *Intervention research: Design and development for human service* (pp. 215–233). Binghamton, NY: Haworth Press.

Scheirer, M.A. (1981). *Program implementation: The organisational context*. Beverly Hills, CA: Sage Publications.

Scheirer, M.A. (2005). Is sustainability possible? A review and commentary on empirical studies of program sustainability. *American Journal of Evaluation*, 26(3), 320–347.

Snowden, D.J. & Boone, M.E. (2007). A leader's framework for decision making. *Harvard Business Review*, 85(11), 68–76. Retrieved from: http://search.ebscohost.com/login.aspx?direct=true&db=heh&AN=27036324&site=ehost-live

Straus, S.E., Tetroe, J., & Graham, I. (2009). Defining knowledge translation. *Canadian Medication Association Journal*, 181(3–4), 165–168. http://dx.doi.org/10.1503/cmaj.081229

Suomala, P. & Lyly-Yrjänäinen, J. (2009a). *Interventionist management accounting research: Lessons learned*. Retrieved from: http://www.gslb.cimaglobal.com/Documents/Thought_leadership_docs/Organisational%20management/cid_ressum_interventionist_management_accounting_research_apr2010.pdf

Suomala, P. & Lyly-Yrjänäinen, J. (2009b, May 13–15). *Interventionist management accounting research: The scope and intensity in three series of empirical research*. Paper presented at the 32nd Annual Congress of the European Accounting Association, Tampere, Finland.

Tucker, B.P. & Parker, L.D. (2013). In our ivory towers? The research-practice gap in management accounting. *Accounting and Business Research*, 44(2), 104–143. https://doi.org/10.1080/00014788.2013.798234

Westley, F.R. (1990). Middle managers and strategy: Microdynamics of inclusion. *Strategic Management Journal*, 11(5), 337–351.

Yin, R.K. (2017). *Case study research and applications: Design and methods* (6th ed.). Thousand Oaks, CA: Sage Publications Inc.

13 Disseminating Your Interventionist Research

"Sharing knowledge generated from research is fundamental to the research enterprise and an ethical obligation of investigators" (Gitlin & Czaja, 2016, p. 453). Intervention dissemination, see Phase 6 of the Interventionist Research Framework (IRF) (see Chapter 5), completes an accounting IVR project through distributing its outcomes in some form or using some channel. This chapter aims to offer guidance on how to present your research, with whom to publish, and where to publish your knowledge produced from your IVR. Publishing new knowledge or knowledge-producing theoretically significant contributions enable interventionist researchers to provide meaningful accounting research with theoretical relevance.

Additionally, we consider writing for and transforming scholarly knowledge into actionable knowledge for sharing with non-academics (i.e., practitioners, non-accounting managers, and community members) in social systems. Here, actionable knowledge may encompass solutions to address real social system problems or to mobilise a range of people and institutions to achieve objectives, sustain their adaptability and survivability, and effectiveness. Here, we provide meaningful accounting research with practical and societal relevance. Disseminating scientific and practical knowledge is consistent with Lewin's duality of IVR output. Our primary message in this chapter is threefold: a) developing thoughtful and meaningful publications is important for accounting IVR relevance; b) selecting a high-quality journal is paramount to further IVR's legitimacy; and c) identifying critical stakeholders, especially non-academics, that your research will impact through dissemination requires careful consideration.

Dissemination—Initial Reflections

Our conversation on dissemination started at the beginning of the book, where we introduced readers to IVR. Specifically, in Chapter 2, we examined the research-practice gap and why this gap persists. Here, we find that the language, terminology, and jargon are fundamental communication barriers explaining why non-academics do not read what we write. Academics have 'private conversations' among ourselves in our journals, at research seminars, and conferences.

Conversely, publishing accounting IVR in high-quality journals is incredibly difficult, as theoretical advancement is always given a higher weighting than the influence or implications of accounting practices. We then consider how accounting scholars and practitioners address the research-practice gap, where we find some scholars argue for leading academic journals to publish accounting research that meets the dynamic needs of society. Conversely, other scholars argue that accounting researchers must go outside their comfort zones and publish in professional journals. Scholars must 'get-out-there' and engage in conversation with non-academics at conferences and professional association events about the implications of our research to enhance social system health and well-being.

In reflecting on dissemination in Chapter 5, we observe that in the context of social work, Thomas and Rothman (1994) view this phase as 'commercial', where they discuss branding, setting standards for use, and establishing a price for intervention akin to creating demand and identifying potential markets; similarly, in the behavioural IVR context (e.g., Beilenson *et al.*, 2016). Our perception of the commerciality of the intervention stems from the fact that IVR in social work and healthcare yields practical interventions that significantly influence health and human service needs across the larger society. Therefore, disseminating critical interventions outside of the intervention context (e.g., ten primary care practices with 250 participants) to satisfy critical needs requires a robust plan and a commercialisation approach with high associated costs.

Anecdotally, as accounting interventionist researchers, we are often confronted by other normative or interpretive accounting scholars on the issue of consulting, and it is hard work to dissuade them that the IVR we conduct is not a consulting practice. Hence, we cannot advocate intervention dissemination in accounting as applied in the health and human services context. We are not saying that accounting scholars must not engage in the commercialisation of their interventions, that is your prerogative entirely; we do offer some insights in Chapter 6 on the matter of intellectual property. Kaplan and Norton (1992), of the balanced scorecard fame, and Eccles and Krzus (2010) and their version of integrated reporting (One Report) are two examples of partnerships between researchers and practitioner consultants that have built their reputations and frameworks by working closely together. Also, in Chapter 5, we state that we view dissemination in the accounting IVR context as publishing in reputable academic journals and professional publications, engaging directly with non-academics, introducing IVR in research courses in higher education institutions, and through doctoral education in academic settings.

Our final reflection is on the meaning of dissemination, which we consider in Chapter 12 on intervention implementation. We find that the terms 'adoption', 'implementation', 'diffusion', and dissemination are subtly different in the IVR context. In the human and services context, dissemination includes the adoption of an intervention, following evidence of an intervention's successful implementation potential, by a variety of settings outside of where the intervention took place (Beilenson *et al.*, 2016). In the accounting IVR context, our interpretation of dissemination for this book refers to the communication of theoretical and practical knowledge about an intervention through a variety of scholarly and non-academic channels.

Publishing IVR in Academic Journals

Communicating the outcomes of scholarly IVR is imperative regardless of the discipline. While the aspects of publishing presented in this section may seem obvious, accounting interventionist researchers must recognise and respect the contributory obligation that we have when conducting IVR—it supports the legitimacy of the methodology. In this section, we focus primarily on publishing an accounting research article as one of the final products of an accounting IVR project. Thus, by knowing the inherent challenges in publishing quality accounting IVR articles, researchers can make informed strategic decisions on what and where to publish (de Villiers & Dumay, 2013, 2014). Thus, Table 13.1 outlines a proposed research strategy based on publishing accounting research and the alignment with the IRF.

Arguably, the interventionist researcher can begin writing the article at any time during the IVR project, but as we outline in Table 13.1, there must be some thought given to planning and enabling the dissemination process during the IRF phases. It is most important to include the publication strategy developed from Table 13.1 as part of the research protocol document developed in Phase 1 and to continually update the strategy and its enablement in the protocol document.

Publication Timeline and Resources

A common error in developing research projects is not devoting enough time to planning for IVR dissemination. IVR dissemination is a complex process and is hard work for several reasons. If you are doing an IVR project to satisfy the requirements of a doctoral thesis, then you have a distinct time allocated for collecting and analysing data and writing the results to meet your submission deadline. Outside of doctoral work, this may not necessarily be the case. If you have a funded IVR project, as with any other funded project, the dissemination of academic work may not be a prime concern of the participants or the social system under investigation. Also, IVR dissemination is usually not a single-authored work and can have multiple authors because IVR teams consist of several people, and several

Table 13.1 Publishing IVR: A Strategic Framework

Strategic Element	Description	Phases
Publication Timeline and Resources	Ensuring that you have a realistic timeline for publishing the article so that you can allocate appropriate time and resources, especially in projects employing research assistants, co-investigators, co-authors, and participants.	Phase 1 & 6
Choosing a Target Journal	Ensuring that you have a realistic idea of where you want to publish an article, and awareness of the minefield associated with selecting a target journal.	Phase 1 & 6
With Whom do I Publish?	IVR is rarely a "one-man-band", and the project will most likely have more than one person involved.	Phase 1, 3, 5, & 6
Article Structure	In accounting, an IVR article is a subset of a case study research article, and therefore all the rules associated with publishing case study research apply. Therefore, you need to get the structure right to tell the story.	Phase 6
Polishing the Rough Diamond	There is nothing worse than submitting an article to a high-quality journal, and the article has a multitude of errors. Copyediting and proofreading are essential before submitting articles.	Phase 6

articles can result from a single project. For example, the Conservatorium of Music project by Dumay (2010a) resulted in conference papers (e.g., Dumay, 2010b), several academic articles (e.g., Dumay, 2011), and a report, and included co-authors from academia (e.g., Dumay & Guthrie, 2012) and from the project (Dumay *et al.*, 2013). Thus, researchers need to plan for a dissemination process that normally takes longer than the actual project and may have multiple authors.

An IVR project can be a lengthy process to complete from inception, and dissemination invariably will occur at the end of (or sometimes, but rarely, during) the IVR project. Typically, one to three years will pass before an article is ready to submit to an academic journal. Before your team submits the article to a journal, you might want to 'road test' the article and present your research at research seminars and conferences before submission; that will add time to the process for submitting the paper. Once the article is under review, then it takes three to six months (or longer) for the first reviews to come in. However, it is almost impossible that the editor accepts the article on the first submission, and if the article receives positive reviews, the research team needs to revise the article and re-submit for another round of review, and this process can take up to a year. Typically, an article will go through three or four rounds of review before being accepted. Last, even after the editor accepts the article for publication, it can take up to two years to appear in print because of a long queue of accepted papers waiting to be published in the journal. However, these days high-quality journals will have an 'In Press' version available shortly after accepting it to attract readers and citations. Thus, the process can take as little as one to two years, or as much as up to seven years from the beginning of the IVR project.

During the time spent trying to publish your article, you also need to consider and budget for the costs associated with developing the article, as we have outlined and discussed in more detail in Chapter 6. As part of the research process, the interventionist researcher needs money to transcribe interviews, analyse documents and other data (research assistants), copy editing and proofreading, and service costs associated with attending conferences. Additionally, if public agencies, such as the United Kingdom Research Council, fund your research, you might need to have money to publish it as a gold open access article, which makes the article free for anyone to read even though it is behind the academic paywall (see Guthrie *et al.*, 2015). Therefore, you must ensure that there is adequate funding for disseminating the research.

Choosing a Target Journal

One of the greatest minefields for an accounting academic and interventionist researcher is where to publish. Unfortunately, the dissemination strategy often neglects to address this question until after completing the research or even writing the first articles. Answering the where to publish question is important because if done with strategic intent, it can help increase the chances of getting the article published in a good journa, and shorten the time it takes to publish.

We call choosing a journal a minefield because if you do not take a strategic approach, you can end up publishing in a non-peer reviewed pay-to-publish journal that can eventually blow up in your face and be detrimental to your academic career. There is no doubt the pressure to publish is so great that some academics (not just accounting academics) might sometimes take a short-cut to publish an article and respond to one of the many emails they receive offering a quick review process and quick publication on acceptance. We must be aware that these offers are not in our interest and are further suspect if the publisher is not recognisable as one of the leading academic publishing houses and does not appear on your university's recognised list of publishers.

While some of these emails may be genuine offers from academics with the right intentions, we have yet to receive one from a journal that offers quick reviews and publication, and a fee. We do of course get invited to write articles, but these are mainly for special issues or for a journal that wants to promote discourse in a specialist area. For example, the Dumay (2010a) article is an article that the editor of the journal invited him to write after seeing him present a paper about the project at an academic conference. However, the article still underwent a full peer-review before being accepted as part of the special issue on IVR published in *Qualitative Research in Accounting and Management* (Westin *et al.*, 2010). Therefore, we do not want to discourage researchers from accepting invitations to write for a journal, but please be wary of the invitation, that it might cost you money, and even damage your reputation.

To avoid the problem, we recommend researchers to consult with their schools about where their discipline is targeting publications. For example, our school uses the Australian Business Deans Council (ABDC) ranking of academic journals as a guideline and encourages us to publish in A* and A-ranked journals. While it is true that many of those journals might not be interested in publishing case-study research because they mainly publish quantitative studies, many are open to publishing case-study research in accounting. Considering the relationship between IVR and case study research, there is no reason why the journals would reject the article just because it is an IVR study. However, you must consider the balance between theoretical and practical contributions based on the journal's intended audience. Academically, you will probably need to err on the side of theoretical over practical contributions. As with all research, if it is of high quality and has novelty, and can successfully argue that it contributes to accounting knowledge, then potentially the article can be published. Table 13.2 presents ABDC ranked academic accounting journals that we recommend might be interested in your research. However, you should always check with your school as to which journals are acceptable.

Arguably, what Table 13.2 also shows is that there is a myth in accounting and amongst interventionist researchers that IVR is particularly difficult to publish. We argue that quality research that includes IVR as a methodology is publishable and faces the same challenges that any other case study article faces in passing by the reviewers.

Our main recommendation to the reader is that they should familiarise themselves with a target journal to understand the issues that appear in the journal, which form the prevailing conversation, and the links between the other articles in the journal. It is important that your research links with these conversations, or is so novel that it makes the article interesting for the journal's audience. Therefore, you should try to publish in journals that you are familiar with and are likely read and cite on a regular basis.

Table 13.2 A Home for Your IVR Research Article

Ranking	Journal Title	Publisher
A*	Accounting Auditing and Accountability Journal	Emerald Group Publishing Limited
A*	Accounting, Organizations and Society	Elsevier
A*	British Accounting Review	Elsevier
A*	Contemporary Accounting Research	Wiley-Blackwell Publishing
A*	Management Accounting Research	Elsevier
A*	The European Accounting Review	Taylor & Francis Online
A	Accounting and Business Research	Taylor & Francis Online
A	Accounting and Finance	Wiley-Blackwell Publishing
A	Accounting Education	Taylor & Francis Online
A	Accounting History	Sage Publications
A	Advances in Accounting Behavioral Research	Emerald Group Publishing
A	Advances in Management Accounting	Emerald Group Publishing
A	Behavioral Research in Accounting	American Accounting Association
A	Critical Perspectives on Accounting	Elsevier
A	Financial Accountability and Management	Wiley-Blackwell Publishing
A	International Journal of Accounting Information Systems	Elsevier
A	Managerial Auditing Journal	Emerald Group Publishing
A	Meditari Accountancy Research	Emerald Group Publishing
A	Qualitative Research in Accounting and Management	Emerald Group Publishing

With Whom Do I Publish?

Answering the above question sometimes gets answered by who you work with on your IVR project. Normally, the first consideration should be putting together a team of the best available to complete the project. However, you must also ensure that members of the research team, including participants, have the capabilities to disseminate research. Additionally, if one of the outlets is a high-impact academic accounting journal, these journals also have gatekeepers and can also be considered social systems that have barriers to entry.

To overcome the barriers, an interventionist researcher must be strategic in how they prepare the journal article for publication. For example, in research by de Villiers and Dumay (2013) that analyses the attributes of successfully published articles in *Accounting Organisations and*

Society, Accounting Auditing and Accountability Journal, and *Critical Perspectives on Accounting,* they find that the majority of articles had more than one author and that first-time authors normally published with another author who had previously published in the journal. Therefore, our advice is to consider your co-authors carefully, and if you want to publish in a high-quality journal, like those listed in Table 13.2, you must ensure that at least one person on the research team has already successfully published in the target journal.

Testing the Waters

While we recommend publishing articles in journals appearing in Table 13.2, it is easier said than done. Therefore, once you have chosen a target journal, you need to be even more strategic in understanding whether the journal is interested in your article. Our first advice in this area is for you to contact the journal's editor or associate editor and pitch your idea for the article. You need to keep in mind that editors are always on the lookout for new and interesting research for their journal. In our experience, we have often written or communicated with journal editors about our research and rarely has one ever not responded to discussing an idea for an article. Usually, quite the opposite is true, and if there is a good idea, they are very encouraging and make helpful comments before sending an article to the journal. Editors like to work with authors on ideas because if they submit an article to the journal that does not match the conversations or the style of research the journal is publishing or is not sufficiently novel, it is a waste of their time and the author's time. Thus, we recommend that you submit an abstract or an outline for an article to the journal editor before you even start writing and get some form of feedback to guide you.

Similarly, you should take your ideas and drafts to conferences and test them with the audience. If you present an interesting article at a conference, you may attract the attention of journal editors. It is a prime event where the editors look for interesting and novel ideas for their journal. It also gives the editors opportunities to meet potential authors and talk to them face-to-face about the research. It is your job as a potential author to look for and talk to journal editors. As indicated above, journals are social systems, and editors are the gatekeepers along with associate editors and members of the editorial boards, who are generally present at these conferences. By becoming involved in that social system of the journals at conferences and other academic events, you will understand better how the target journal attracts high-quality articles, the types of topics, and the novelty your research must have to have a better chance of being accepted.

Another key to testing the waters is to use trusted friends and colleagues to give you feedback on the article. By enlisting a subject matter expert who is familiar with your target journal to read your article before submitting to a journal, you can help identify what reviewers might be looking for in your article, and this person might be able to give you good advice on any major defects or flaws that your article has. Also, you might give the article to a non-academic and ask them to read it to see if they can understand your logic and argument. If a non-academic can engage in understanding your arguments, the article will be more engaging for the reviewers and hopefully the eventual target journal's readers. For example, you can get your spouse to read the article to see if they comprehend your argument and understand your story. By working hard at getting your journal article to a stage where the arguments flow and can be understood by others can significantly help in the review process. The last thing you want is a reviewer saying they do not understand the point of your article.

Article Structure

How you present your research is most important because what you're trying to do is tell a story about your IVR project and to justify its academic contribution, along with contributions to management practice and even public policy. One key question always asked by both students and colleagues is how they should approach writing an academic accounting article. This is because there appear to be no rules, or the rules given to them are often contradictory and based on more quantitative methodologies, which are not related to case study research and thus not to IVR. Recently, there have been studies published on the structure of accounting academic articles and another article giving general advice on how to write an academic accounting article (de Villiers & Dumay, 2013, 2014). Another book chapter that outlines good general advice is by Guthrie *et al.* (2004). We recommend you read these resources in conjunction with this book.

To assist interventionist researchers in writing up an academic article, we have outlined the proposed structure of an article, much like a recipe that you will find in a cookbook, in Table 13.3. However, like any good recipe, you do not have to stick precisely to the instructions because each time you prepare a meal, you might have slight variations depending on the conditions and ingredients available. Thus, writing an academic article is similar because no two IVR projects are the same, and there will always be variations in the way that you can prepare the article and still come out with a very good outcome. However, if you were to stick to the major parts of the recipe and then have variations in how you implement the individual sections, then you will be more likely to have the structure that the reviewers will find easy to follow, and thus enhance the chance of having a paper accepted. It's not the story, but how you tell it.

We hope that you find Table 13.3 informative and helpful in developing your IVR academic article. For a more comprehensive description on

Table 13.3 A Recipe for a Proposed IVR Academic Article

Major Section	Individual Section	Description
The Front End	Abstract	Presents an overview of the article in 100–300 words identifying a summary of the article's purpose, methodology, findings, conclusions, and limitations.
	Introduction	Presents a more detailed overview of the article designed to spark interest to read further. At a minimum, it summarises the development of the research question and outlines the novelty of the article. In some cases, it includes a more detailed summary of findings and a road map paragraph outlining the remaining structure of the article. Word Limit: 1,000
	Literature Review	Presents a critical (the good and the bad) overview of the contemporary literature related to the topic or theme of the research. It identifies the gaps in the literature that, in turn, justify the research questions. Word Limit: 2,000
	Context	In some accounting articles, this section is not present. As we are writing about an IVR project situated within a social system, this section is essential. Therefore, the context where the research is situated needs to be defined, for example, the details and history of a case study social system (organisation) and the problem that needs resolving, and how the researcher(s) became involved with the social system. Word Limit: 1,000
Methodology	Interventionist Research	Considering that IVR is a specific methodology based on case study research, the opening of the methodology section should include a brief description and reasoning behind interventionist research, as you would any other article. For example, Yin's (2017) methodology would outline and justify its use to answer the research question. Word Limit: 300
	Methods	Describes the steps involved in collecting and analysing the research data. Includes justification for using the method to collect data to answer the research questions. When undertaking a case study, you should how you develop reliability and validity

Major Section	Individual Section	Description
		(see Chapter 8). Also, an IVR project can use many different theories, especially when switching between emic and etic. You may need to explain theory when developing the methods and provide detailed descriptions of a major theory used to frame the results. Word Limit: 1,000 to 2,000
	Theory	To achieve duality of IVR output, specifically theory, this section is also very important. Here, you need to outline the major theory used as the basis of the analysis that is unfamiliar to readers of the journal. This section should give a brief outline of the theory's elements used. It must explain how the theory links with answering the research questions, and how it contributes to framing the results, discussion, and the contribution of the IVR project to academic research. Word Limit: 1,000 to 2,000
The Back End	Analysis and Results	The dissemination of the analysis must directly link with answering the research question. Here the authors should pay attention to demonstrating how reliability and validity are applied to the analysis and thus develop reliable and valid results.
	Discussion	Shows how the authors contribute to the research question with clear links to theory or theories employed. This section normally outlines the significance, meaning, and relationship of your research to findings in prior studies identified in the literature review. Here, we recommend the authors address the issue of generalisability and demonstrate how the findings can be generalised using theoretical and naturalistic generalisations (see Chapter 8). Word Limit: Variable from 1,000 to 5,000 words or more
	Conclusion	This section provides a final commentary on how the author(s) answer the research question. Here, authors should first outline the implications for contemporary practice, policy, and future academic research. As with the discussion, there should be clear links to the issues raised in the literature review. Finally, any limitations of the IVR project should be listed. Word Limit: 500 to 1,000

(Continued)

Table 13.3 (Continued)

Major Section	Individual Section	Description
Supporting Evidence	Notes	These are represented as either footnotes or endnotes, depending on the style adopted by the journal. Should be used sparingly only for information that does not generally flow with the context of the document or the article's arguments. For example, the definition of a common term as to how it might be used in the article, if inserting the definition would break the flow of the argument.
	Appendix	Used to display large amounts of data that may have been summarised or utilised in other sections of the document. For example, a survey instrument. Again, these should be used sparingly and generally only if your target journal requires it.
	Acknowledgements	Some journals require some form of acknowledgement of the contribution of significant others who may have assisted with or reviewed previous versions of the article. As the IVR project requires the interaction of other people from other social systems, it may be prudent if your ethics allow it to thank the other participants directly. In this section, the authors also can make a note of the funding source for the IVR project. Word Limit: 100 words or less
	References	A list of the academic sources and external resources cited in the articles from secondary sources, such a publicly available journal articles, books, webpages, etc.

Source: Adapted from Guthrie *et al.* (2004, p. 214), de Villiers and Dumay (2014, pp. 333–345) and our experience as IVR authors.

how to write an accounting academic article, we refer you to de Villiers and Dumay (2014, pp. 333–345). In Table 3.3, we make specific references to how the structure of an academic article links to IVR research, which may be different to writing up a case study for a general accounting academic article.

Our main advice is not to follow the Table 13.3's structure from beginning to end but start with the literature review and begin to write that first so that the objectives of the research are clear from the onset. Thus, we recommend starting your literature review in conjunction with Phase

1 and/or 2 of the Interventionist's Framework and include an initial summary as part of your research protocol document. Our experience as researchers and authors tell us that writing an academic article is very much an iterative process, very much like the emic and etic processes of IVR. While it is nice to have a recipe, we are almost invariably going in and out of the article and preparing different sections at different times depending on our reflections of the project and where what we are writing about fits. Thus, we advocate to leave writing the introduction and then the abstract last, because you need to know the implications and conclusions beforehand, and because you need to transfer these as a summary and precis to these sections.

Polishing the Rough Diamond

One last piece of advice is to ensure that any research you present to a high-quality journal is a highly polished piece of work. The pressure to publish in academia is so great that often we take a shortcut and present work to journals that is not ready for review and can contain many errors or omissions. Our previous advice to enlist an expert or trusted colleague to read your draft article is the first step in polishing what we refer to as the rough diamond. Similarly, presenting your draft as a paper at a conference is also highly recommended to get the feedback. You can also outline in your letter to the editor the steps that you have taken to ensure the quality of your article. An article submitted with such a pedigree is more likely to receive a good response from the editor and not be desk rejected. In high-quality journals, the rejection rate can be as high as 95%, and in highly prestigious journals even more. Thus, you need to ensure your article is a polished diamond before sending to the journal for review.

One last line of defence before sending your paper for review and to polish the rough diamond is to use the services of a copy editor or proofreader. First, copy-editing is essential to pick up small errors, such as incorrect punctuation, spelling, and numbering of tables and figures. Copy-editing ensures that the style and formatting of your article also fit the journal's requirements. However, proofreading is also essential because proofreading looks at structure, and ensures that your research is written in a comprehensible manner and makes suggestions on how you can improve the clarity of your article's presentation. We recommend that every article you submit should be subjected to proofreading by an expert academic proofreader familiar with your subject matter. Their recommendations come from years of experience in proofreading articles for high-quality journals. Therefore, especially for students and early career researchers, the use of a proofreading service can be very informative to developing your writing skills because you will learn from the proofreader's feedback.

Disseminating to a Practitioner Audience

From an academic perspective, writing for a high-quality journal is one primary outcome; you also have another but equally important outcome—the prospect to write for a practitioner audience. Hence, here we focus our discussion on writing for a practitioner audience and working with professional organisations to disseminate IVR outcomes to non-academics.

Writing for Practitioners

In our careers, we have written for professional and online magazines, news articles, blogs, and social media outlets such as LinkedIn. Publishing for a practitioner audience allows for our research to reach a wider audience beyond what is sometimes known as the academic paywalls of journals, where your high-quality research article is only accessible to people, most likely academics, who subscribe to the academic journal publishing houses subscription services (see Chapter 2). For example, *The Conversation* online magazine is a popular outlet for academics to disseminate their research findings that are of interest to academics and the wider community (e.g., Dumay & Guthrie, 2018; Dumay *et al.*, 2018). Thus, using these external publication outlets, you can reach an audience who may never have had the opportunity to read your work, and through communicating the potential generalisations from your research, it may influence future practice.

Disseminating your research to a wider audience appears to be more important now than ever because if practitioners use the generalisations, it demonstrates that your research has an impact on society. For example, in Australia, the Australian Research Council (ARC) has recently announced changes in how it conducts its Excellence in Research Australia (ERA) assessment exercise by including an assessment of engagement and impact (see www.arc.gov.au/engagement-and-impact-assessment). Similarly, in the United Kingdom, they have a well-established research impact assessment framework to judge how academic research interacts with, and impacts on, society beyond academia, where universities must develop research impact case studies as a measure of academic performance (see https://re.ukri.org/research/ref-impact/). Thus, academic performance is starting to reach beyond the academic paywalls to demonstrate how it has an impact on society. As we have outlined in Chapter 2, research impact is highly desired by governments and funding agencies. In the end, future research funding will be allocated on its potential economic and social benefits, not just good ideas (see Martin-Sardesai *et al.*, 2019).

The challenge with disseminating research to a wider audience is that we are too ingrained in writing academic research with other academics as our primary audience. We academics tend to have our own language when writing articles that non-academics can find difficult to unravel and understand. Writing for a non-academic audience means that researchers must have the appropriate qualities that include competences in writing for non-academics. If academics do not have practical experience because they only write for other scholars, then this is something they must add to their toolkit for disseminating the results of an IVR project. The following are some guidelines from *The Conversation* for writing for a practitioner and general audience (Hansen, 2018):

> Our readers are engaged and intelligent, but most of them are not academics. When writing, imagine you're talking to a clever friend or relative—not a colleague. This means no jargon, just plain English. Our favourite saying at The Conversation is that you'd never alight an automobile when you can get out of a car.
>
> Keep it snappy—our pieces are 600–800 words, so get to your point fast.
>
> It's also important to remember we're here to inform people, not to convince them of anything or to preach. Aggressive or patronising tones turn off readers—we aim to present people with information to help them make up their own minds, not tell them what they should think.
>
> In an age when journalism is suffering from a lack of trust, we want all the information we share with readers to be verifiable. Whenever you mention a fact or statistic make sure there's research or data to back it up, and include a primary reference in the form of a hyperlink.

We also recommend one thing to remember when writing up your research for a practitioner and a general audience—they are more focused on the practical outcomes than the theoretical. Writing about practice is more likely to engage with your reader than writing about theory. As with academic writing, you need to learn and to practice getting it right, because when you do, you never know how many more people you can reach.

Working with Professional Organisations

Another mode of the dissemination is to work with and present your findings to professional organisations. For example, at our university and other universities in Australia, the accounting departments have a strong relationship with the Certified Professional Accountants (CPA) and the Chartered Accountants of Australia and New Zealand (CAANZ). These professional associations, in collaboration with universities, host regular 'town and gown' sessions, where accounting researchers present their latest findings to practitioners. As with writing for a professional audience, these presentations need to be practical so that professionals can understand them. Thus, a standard presentation for an academic conference is inadequate for this purpose. As with writing, you need to know your audience.

Another avenue for dissemination is to conduct workshops in conjunction with the professional accounting organisations. For example, all accountants need to maintain their professional qualifications, and they do this by attending training that qualifies as part of the professional development hours. Hence, you can work with professional organisations in developing these workshops. Again, these need to be practically relevant and would be quite different to what you would teach in a classroom.

Writing the Social System Report

Another important mode of dissemination that is very important is writing the report for the organisation or community that you are involved with during the research. This step is most important in bridging the research-practice gap, see Chapter 2, because we can now demonstrate to practice that academics are contributing to solving real-world problems and are not sitting still in our ivory towers. As discussed in the previous sub-section, you are writing about a direct outcome of the IVR project, and you must write this in a manner that is understandable by the participants. Therefore, we recommend that any report you write involves the feedback of the participants, and even better yet, involves them in writing the report. As we outlined in Chapter 8, getting the feedback and involvement of participants is essential to the validity of the research outcomes and supports developing the eventual quality and outcome of the intervention (Dumay, 2010a).

As with academic articles, a report for an organisation or community needs to be highly polished because your audience will often be senior managers and or people in society, such as politicians, policymakers, standard setters, and so on. These people are busy and need to have results disseminated to them professionally and concisely. These are often skills lacking in an interventionist researcher, as we normally write for an academic audience, not senior managers and members of society. Therefore, the use of professionals, such as proofreaders, graphic artists, desktop publishers, and even public relations companies, is at times needed for developing and disseminating the report. Therefore, if a report is an essential outcome of the IVR project, it should be planned for from the onset of the research protocol. Additionally, you should allocate adequate resources and budget for producing the report in conjunction with the social system (organisation).

In Summation

In summary, we want to emphasise the need for producing high-quality outputs when disseminating research. You need to be aware that dissemination does not stop with an academic article but needs to extend also to practitioners and the social system. We highly recommend that all IVR includes all three forms of dissemination, and that dissemination reaches beyond just the printed word via presentations and workshops for accounting professionals. Doing so will ensure that IVR does not end up on a shelf behind an academic paywall but has both academic and managerial outcomes that have an impact on society.

References

Beilenson, J., Gitlin, L.N., & Czaja, S.J. (2016). Disseminating proven behavioral interventions. In L.N. Gitlin & S.J. Czaja (Eds.), *Behavioral intervention research: Designing, evaluating, and implementing* (pp. 399–416). New York, NY: Springer Publishing Company.

de Villiers, C. & Dumay, J. (2013). Construction of research articles in the leading interdisciplinary accounting journals. *Accounting, Auditing & Accountability Journal*, 26(6), 876–910.

de Villiers, C. & Dumay, J. (2014). Writing an article for a refereed accounting journal. *Pacific Accounting Review*, 26(3), 324–350.

Dumay, J. (2010a). A critical reflective discourse of an interventionist research project. *Qualitative Research in Accounting and Management*, 7(1), 46–70.

Dumay, J. (2010b, April 24). *Intellectual capital and strategy development utilising narrative: An interventionist approach*. Paper presented at the 12th Alternative Accounts Conference and Workshop, Toronto, Canada.

Dumay, J. (2011). Intellectual capital and strategy development: An interventionist approach. *VINE*, 41(4), 449–465.

Dumay, J., Evans, R., Walker, K., & Bodrova, O. (2013). The case for a global eConservatorium of music based in Australia. *Academic Leadership Series Volume 4: The Virtual University: Impact on Australian Accounting and Business Education*, 4(1), 57–65.

Dumay, J. & Guthrie, J. (2012). Intellectual capital and strategy as practice: A critical examination. *International Journal of Knowledge and Systems Science*, 4(3), 28–37.

Dumay, J. & Guthrie, J. (2018). The modern Slavery Bill is a start, but it won't guarantee us sweeter chocolate. *The Conversation*. Retrieved from: https://theconversation.com/the-modern-slavery-bill-is-a-start-but-it-wont-guarantee-us-sweeter-chocolate-102765

Dumay, J., Nadeem, M., & Massaro, M. (2018). To value companies like Amazon and Facebook, we need to look beyond dollars and assets. *The Conversation*. Retrieved from: https://theconversation.com/to-value-companies-like-amazon-and-facebook-we-need-to-look-beyond-dollars-and-assets-94578

Eccles, R. & Krzus, M. (2010). *One report: Integrated reporting for a sustainable strategy*. Hoboken, NJ: Wiley & Sons.

Gitlin, L.N. & Czaja, S.J. (2016). *Behavioural intervention research: Designing, evaluating and implementing*. New York, NY: Springer Publishing Company.

Guthrie, J., Parker, L.D., & Dumay, J. (2015). Academic performance, publishing and peer review: Peering into the twilight zone. *Accounting, Auditing & Accountability Journal*, 28(1), 3–13.

Guthrie, J., Parker, L.D., & Gray, R. (2004). Requirements and understandings for publishing academic research: An insider view. In C. Humphrey & W. Lee (Eds.), *The real life guide to accounting research: A behind-the-scenes view of using qualitative research methods* (pp. 411–432.). Amsterdam: Elsevier.

Hansen, A. (2018, October 30). *How to pitch to the conversation.* Retrieved from: https://theconversation.com/how-to-pitch-to-the-conversation-105850

Kaplan, R.S. & Norton, D.P. (1992). The balanced scorecard: Measures that drive performance. *Harvard Business Review*, 70(1), 71–79. Retrieved from: http://search.epnet.com/login.aspx?direct=true&db=buh&an=9205181862

Martin-Sardesai, A., Guthrie, J., Tooley, S., & Chaplin, S. (2019). History of performance measurement systems in the Australian higher education sector. *Accounting History*, 12(1), 40–61.

Thomas, E.J. & Rothman, J. (1994). An integrative perspective on intervention research. In J. Rothman & E.J. Thomas (Eds.), *Intervention research: Design and development for human service* (pp. 3–23). Binghamton, NY: Haworth Press.

Westin, O., Roberts, H., & Roberts, H. (2010). Interventionist research: The puberty years: An introduction to the special issue. *Qualitative Research in Accounting & Management*, 7(1), 5–12.

Yin, R.K. (2017). *Case study research and applications: Design and methods* (6th ed.). Thousand Oaks, CA: Sage Publications Inc.

14 Synthesis and Future Directions

Overall, this book addresses the complexity associated with designing, constructing, and implementing accounting interventions. Additionally, using sound methodological foundations and insights on IVR design, we exemplify IVR's legitimacy to help accounting scholars generate accounting research with theoretical, practical, and societal relevance. In turn, this will help address the need presented by the research-practice gap, where academics and non-academics need to collaborate to solve problems and enhance social system competence and effectiveness in a dynamic global environment. We highlight and cover a broad range of topics, including strategies to address: IVR's challenges, research participant selection and retention, selecting and managing an intervention team, planning your IVR project, and addressing IVR's 'bad' and 'ugly' aspects. Our aim is to provide helpful and vital insights into issues for advancing Interventionist Research to enhance the probability that interventions will have an optimal impact on a range of social systems.

To conclude our book, we have decided to reflect on two issues that we have discussed which we feel are exceedingly important to forge a future path ahead for IVR, being the research-practice gap and impact. As we have outlined in Chapter 2, the research-practice gap needs to be addressed, and IVR is a methodology that can help address that urgent need. Similarly, as discussed in Chapter 2, the impact of our research is becoming more and more important as universities grapple with the changing educational environment, different funding models, and the need to attain recognition as high-quality learning institutions. IVR is well-placed to deal with these issues.

In dealing with these issues, we academics must also be wary of our responsibility not just to do accounting research but also to become accountable, because there is no accounting without accountability. In completing this book, we count the book as a publication. We have done our job as accounting researchers, and we have met one of our key performance indicators so we can avoid the vulgarities of the publish or perish mentality that currently pervades in many universities (de Villiers & Dumay, 2014; Martin-Sardesai & Guthrie, 2018). But how do we become accountable, and what is the impact of our accountability?

The key to understanding the impact of our efforts to bridge the research-practice gap is the term 'social systems', which we use throughout this book. When you, the reader, think about IVR as we outline in this book, you would more likely associate an organisation or a company as the social system under research because most of the examples presented in this book are readily associated with a specific organisation. If we look at the early IVR in accounting, many of these studies also concentrate on management accounting in specific companies, and the impact is managerial and mainly benefits the company. The managerial approach to accounting research has some impact because it allows us to reflect upon and generalise the lessons learned (Parker & Northcott, 2016). But to us, this is a narrow view of a social system and is confined to the strict boundaries of a business-based organisation.

The problems that many businesses and organisations are facing these days exist well beyond their boundaries. For example, they would be remiss these days if they did not recognise climate change as a critical issue facing the world. Whether you are a climate change believer or sceptic, the topic continues to pervade in the news. It is the topic of debate as government and society grapple to find a solution. Similarly, the United Nations Sustainable Development Goals are another example of external issues that many organisations, both public and private, are attempting to resolve. However, a single organisation or researcher cannot resolve these issues or problems. They need to be addressed collectively by involving companies, non-government organisations, expert practitioners, and accounting scholars. We must move from being interdisciplinary to transdisciplinary and form new social systems that enable us to collaborate to solve the problem.

Many of these worldly problems are known as "wicked" problems (Jacobs & Cuganesan, 2014; Rittel & Webber, 1973). These problems are wicked because there are no easy solutions, as opposed to tame problems which can be solved using technology and science, such as accounting. However, if we use IVR just to tackle tame managerial problems, then all we are doing is limiting our impact to the accounting practice within strict organisational boundaries. Thus, for IVR to move forward, we must also consider its use beyond organisational boundaries, and ask ourselves how we can become involved in social systems that tackle wicked problems.

We must also become aware that due to the wicked nature of these problems, we are not always going to find solutions. While it would be nice to find a solution to every problem, it is an impossibility. But as accounting researchers, our contributions can reach beyond accounting as a technology to help improve organisations, to using accounting as a technology that can improve society, being the ultimate social system. Therefore, we call on our readers to make sure that when they think about IVR, they are not constrained by accounting as a technology to solve tame problems but to think also about accounting to help address the wicked problems that face us all.

To enable accounting to help better resolve wicked problems, we also have to think about the resources required to undertake such a huge challenge. As we have outlined in this book, there are many skills that an interventionist researcher must have and develop to undertake IVR. Many of our colleagues do not have the confidence or skills to tackle IVR projects, and rightly so, because a researcher without the confidence to conduct research to solve a problem can sometimes do more harm than good. So, we as experienced interventionist researchers also must ensure that we train our doctoral students and our early career researchers in IVR as an acceptable methodology for research. Thus, our responsibilities are twofold: we must continue to develop our IVR projects beyond organisational boundaries, and we must take along and train those who will be the future of accounting research—a new generation of practice-oriented academics.

So, while we, as accounting researchers, have ticked the box and published this book, we hope that what we outline can also inspire IVR projects in accounting to expand more towards solving wicked problems. Only then can we claim to have become accountable, and that we are addressing the need presented by the prevalence of the research-practice gap by truly achieving an output that has an impact on the wider social system of society rather than just the narrow boundaries of an organisation.

References

de Villiers, C. & Dumay, J. (2014). Writing an article for a refereed accounting journal. *Pacific Accounting Review*, 26(3), 324–350. doi:10.1108/PAR-08-2012-0033

Jacobs, K. & Cuganesan, S. (2014). Interdisciplinary accounting research in the public sector: Dissolving boundaries to tackle wicked problems. *Accounting, Auditing & Accountability Journal*, 27(8), 1250–1256.

Martin-Sardesai, A. & Guthrie, J. (2018). Human capital loss in an academic performance measurement system. *Journal of Intellectual Capital*, 19(1), 53–70. doi:10.1108/jic-06-2017-0085

Parker, L.D. & Northcott, D. (2016). Qualitative generalising in accounting research: Concepts and strategies. *Accounting, Auditing & Accountability Journal*, 29(6), 1100–1131.

Rittel, H.W.J. & Webber, M.M. (1973). Dilemmas in a general theory of planning. *Policy Sciences*, 4(2), 155–169. Retrieved from: www.jstor.org/stable/4531523

Index